M000201891

"*When the Soul Awakens* is a rare and welcome book. The authors have done the near impossible—they have distilled the meaning of centuries of spiritual wisdom from a multiplicity of sources—familiar and unfamiliar—and presented it in clear and succinct language. Their exceptional facility for synthesizing deep and complex knowledge is a rare gift for those familiar with the knowledge, as well as for those approaching it for the first time."

Lamar Carter – past president, International Center for Integrative Studies

"This book deserves to become a classic in esoteric philosophy. It's thrilling to see how the authors have woven together the esoteric and ageless wisdom traditions with the arts and letters of the ages. From Emerson and Steiner to the Buddha and Rumi, the Kabalah and yoga, Plato and Dante, St. Francis and John Paul II, Tolstoy and Dostoevsky – there is a taste of wisdom from each major branch on the tree of knowledge. This is the best book showcasing the modern wisdom teachings that I've read to date."

J.S. Bakula, Ph.D. – psychologist, author and lecturer

"Among countless attempts to bring awareness of the spiritual underpinnings of life to the thinking public, *When the Soul Awakens* is outstanding. It builds a bridge to intellectuals of goodwill who are on the verge of awakening or have recently found the Light. This book is a must-read for closing gaps in understanding and lending confidence to those who are finding their way into the uncharted but irresistible new territory of the Soul. The authors will attract the gratitude of many for years to come."

Gloria Crook – president, School of Ageless Wisdom

"*When the Soul Awakens* is an affirmation of the real spiritual potential that is within each of us and within the world. Most important it emphasizes the experience of the oneness of life that belongs to spiritual awakening. It also takes us beyond individual awakening to the evolution of global consciousness, a new era of oneness that is awaiting us. This book sends a message of joy and hope to the soul."

Llewellyn Vaughan-Lee – Sufi teacher and author

"This book presents an exciting and unique perspective on the human soul and the spiritual path. It offers a rich experience to the reader, as the authors draw on a great variety of sources about the deeper truths of existence. The book offers a vision of both the great diversity and the universality of humanity's experience of the soul and its evolutionary journey. For readers new to esoteric wisdom it will be interesting, challenging, and highly rewarding."

Irene Seeland, M.D. – psychiatrist and author, Fire on the Mountain

"This work is truly soul food for people who are hungry for spiritual truth. The authors tackle the compelling question of what it means to be alive at this moment in history, bringing to light the genuine opportunity for spiritual seekers. They have synthesized the essences of the Ageless Wisdom in a way that invites and informs people new to the teachings as well as long-time students. This book will fuel the powerful undercurrent of transformation in the world today."

Susan MacNeil, Ph.D. – psychologist

"*When the Soul Awakens* provides a rich introduction to esoteric teachings known broadly as the Ageless Wisdom. The mind and heart of humanity are undergoing a profound transformation at this time. The insights of esotericism give a unique perspective that can help us deepen our cooperation with the evolutionary changes. This book has much to say to the modern seeker who, inspired by the wholeness vision which comes from the soul, wants to enter into that vision."

Steve Nation – writer and co-founder, Intuition in Service

"This book is fascinating and enlightening. It's a treasure trove of information that demystifies the nature of the soul and spiritual experience. It is so informative, and so carefully and thoughtfully laid out, that it could be used as an introductory text in a course on the Ageless Wisdom. For many seekers who are moving from the realm of the rational, concrete mind into the more mystical realm of intuitive knowing, it will provide much needed validation. This book not only informs, it also inspires."

Nancy Wait – artist and writer

"*When the Soul Awakens* makes a wonderful contribution to the current of spirituality that is sweeping the modern world. The authors draw upon ancient teachings, religion, science, and literature to present an exciting view of humanity's expanding consciousness. Particularly valuable is the integration of ideas from 19th- and early 20th-century Russian literature which, in many ways, were prophetic of the new spirituality of the 21st century."

John F. Nash, Ph.D. – historian and author, The Soul and Its Destiny

"*When the Soul Awakens* is engaging, intelligent and highly informative. It takes an inclusive approach to spirituality that breaks down the barriers between religions and highlights what is universal. The authors enrich our lives with their presentation of the ageless wisdom."

Jackie Durham – science editor

"*When the Soul Awakens* presents a vast range of information about the spiritual path in clear and understandable prose. It is an accurate and well-researched overview of the thinking of many of the world's great mystics, dealing with subjects like karma and reincarnation in a way that makes it apparent that these beliefs are not wacky and eccentric, but genuine spiritual principles widely followed throughout the ages by many different cultures. The book's non-dogmatic and objective approach to truth, and its analysis of world developments through 'an esoteric eye,' make it worth reading more than once. It is ideal for sharing the experience of the Path with others."

Christine Townend – author and artist

"This extraordinary work is just what is needed by those awakening to a higher stage of consciousness. Through the perspective of the Ageless Wisdom, the authors illuminate the mysteries of spiritual evolution in a way that reassures those who are starting their journeys that they are following in an ancient tradition; that there is a growing body of seekers who are on the same path; and that it is the birthright of all human beings to become co-creators with God."

Jean Boston – publisher, Willow Way Press

"…This book will expand the reader's understanding of the conditions by which the Way can be followed. It is particularly suited to the intelligent, searching inquirer but even those who consider themselves well-read in esotericism will find illumination in the many insights expressed with precision and thoughtful understanding of the joys and challenges of the spiritual Path."

The Beacon – *a magazine of esoteric philosophy*

WHEN
The SOUL
AWAKENS

The Path to Spiritual Evolution and a New World Era

SECOND EDITION

NANCY SEIFER AND MARTIN VIEWEG

Gathering Wave Press

Reston, Virginia

When the Soul Awakens:
The Path to Spiritual Evolution and a New World Era, Second Edition

Published by
Gathering Wave Press
P.O. Box 2185
Reston, VA 20195-0185
www.whenthesoulawakens.org

ISBN: 978-0-9820047-0-8
(previous edition 2008—ISBN 978-0-595-46580-4)

Library of Congress Control Number: 2008934566

Printed in the United States of America.

Cover design by Mayapriya Long / Bookwrights
Text design and production by Bookwrights

TO ALL WHO RECOGNIZE
THE INHERENT ONENESS OF LIFE ON OUR PLANET
AND SEEK TO MAKE IT MANIFEST IN OUR WORLD.

The things we now esteem fixed shall, one by one,
detach themselves like ripe fruit from our experience and fall.
The soul looketh steadily forwards,
Creating a world before her, leaving worlds behind her.

~ *Ralph Waldo Emerson*

Everything on earth is subject to the laws of evolution,
And this is particularly true for the human soul.

~ *Rudolf Steiner*

CONTENTS

ACKNOWLEDGEMENTS

WE WOULD LIKE TO express our gratitude to everyone who read the manuscript of this book with an eye toward its improvement: Jean Boston, Jackie Durham, Susan MacNeil, Dominique Mazeaud, Nina Miller, John Nash, Steve Nation, Nancy Roof, Irene Seeland, and Nancy Wait.

Their encouragement helped us through the revisions, and their suggested changes substantially enhanced the final result.

PREFACE

A YEAR HAS PASSED since the manuscript for the first edition of this book was completed. In the space of that year, the modern wisdom teachings—which form the basis of this book—have become an increasingly practical guide to living. One of the gifts of these teachings is a vision of the future linked to the spiritual awakening of humanity. This vision makes it possible to see beyond the pall of darkness hovering over our planet to the rays of light emerging everywhere. And it becomes clear, from this perspective, that the intensifying pressure of living through these darkening times is serving to evoke the light of the soul.

Philosophers long ago pointed out that any extreme condition tends to evoke its opposite, leading to a state of chaos until a higher level of order is attained. Over the past year, the contrasts in our world have become more extreme than ever. Not only is the middle ground between good and evil, truth and falsity, diminishing rapidly, but the gap between rich and poor grows ever more glaring. And now, the perilous ramifications of this material gap are creating a new openness to spirituality. Progressive thinkers are realizing that one of the greatest threats to life on Earth is the spiritual impoverishment of much of "the modern world."

In our electronic age, dramatic contrasts and polarities besiege our psyches daily. Ubiquitous images of material indulgence in wealthy countries are punctuated by indelible images of human suffering that has reached epic proportions in poor regions of the world. It is no longer rare to see starving people reduced to eating mud cakes to stave off hunger pangs, or families baking in the desert sun with virtually no shelter, food, water or hope. And yet the escalation of extreme suffering seems to have evoked a corresponding outpouring of goodwill, as witnessed increasingly on our television screens.

Stories of altruism and compassion swelled during the summer of 2008, offsetting a relentless tide of bad news. Among the heroes of these stories, children and adolescents figured prominently. One 8-year old girl, upset by the plight of pets abandoned by their owners in the wave of mortgage foreclosures, created a program to help these creatures stay alive until new homes could be found. She started a website to collect donations of pet food for animal shelters. A 16-year-old boy stayed awake at night thinking about people whose homes had been destroyed by floods halfway across the country. Finding a way to travel there, he spent his summer vacation leading teams of volunteers to refurbish the mold-infested houses and lift their owners' spirits.

In small ways and large, individuals and groups have been responding to the crises of our times—not waiting to be asked, not asking anyone for permission. Acting under the authority of their own souls, they have voluntarily assumed responsibility in dire situations where a void of leadership exists. As old systems sink under the weight of greed and corruption, and masses of people are left to fend for themselves, soul-inspired individuals and groups are stepping into the breach to help people in need at all levels—local to global.

To fill a leadership void on the planetary level, the Coalition for the Global Commons came into being in 2008. Its aim is to counteract the destruction wrought by "market states," and the transnational corporations that finance them, by creating a worldwide force to protect the rights of *all* human beings, the diversity of cultures, and the health of our oceans, forests, rivers and wildlife. The founders are calling upon organizations around the globe, including the body of non-governmental organizations at the UN, to join forces to protect the common good and to redefine themselves as a "third sector"—neither public nor private but one that underlies both. Their vision is to create a global "superpower" that can act for "the well-being of everyone on the planet."[1]

To address the intractable situation in the Middle East, another ground-breaking initiative took form in 2008. The Global Conference on Dialogue—an interfaith gathering of religious leaders—was held in Madrid at the invitation of the King of Saudi Arabia. The aim of the conference was to dissolve ancient stereotypes and encourage religious leaders to join forces around values they hold in common—tolerance, compassion, justice, and love. A progressive American rabbi who took part in the event saw it as an effort to create a moderating influence in the Islamic world.[2] Noting that the King's idea had drawn resistance from Saudi Arabia's conservative Islamic leaders, the rabbi likened the historic significance of this meeting to Gorbachev's declarations of *glasnost* and *perestroika*, which led in time to the dismantling of the Soviet regime.

In the light of the wisdom teachings, all of these initiatives are signs of the Soul of humanity entering our world. It is the soul, the higher Self of a human being, whose awareness transcends borders and whose impulse is to heal and make whole. Increasingly, awakened souls from distant corners of the globe are connecting with each other and finding greater affinity with one another than with those born into the same tribe, nation, religion, or race who do not share this unfolding awareness. Paradoxically, even as our present human civilization appears headed toward an irreversible tipping-point, the light of the soul continues to emerge into greater evidence.

During the course of this past year, the acceleration of change on our planet has become an established fact. Many things are happening more rapidly than expected: the melting of Arctic ice sheets, the disappearance of species, the drying up of once fertile lands. At the same time, breakthroughs in the realm of consciousness are also speeding up, and the causal relationship between material and spiritual changes is ever more apparent. The rapidly shifting foundations of our material reality have created a state of uncertainty in which many people, feeling less firmly anchored on the material plane, have begun searching for underlying causes of present perils and looking for answers to ultimate questions.

The urgency of these times is acting as a "forcing process" that is quickening the evolution of human consciousness. The challenges of our increasingly tight-knit world of interlinking crises seem to be calling forth the next stage in our conscious unfoldment as a species: a realization of our true identity as souls and our inherent unity as a human family. Numerically, perhaps only a tiny fraction of the human species has reached this stage of awareness as yet. But there is growing evidence that a spark of spiritual awakening is spreading rapidly, igniting the opening of hearts and penetrating the minds of individuals who have the potential to influence events for the greater good.

Decades ago, this turning-point in human evolution was foreseen by Buckminster Fuller (1895-1983)—philosopher, architect, inventor and visionary. Shortly before his death, Fuller noted that in the space of his lifetime, the literacy rate of humanity had risen from 5% to 65%. For the first time in history, a majority of human beings could obtain information freely, independent of political and religious leaders. The next step, in his view, was for a critical mass of individuals to reflect on that information honestly and decide to act on it. "Our power," he counseled, "is in our ability to decide."

Fuller foresaw "a new moment of integrity" on Earth, when humanity could enter into a new relationship with the universe. For him, integrity was everything. It meant a system of values flowing from a recognition of the integrity (wholeness, completeness, inclusiveness) of the universe and the oneness of humanity. He urged people to see our world as it *truly* is—a small planet whose life is intricately interwoven, revolving around a much greater body—and to think and act in light of these realities. To Fuller, questions of race, religion, nationality, region amounted to an illness he called "categoryitis." By the 21st century, he cautioned, either humanity will have become aware of the "absurd and anti-evolutionary" nature of such questions, or it will no longer be able to survive on Earth.

The wisdom teachings sound the same note in describing this pivotal moment in evolution. What is intended at this juncture, we are told, is that the intelligence flowering within humanity—in response to increasingly available knowledge—be turned toward serving the greater good of *all* lives on our planet. Up until now, observers have remarked, many of us have lived like self-centered adolescents, heedless of the consequences of our actions. Now we are being jarred awake as a species, standing on the threshold of adulthood, impelled to take responsibility for ourselves and for one another.

From an esoteric view, the opportunity inherent in this planetary crisis is a great soul awakening. As the light of the soul dawns, individually and collectively, we will learn to see beyond self-interest and look towards the welfare of the whole. Over the course of this new century, and millennium, it will become increasingly evident that each of us is a unit of consciousness that lives, moves, and has its being in a vast but unified ocean of consciousness. Once we come to know ourselves as souls, part of the one Oversoul, it is inevitable that a new era will dawn on our small planet.

August 2008

NOTES

1   James Bernard Quilligan, "Making the Great Adjustment: Coalition for the Global Commons," *Kosmos*, Spring / Summer 2008, 67-69.

2   Rabbi Michael Lerner, editor of *Tikkun* magazine, distributed a report to his email list in July 2008 entitled, "My Talk with the Saudis, and What I Learned from Them."

A Note to the Reader

WHEN THE SOUL AWAKENS is based on a set of teachings about the soul and the spiritual path known as the Ageless Wisdom.[1] These teachings, relatively recent in their present form, are actually both old *and* new. Many of the truths they contain were long ago perceived by knowers and seers who managed to penetrate the veil of appearances and touch the reality of Spirit.[2] These rare individuals were able to tap what the ancient sage Patanjali called "the raincloud of knowable things"—the fount of wisdom and truth that has inspired mystics, poets, and prophets from time immemorial.

As evolution proceeds, however, the substance of this "raincloud" grows and expands accordingly. The newer content of the Ageless Wisdom concerns that which is most relevant for seekers of truth during this transition from one era to another: knowledge about the evolutionary plan for humanity and the spiritual principles governing the evolution of consciousness. Thus the modern wisdom teachings[3] present both divine truths that have "stood the test of time" and newly revealed esoteric ideas concerning a new age—a new stage in consciousness that will see the flowering of the human soul.

Many ideas in this book may be familiar to the reader, while others may be new either in content or in context. Through the lens of the wisdom teachings, spiritual truths that originated in the East or the West, formerly perceived in isolation, are seen as complementary facets of a whole. Brought into living relationship, viewed as integral parts of a single body of spiritual wisdom, the deeper meaning of seemingly disparate principles stands revealed. Woven together, they form a solid platform of understanding on which the newer truths for our times can be more readily assimilated.

One of the core truths of the Ageless Wisdom teachings is that consciousness evolves through experience, sometimes slowly, sometimes rapidly. We are living in a time when the pace of evolution has been accelerated, and its direction has become clear. Countless phenomena occurring on our planet—in the world of form and in the realm of consciousness—point toward universality. Through the prism of universality, spiritual truths that emerged in earlier epochs can be seen as integral to the progressive unfoldment of *human* awareness. Separate "pieces of the spiritual puzzle," contributed by different traditions, together reveal the light of universal truth.

For some readers, ideas presented in these pages may be too unfamiliar to be easily assimilated. Yet if approached with an open mind, they may help to illumine the reader's chosen path. Experiences related to soul awakening may initially sound strangely mystical, as they involve levels of consciousness that transcend the concrete mind. Awakening brings, for example, a growing realization of being part of a greater life that is both visible and invisible; a state of awareness that extends beyond the normal boundaries of space and time to include subtler planes of reality; a dawning recognition that we have lived before and with it, a greater sense of responsibility for our lives.

If such ideas *are* unfamiliar, we would like to suggest a new way of gauging their validity. Rather than relying upon the analytical lens of science to discern the truth of spiritual teachings, we would invite readers to use a spiritual measuring tool—the lodestar of their own souls. There is no better arbiter of truth than the human soul, as Ralph Waldo Emerson affirms:

> The soul is the perceiver and revealer of truth. We know truth when we see it, let skeptic and scoffer say what they choose... We know truth when we see it, from opinion, as we know when we are awake that we are awake.[4]

Because the intangible reality of the soul contrasts markedly with that of the concrete world in which we live, parts of this book may call upon readers to take a stance that differs from the one usually taken in reading a book. To make the picture whole, the spiritual eye—the synthetic eye of the intuition—will be needed *in addition* to the analytical lens of the concrete mind. We invite readers to reflect upon the ideas presented through this expanded awareness, in the hope that we may realize—individually and collectively—a fuller measure of our potential to live as souls and thus to create a new reality on Earth.[5]

NOTES

1   See Glossary.
2   Certain words in this book, such as "spirit" and "soul," are often capitalized in metaphysical literature to denote spiritual significance. Since the constant use of capitals may inadvertently create the opposite effect, we have chosen to avoid capitalization for the most part, allowing for occasional usage where emphasis seems necessary.
3   "The wisdom teachings" is a term for the greater body of Ageless Wisdom, inclusive of the many offshoots of the main teachings described in the Introduction to this book and in the Glossary.
4   Ralph Waldo Emerson, "The Over-Soul," *The Best of Ralph Waldo Emerson*, 213.
5   "Earth" will appear capitalized when referring to the name of our planet, but in lower case when referring to the physical realm in which we live.

INTRODUCTION

What you are searching for is what is searching.

~Saint Francis of Assisi

TO BE ALIVE NOW, and sensitive to the state of the world, is to realize that an old order is passing away. With every year of the new millennium, there are growing indications that a cycle of history is ending. Unfathomable though it may seem, we are actually in the midst of the Great Turning of the Ages that many religious and esoteric teachings have long predicted: the much anticipated moment when humanity will move out of an age of spiritual darkness and into an age of light.

Living through this transitional time, bombarded by signs of "the end,"[1] we are challenged to focus on what lies ahead while making use of the opportunity at hand. The idea that opportunity can be the flip side of danger is graphically expressed in the epigram of our times—the Chinese character for "crisis" linking danger and opportunity. The danger inherent in any crisis lies in pursuing the same course of action, while opportunity lies in changing course. Given the scale of our current world crisis, however, it appears that more is needed than a simple change in course. There is a need for action flowing from a higher level of consciousness.

The opportunity now facing us is a spiritual one, involving a shift to a higher dimension of awareness. With the daily shattering

1

of illusions about the material world, growing numbers of people around the globe have felt impelled to search for higher truth. For many, this search had already begun in the 1960s and 70s, with the first wave of spiritual awakening sparked by the energies of Aquarius.[2] But events unfolding since 2001 have accelerated and intensified a *collective* search for what is genuine and real. Millions of people are now engaged in a spiritual quest that is, at its core, a quest for the Soul.

Inevitably, all who embark upon this journey are confronted with mystery, as reflected in Saint Francis' paradoxical allusion to the soul as *both* that which is searching and that which is being sought. The true nature of the soul, which Plato called "a divinity," has been shrouded in mystery for millennia and remains so, despite the recent outpouring of popular books on the subject. What informs most of these books is a consensual reality based on material science—a form of science that recognizes only the tangible, measurable, visible, concrete dimensions of existence.

In the last century, a new kind of science came into being—a "science of the soul." Though little known in mainstream culture, it has served to fuel the spiritual awakening now occurring around the globe. Esoteric in nature, this new science has furthered human understanding of the invisible, subtle, spiritual dimensions of existence that lie behind the dense material world. It has been put forth in a set of teachings known collectively as the Ageless Wisdom, a blend of truths from East and West. These teachings form a body of knowledge that holds keys to many of the great mysteries that continue to surround the human soul.

Although this "science of the soul" has been available for some time, it has thus far been embraced by a relatively small circle of seekers. There are two apparent reasons for this. One is that the teachings contain many highly complex, fundamentally new concepts, presented in language that is often abstruse and exceedingly difficult to penetrate. The density of many of the texts can discourage all but the most stalwart students of esoteric wisdom (who nevertheless are estimated to number in the hundreds of thousands).

Another reason for limited readership is the source of these teachings, which tends to strain the credulity of the scientifically minded. The Ageless Wisdom originates from a plane of consciousness higher than the analytic mind, beyond the scope of purely *human* awareness. The supra-human source of the teachings can be discerned in their extraordinary power of illumination. The revelations they contain cast new light on the religious assertion that a 5th kingdom in nature exists—a spiritual kingdom—in addition to the mineral, plant, animal, and human kingdoms. Within the spiritual kingdom are Masters of Wisdom, initiates of universal truth, who guide the evolution of humanity.[3] It is they who transmitted the wisdom teachings in the goal of accelerating the evolution of human consciousness at this time.[4]

To comprehend the nature of these spiritual beings requires only an expansion of an idea that has now become widely accepted: the idea that human consciousness unfolds in stages. If we take that notion a step further and allow for the possibility that consciousness can evolve not only from one *human* stage to another, but also *beyond* the strictly human dimension, it becomes possible to conceive of a higher kingdom in nature. The beings who transmitted the wisdom teachings to humanity (by telepathy to advanced human beings), are individuals who have passed through all stages of human evolution and mastered the human experience. Having moved on to a higher plane of consciousness, or kingdom, they serve the divine evolutionary Plan by fostering the development of those who follow after them.

According to these masters of wisdom, we are currently in transition to a new world era. At its zenith, it will bring forth a flowering of the Soul of humanity—the result of many souls awakening and finding their way to the spiritual path. This Path is the way of transformation—the means by which we evolve beyond ordinary human consciousness, beyond that which we recognize as "human nature." It is likewise the means by which a segment of humanity will collectively evolve a new civilization in the Aquarian age. With the shifting of the ages, we will be moving from one dimension of consciousness to another. This new dimension is a spiritual one—the realm of the Soul. Our passage into this realm begins *when the soul awakens.*

It was the awakening of a significant number of souls, starting in the late 19th century, that elicited the new esoteric teachings with their new science. The masters of wisdom deemed that the time had come to reveal knowledge that had long been hidden from most of humanity. To catalyze the process of conscious evolution, it was decided that esoteric wisdom, once closely guarded, be made *exoteric*—available to all who search for it. This book has been written in the hope of contributing in a small way to this ongoing process, by presenting core truths about the reality of the soul to an expanding circle of spiritual seekers.

While this book is deeply rooted in and informed by esoteric knowledge, it is not about the Ageless Wisdom, per se. This is a book about the unfoldment of human consciousness, for which the wisdom teachings provide an essential framework of understanding. These teachings have given us a lens through which to see where we now stand on the path of evolution, as a human race, and where we are headed in the future as souls awaken to their true nature and forge a path into an age of Spirit.

From an esoteric viewpoint, what most distinguishes the new era from previous ones is that *many* seekers are now being drawn to the path of spiritual evolution. In the past, it was only rare individuals, widely scattered across the pages of history, who sought the light of higher truth. Recognized as saints and sages, poets and philosophers, mystics and enlightened teachers, they were known for the gifts they left to humanity. Now, through the prism of the wisdom teachings, we can also see them as fellow seekers who have traveled the path before us. Their insights take on vitally new meaning in light of the realization that we are following in their footsteps.

In the pages of this book, the reader will find a tapestry of illumined thoughts of those who have preceded us, woven together on a loom of understanding provided by the wisdom teachings. The golden thread in the fabric is the reality that the soul, an individual "unit of consciousness," is on an evolutionary journey toward the light of Spirit. Through the words of seekers across time, from all corners of the globe, we come to realize the inevitability of this journey, as well as the universality of its essence.

Awakening, as the word implies, is only the first stage in a long and challenging process of transformation. The soul's initial glimpse of its true identity is not the path itself, as is sometimes inferred, but rather the impulse that sets the journey in motion.[5] This book attempts to expose the full breadth of the Path of Return—from the soul's first gleaning of a higher reality, to the drive to discover what lies behind the transitory world of form, and the ensuing struggle to reorient our awareness from the plane of matter to the plane of spirit. It is this path that transforms and enables us, over time, to fulfill the true purpose of our existence on Earth.

As students of the wisdom teachings and grateful beneficiaries, our aim in writing this book was to share the fruits of what we have learned with other seekers. In formulating the book's contents, the process sometimes had the feel of dismantling a richly jeweled crown in order to reveal the beauty of the individual gems. By placing each jewel of higher truth in its own unique setting, the luminosity of each one could be more readily appreciated. In crafting these settings, we have tried to lead the eye from the familiar to the unfamiliar—from knowledge already available to that which has been largely hidden from view.

Two gems of higher truth are central to this book: the fact that the soul never dies and the fact that the soul's evolution is continuous. The soul truly *is* eternal, evolving through lifetimes of experience and gradually, over time, accumulating knowledge, insight, and wisdom. Awakening occurs—in one incarnation or another—when the individual soul becomes satiated with material living and feels compelled, by a deep inner urge, to discover the truth that lies behind the outer world of appearances.

The great promise of our time is that we are arriving at this stage in consciousness *en masse*. As the body of serious seekers around the world continues to expand, so does our collective potential to manifest a new reality on our planet. The soul, innately aware of the oneness of life, is a force for universality and thus for peace. Alive to the spirit within the form, the soul sees beyond outer differences. Increasingly, as soul awareness moves into the foreground of human consciousness, religion, culture, race, and nationality will become symbols of diversity rather than forces of cleavage.

This book is dedicated to the spirit of universality that heralds a new era of world peace. Its premise is that the spiritual path is the common thread uniting seekers of all backgrounds. Enlightened souls throughout history have testified to the commonality of this path and the realizations to which it leads: there is one God or Life Force that ensouls all forms; there is one spiritual realm from which all souls emanate and to which all return; there is a spark of divine consciousness within every human soul, lying dormant until it awakens and begins the journey of return. That turning-point in awareness is the focus of this book.

The contents of *When the Soul Awakens* are loosely divided into two sections. The first part takes a longer view of the soul and its evolutionary unfoldment, exploring the more timeless aspects of both. The second part looks more closely at the ways in which the evolution of human consciousness is becoming manifest in our world today. It explores many contemporary developments that signal an acceleration of spiritual awakening on our planet.

Part One, consisting of five chapters, explores: the meaning of being human, body *and* soul; the nature of the soul—the higher Self; the experience of awakening; the functions of karma and reincarnation in spiritual growth; and the human evolutionary journey—spanning eons—from immersion in the world of form (and the experience of separation) to awakening and discovering the path to union with God and all of life. Part Two, also consisting of five chapters, examines: suffering as a catalyst in spiritual growth; the characteristics of soul awareness; the universality of the spiritual path; the higher stages of consciousness to which the path leads; and the unfolding plan of evolution.

In writing this book, the works that influenced us more than any other single source were those of Alice A. Bailey. As with many who awaken spiritually, our individual journeys led us to varied teachers and teachings, until we came upon these books. There, among the twenty-four volumes, we found a comprehensive presentation of the stages of the path, explaining the challenges we had faced and were facing. The clarity and precision with which our personal journeys were reflected in the pages of these books made it evident that our experiences were not unique, but were universal to all seekers—as is the progression from belief, to conviction, to inner knowing that occurs as the path unfolds.

It was a Master of Wisdom named Djwhal Khul, often referred to as the Tibetan master, who telepathically transmitted to Alice Bailey all but five of the books published in her name. At the start of each of his volumes he states that his purpose is "to teach and spread the knowledge of the Ageless Wisdom wherever I can find a response." He cautions that the contents are true and useful only to the degree that the reader ascertains them to be so, based on intuition and on their practical value in living a spiritual life.

In this same spirit, we offer insights garnered from the living of our own lives in the light of these teachings. We have tried to faithfully render fundamental truths of the Ageless Wisdom, making them as useful to other seekers as they have been to us. If what we say finds resonance with readers, and helps them to strengthen their intuitive grasp of spiritual reality, then our efforts will have been worthwhile. It is our fondest hope that this book will encourage those who come upon it to step more firmly onto the Path of Return, thereby quickening their own journeys and furthering the collective passage of humanity into the new age.

NOTES

1 Millennialists point to floods, fires, earthquakes, wars, and plagues as "signs of the end." Scientists point to changes in our Earth such as shifting magnetic fields, disappearing species, melting glaciers, and unsustainable patterns of human consumption as signs of the end of a cycle of human civilization.

2 The earth is slowly beginning to enter into the energetic sphere of influence of the constellation Aquarius. See Chapter 2 for an explanation of this process, and a further mention in Chapter 10.

3 See the Glossary for definitions of this and other terms appearing throughout the book.

4 See Chapter 9 for an explanation of the unfoldment of consciousness leading to the stage of mastery.

5 The soul referred to here is the soul incarnate in the world of form, awakening to the reality of its spiritual existence on subtler planes. See the Glossary for further clarification of the dimensions of the soul.

CHAPTER ONE

THE REAL HUMAN BEING

There is one spectacle grander than the sea, that is the sky;
There is one spectacle grander than the sky;
That is the interior of the soul.

~Victor M. Hugo

THE IDEA THAT HUMAN beings have souls—or that we fundamentally *are* souls inhabiting physical bodies—remains foreign to the materialistic culture of modern civilization. In the West, in particular, there are many who might still wonder why such a seemingly impractical, scientifically improvable notion should matter at all to contemporary human beings. Others would argue that the soul's reality matters now more than ever. An expanded perception of who we are has profound and immediate consequences for all of life on Earth.

Who we *think* we are has everything to do with how we live our lives on this planet. People who believe they are basically physical beings, entirely separate from other physical beings, hold a very different set of values than people who believe they are spiritual beings, vitally interconnected with all other living beings. Since beliefs determine values, and values determine choices and actions, it follows that human lives based on a material worldview will be conspicuously different from lives rooted in spiritual values.

It has long been evident that how we *feel* about ourselves determines how we act toward others. Feelings of being loved or unloved, safe or unsafe, are indicators of human behavior that cut across all cultural lines. Some of the best evidence of this can be found in children's drawings about their feelings, used by psychologists to predict behavior. Drawings containing symbols of fear, anger, and violence are known to reveal the potential for harmful actions towards others. Those that contain symbols of well-being, security, and love are reliable predictors of benign behavior.

Even more far-reaching than the consequences of our feelings are the consequences of our *beliefs* about who we are. Given that beliefs determine values and actions in *all* spheres of life, and given that all lives on our planet are increasingly intertwined, understanding the basis of our beliefs becomes increasingly essential to our collective well-being. The future of our own species, and of many others, may well depend on how we answer such existential questions as: Who are we? What does it mean to be a member of the human race? What is the purpose of our existence?

In the past, people generally turned to religion or philosophy for answers to questions such as these. With the Age of Reason, however, science emerged as the principle arbiter of reality in the modern world.[1] Through the lens of science, humans are biological creatures. Like all other living organisms, we are born, we grow, mature, and die. Our species is part of the sub-order of primates named *anthropoid* (humanlike), denoting the resemblance between us and our fellow primates—gorillas, chimpanzees, and others of the lesser and greater apes. The awesome extent of that resemblance has now been quantified by genetic researchers: we share ninety-seven per cent of our DNA with gorillas and ninety-eight per cent with chimpanzees, our two closest relatives.

According to our reference books and texts, a human being is, first of all, a member of the genus *Homo* and the species *Homo sapiens*; and secondarily "a person," as distinguished from other animals. The name of our biological genus, *Homo,* refers to the fact that we are bipedal primates, i.e., we can stand on two feet. The name of our species, *Sapiens,* derives from the Latin verb "to know." *Sapiens,* often translated as "intelligent," is linked to the size of our brain. The most common definition of who we are is *bipedal primates with large brains.* Scientifically, we are distinguished from other primates most of all by our enlarged cerebral hemispheres.

In the view of science, our larger and more highly developed brain is the major cause of our evolutionary progress beyond other primates. It is believed that our brains have given us the capacity for both language and logic. The ability to use words, the symbols that comprise language, has resulted in the capacity for abstract reasoning, which is based on word and number symbols. We also have more advanced binocular (two-eyed) vision than our closest primate relatives. It was the combination of our larger brains and our advanced vision, plus an erect body carriage that frees our hands, which gave us the capacity to create and use complex tools.

Anyone who consults a text or reference book to learn about the nature of a human being will discover that we are large-brained primates capable of creating and using complex tools. That is who we are from the perspective of modern science. But who are we *really*? What about hopes and dreams? What about the spiritual dimension of ourselves? How do we account for inspiration and imagination, forgiveness and love, courage and altruism, compassion and empathy? Do such qualities derive from the physical brain, as most scientists still believe, or might they have a different origin?

While pondering such questions, it is instructive to recall that there was a time, not all that long ago in the greater scheme of things, when the most advanced thinkers in the world held a far more holistic view of the human being. The philosophers of ancient Greece believed that human beings were composed of body *and* soul, and they attached by far the greatest importance to the soul. Plato (427–347 BCE), who has been called the "determiner of Western thought,"[2] viewed the soul as the supreme feature of the human being.

In Plato's understanding, the soul was "the divinity of each one," the part of us that linked us to the *realm* of divinity. Every human being was innately endowed with a rational soul, but this divine endowment did not automatically reveal itself. Each individual was destined to engage in a struggle for the rational soul (the highest of three aspects of soul in Plato's schema) to control the lesser, more animal-like aspects of our being. In his view, the advantage of our upright posture was "to facilitate the victory of the rational soul." In the *Timaeus*, he uses metaphor to explain the soul's position in the body.

> God gave the sovereign part of the human soul to be
> the divinity of each one, being that part which, as we
> say, dwells at the top of the body, and inasmuch as we
> are a plant not of the earthly but of a heavenly growth,
> raises us from earth to our kindred who are in heaven.
> The divine power suspended the head and root of us
> from that place where the generation of the soul first
> began, and thus made the whole body upright.[3]

In a more pragmatic sense, Plato saw our upright posture as enabling us to look upward toward the heavens. He believed that by observing the motions of celestial bodies we would "behold the course of intelligence in the heavens." Recognizing the divine intelligence behind the movements of the stars and planets, we would be inclined to try to understand the *source* of that intelligence. To him, this was the purpose of philosophy, whose literal meaning is "love of wisdom."

Philosophy for Plato was the bedrock of human society and its highest good. It was a gift from the gods, bestowed upon mortal men for the purpose of learning to express our divine nature in society. Beyond philosophy, he wrote, "no greater good ever was or will be given by the gods to mortal man."[4] "True philosophy" was, in his view, "the only hope of finding justice for society or for the individual."[5] The essential goal of philosophy was to turn the mind upward to the Truth, which "heads the list of all things good, for gods and men alike." And it was the rational soul within each human being that held the power to turn the mind upward to the Truth.

The soul, "a divinity," was seen by Plato as the mediator between our higher and lower natures—between "the gods and the beasts" within us, and between our immortal and mortal selves. He saw the rational soul as having the power to determine everything in the life of an individual or a society, because the rational soul determined whether our thoughts would be of a higher or a lower nature. The notion that "energy follows thought," increasingly popular in our time, was explained by Plato as follows:

> When a man is always occupied with the cravings of desire and ambition, and is eagerly striving to satisfy them, all his thoughts must be mortal, and, as far as it is possible altogether to become such, he must be mortal every whit because he has cherished his mortal part. But he who has been earnest in the love of knowledge and of true wisdom, and has exercised his intellect more than any other part of him, must have thoughts immortal and divine, if he attain truth, and in so far as human nature is capable of sharing in immortality, he must altogether be immortal.[6]

The vastness of Plato's influence upon Western civilization was encapsulated in a few words by Alfred North Whitehead (1861–1947), one of the 20th century's most prominent philosophers. Whitehead wrote that the European philosophical tradition consisted of merely a "series of footnotes to Plato." It was that same philosophical tradition, shaped by Plato, that inspired the founding fathers of America to create a modern democracy, which in turn inspired the establishment of many other democracies around the world. Yet along the way, the heart of Plato's philosophy—the divinity of the human soul—was lost.

What was it, we might well ask, that caused the dictionary definition of "human being" to stray so far from Plato's lofty notion of who we are? Starting out as souls of divine origin, with the potential to manifest goodness, truth, and beauty in our lives, our self-definition as a species devolved into that of biological entities, chiefly distinguished by the ability to create and use complex tools.

To be fair, if the search for definitions of "human being" is pursued far enough, it will lead to adjectives such as "wise" with regard to our species of primates, *sapiens*. But that is as close as we come to any hint of a higher nature.

"Soul" exists in a category all its own in reference books. By contrast with *Homo sapiens*, which is uniformly defined in the terms of science, definitions of "soul" vary greatly. At one end of the spectrum soul is equated with spirit; at the other end it is equated with sentiments. A sampling of entries for "soul" in various dictionaries and encyclopedias includes the following: the spiritual principle embodied in human beings; the immaterial, animating principle of an individual life; the principle of life, feeling, and thought regarded as separate from the body; the part of the human being that partakes of divinity and is believed to survive the death of the body; the moral-spiritual part of human beings; the moral and emotional nature of human beings; the seat of human feelings and sentiments.

This wide assortment of definitions appears to reflect the myriad views of the soul held by philosophers, theologians, and scholars of different eras, cultures, and religions. From the ancient Egyptians, Chaldeans, and Chinese to the early Hebrews and Christians, beliefs differed substantially about the nature of the soul, its origin, its relationship to the physical body, and whether it existed at all. Some beliefs about the soul that are now divergent actually share common origins. Although Buddhism emerged from Hinduism, the Hindu concept of the soul was altered substantially by Buddhists. Likewise, Christian beliefs about the soul, once strongly influenced by the philosophers of ancient Greece, took some very different turns.

In the West, from the time of ancient Greece through the Middle Ages, it was commonly accepted that human beings were endowed with an immortal soul. With the Renaissance, beginning in the 14th century, the ideas of ancient Greece were revived along with a new philosophical quest to understand the nature of the soul. But with the Enlightenment and the scientific revolution that followed, the existence of the soul was thrown into doubt. In time, philosophers gave up arguing Plato's notion that soul precedes form—that the soul is the life principle animating the physical body, and that the body cannot exist without the soul. In the scientific worldview, for something to be real it had to be proven empirically. The soul, not being subject to such proofs, was split apart from the body and cast aside.

The figure initially responsible for this split, quite unintentionally so, has long been recognized as "the father of modern philosophy"—René Descartes (1596–1650). Nearly two millennia after Plato, Descartes undertook a parallel pursuit, but from a different angle. Whereas Plato and his teacher, Socrates, were the first philosophers to draw a distinction between soul and body, Descartes became the first to attempt to systematically analyze the *relationship* between the two. He sought to find a rational, scientific explanation for the way they interacted. But early on in his quest, Descartes found himself at an impasse. Resolving this impasse—which became known as the "mind-body dilemma" or "mind-body duality"—was to absorb the minds of philosophers for centuries thereafter.

The fact that Descartes' best-known legacy to the world was his pronouncement, "I think, therefore I am," turns out to have been a great historical irony. Deeply embedded in Western culture and imprinted on the minds of philosophy students everywhere, this dictum came to define the human being as *a thinking being,* above all. Paradoxically, Descartes had set out on his philosophical quest with a very different concept of the human being. A devoutly religious Catholic, he had sought to prove the existence of God and the immortality of the soul.

As his search unfolded, Descartes ran into difficulties, recorded in his *Meditations on the First Philosophy.* The source of his difficulties appears to have been twofold: the methods he used, plus the narrowing scope of philosophy by the 17th century. In the time of Socrates and Plato, the purpose of philosophy had been the pursuit of wisdom and truth—in the goal of creating a just and virtuous society. In the age of enlightenment, philosophers sought above all to eradicate the ignorance and superstition of the Dark Ages. They attempted to discover that which was irrefutable by the use of reason. To know a thing with certitude became more important than penetrating underlying meanings and causes. Thus the question of *how* the soul and body were interrelated became more important than conjecturing about which came first, or about what might have been in the mind of the Creator.

Descartes was a scientist before turning to philosophy. He had set out to penetrate "the world created by God" by finding out *how* "the individual consciousness comes to know itself, its God, its world."[7] His method, adapted from science, was to rigorously doubt every philosophical notion that he could not absolutely prove by reason alone. It turned out, however, that his approach was incompatible with the metaphysical subjects of his inquiry. Increasingly, as his *Meditations* progressed, the initial aims—to prove the existence of God and the immortality of the soul—fell by the wayside.

In the end, there was only one truth that survived Descartes' rigorous method of challenging everything that was not provable by logic and reason. The single reality that he was unable to doubt, in any measure whatsoever, was the fact of his own existence. Since he had arrived at that unquestionable fact by means of thought, he made the logical deduction that he was "a thinking thing." And thus was born the celebrated dictum, "I think, therefore I am."

Having demonstrated to his own satisfaction that he was a thinker, Descartes went on to grapple with the question of *how* his thinking self was related to his physical self. For him, thinking was the defining attribute of the soul (a word he used interchangeably with mind), and the nature of the soul was spiritual. By contrast, the body was of a substance that he called "extension"—it extended into space. Descartes thus posited that human beings were "spirits that occupy a mechanical body made of extended substance."[8] But how were these spirits and their mechanical bodies connected? His question framed a philosophical enigma that endured for centuries and assumed his name—"the Cartesian impasse."

Interestingly, in Descartes' personal belief system there was no doubt or uncertainty. The main tenets of his belief were much like Plato's: soul and body were united by God in an intimate union, the soul animated the body, and the two were inseparable. He even theorized about the *locus* of the interaction of soul and body: the pineal gland in the brain. But because his beliefs could not be substantiated by his philosophical methodology, he was forced to conclude that soul and body were made of different substances—one gross and the other subtle—and that they were in fact *separable*. At the time of death, while the body was subject to destruction, he maintained that the soul was not.

Thus it happened that while Descartes had set out to discover the relationship between soul and body, he ended up splitting them apart and finding it impossible to reunite them in a way that explained their interrelationship. The Cartesian impasse became the preoccupation of countless philosophers between the 17th and 20th centuries. Thinking became accepted as the primary attribute of the human being, from Descartes onward. But the burning question remained: *how* does thinking or thought interact with the physical body, which appears to be made of entirely different substance.

Endless philosophical theories sprang forth about the mechanism behind the mind-body relationship. In the metaphysical atmosphere of the 17th century, it was still widely assumed that God was the causal agent. With the 18th century's Enlightenment, the need for rational proofs of philosophical arguments diminished the certitude that God was responsible. By the 19th century, the influence of scientific materialism had begun to displace both God *and* philosophy. For many modern age scientists, the soul simply had no reality. The primacy of philosophy—once deemed "the science of all sciences" because it had sought to unravel the mysteries of life—was challenged by physical science, which sought to prove what was verifiable by repeatable experiments.

What was empirically verifiable about the human being, for modern scientists, was the physical body—the biological aspect of ourselves proven to exist through the physical senses and physical tools of measurement. This perspective dovetailed perfectly with the findings of English naturalist Charles Darwin (1809–1882), whose seminal work, *On the Origin of the Species*, posited that humans shared a common biological ancestry with animals. Darwin came to believe that the human species, *Homo sapiens*, was purely the result of biological evolution; our species had emerged from animal species by means of "natural selection."

With the waxing influence of the scientific worldview, in the 19th century, there occurred a waning of academic interest in the soul. The part of ourselves once seen as an aspect of divinity came to be equated with the mind, which was seen as the organ of consciousness. Later, the mind became loosely equated with the brain, the physical organ that humans share with animals. Psychology, the new science of the mind that emerged in the 19th century, focused mainly on the *physical* aspects of consciousness linked to the brain and nervous system. In the end, the divine soul became a casualty of the worldview of empirical science.

Centuries of philosophical ruminations about the relationship between body and soul culminated with the work of William James (1841–1910), the preeminent American psychologist and philosopher of his time. It was James, who had studied physical sciences and medicine at Harvard, where he also taught physiology, psychology, and philosophy, and where he established the first laboratory of psychology in the United States, who brought the quest initiated by Descartes to its logical end. His own investigations led him to conclude that unraveling the mind-body mystery was beyond the capacity of science.

James was the last in a long stream of philosophers who had devoted their lives to understanding how the invisible dimension of the human being related to the visible one. His main contribution to this field was *Principles of Psychology* (1890), an effort to integrate science, philosophy, and introspection. It included an examination of all theories about the mind-body interaction, such as the "mind-stuff theory," which posited pieces of "mind-stuff" common to mind and brain that allowed them to interact. When all such hypotheses fell apart under his rigorous analysis, he set forth his own unique theory. James asserted a direct correspondence between states of mind (states of consciousness) and brain processes. In the end, however, unable to account for the connecting mechanism or to prove his theory empirically, he was forced to concede intellectual defeat.

For a span of more than two centuries, from the time that Descartes had first formulated the problem, many of the best human minds had struggled to comprehend the mind-body duality but had come up empty-handed. James sensed that the duality was more apparent than real. He knew there had to be a solution to the dilemma, but realized that finding the solution required a greater capacity of perception than that which existed in his time. Given that the academic world was dominated by the "finite and separatist view of things," he predicted that the philosophical quandary would remain unsolved for generations.

Just as James had foreseen, that "finite and separatist view" reigned throughout most of the 20th century. Mind-body studies were divided into separate spheres, then subdivided further into specialties and sub-specialties. Based on the Newtonian model of the universe-as-machine, mind, body, and bodily parts were perceived as separable elements to be disassembled and treated in isolation from the whole. Freud (1856–1939), who came to realize that the mind could create physiological symptoms, vastly expanded the frontiers of mind to include the unconscious dimension. Jung (1875–1961) gravitated toward the realm of higher consciousness in search of the soul. But in keeping with the medical model of psychiatry and the pragmatic thrust of modern science, most studies of the mind were geared toward treating illness.

The aspect of mind once seen as emanating from divinity had been exiled from academia by the late 19th century, with the exception of departments of theology. Virtually alone in bucking this trend was William James, whose most enduring legacy may have redounded to the benefit of spiritual seekers. Admittedly unable to explain the mind-body interaction with the tools of science, James had nevertheless refused to entirely abandon the quest. Instead he took a different tack and set out to validate the soul on its own terms. Rather than pursuing the question of *how* the soul affected the body, he decided to demonstrate the fact that it did so. In *The Varieties of Religious Experience* (1902), his classic study, he sought to illustrate the "efficacy" of the soul through the lives of individuals who had been permanently "converted"—or transformed—by spiritual experiences.

James had been uniquely prepared for this task—both by personal experience and by family history. In his late twenties, he had undergone a prolonged episode of suicidal depression from which he had emerged by an act of sheer will, after having read an essay on free will. His own ability to transform an emotionally crippling condition into a state of optimism had served as proof to him of the limits of "scientific determinism." Fatefully, the soil of that experience had been cultivated by his having come of age in a household permeated by metaphysical discussions of God, the nature of the soul, and the spiritual world.

James' father, Henry James, Sr., was a philosopher and social theorist who had been actively engaged in the religious ferment of his age. In mid-19th century America, many philosophers and theologians were absorbed in a dynamic quest to understand the living reality of the soul—the spirit of a human being—apart from the tenets of faith set forth by organized religion. Among the acquaintances of James' father was Ralph Waldo Emerson (1803–1882), founder of the New England Transcendentalist movement. As it happened, Emerson had been visiting the James' home on the day of William's birth and, by one account, became William's godfather.

Emerson, who had begun his career as an ordained minister, had come to reject all religious doctrines and institutions. He believed that God could be found in the human soul, which he saw as a portion of the "divine oversoul"—the source of spiritual wisdom that pervaded all of created life. Emerson's famous doctrine of self-reliance grew out of his belief that God was directly accessible (internally, in the form of spiritual guidance) to every soul who made the effort to realize his or her spiritual potential. Along with Thoreau and other transcendentalists, he viewed the individual's awakening to the soul's reality and divinity, through spiritual experience, as the source of inner peace and harmony.

One of the strongest influences upon American transcendentalists, such as Emerson and James' father, was Emanuel Swedenborg (1688–1772)—the Swedish scientist, mystic, philosopher, and theologian. Swedenborg's writings, based largely on his inner perceptions of the world of spiritual realities, stressed the absolute unity of God, the divine origin of all created forms. The separation between man and God, according to Swedenborg, had resulted from man's misuse of free will. It was, therefore, up to human beings to reestablish the human-divine relationship through the right use of will, by following the example set forth by the Christ.

Unlike Swedenborg, Emerson, and other American transcendentalists, William James was not a mystic by nature. Though he shared their conviction of the dynamic potency of the human soul, he was fundamentally a man of science—one who resonated deeply with the pragmatic thrust of the Age of Reason.[9] What interested him most about the soul, the human spirit, was its "efficacy." He wanted to discover *how* a person's experience of God affected that person's experience of life, and whether such spiritual experience transcended differences in religious belief systems.

James defined religion in the broadest and most universal terms. Religion, he wrote, "consists of the belief that there is an unseen order, and that our supreme good lies in harmoniously adjusting ourselves thereto."[10] He was interested only in what he called *personal* religion, or direct personal communion with the divine, as distinct from institutional religion. In personal religion, as he defined it, "the relation goes direct from heart to heart, from soul to soul, between man and his maker."[11] This, he asserted, was the religion of the Christ, the Buddha, and Mohammed—of the founders of all world religions and major sects.

Autobiographical accounts of this type of "personal religion" fill the pages of *The Varieties of Religious Experience*. James refers to many of the individuals he investigated—mystics and saints of different epochs and cultures—as "geniuses in the religious line." They were, in his view, the "ripe fruits" of all religions. By documenting innumerable instances of lives that had been permanently transformed by religious experience, he felt he had presented irrefutable evidence of the influence of the Divine upon human beings.

So persuasive was the evidence gathered by James, he believed that science could not reasonably ignore it. While spiritual phenomena could not be explained, as yet, he had compiled voluminous documentation that a higher power *was* capable of transforming human consciousness. In the hope of eventual validation, he proposed a new "science of religion" that would objectively assess the evidence. Though he never lived to see that kind of validation, the influence of *Varieties* has been incalculable—particularly *outside* the walls of academia. James' seminal work substantiated the reality of Spirit in a way that provided solid footing for countless spiritual seekers throughout the 20th century.

Although ahead of his time in many ways, James was also a man of his age. "The greatest discovery of my generation," he wrote, "is that human beings can alter their lives by altering their attitudes of mind."[12] Starting in the late 19th century, explorations of mind and spirit ranged far and wide. Educated Westerners were increasingly drawn to controversial metaphysical phenomena ranging from hypnosis to spiritual séances. The "new thought" movement, also known as "mental healing," attracted significant attention. Based on the principle of "mind over matter," its various branches—from Christian Science to Religious Science—taught that the mind could *heal* the physical body, the inverse of Freud's realization that the mind could make the body ill.

And then, toward the end of the 19th century, a different stream of thought began to enter the world, offering answers to many of the quandaries that had long preoccupied philosophers and seekers of truth. Known as the Ageless Wisdom, this vast body of knowledge provided keys to the most elusive mysteries confronting the human mind. This knowledge originated from a higher plane of reality than ours: it issued from the subtle realm of consciousness that constitutes the Spiritual Kingdom.[13] Masters of Wisdom dwelling in this 5th kingdom in nature transmitted the teachings telepathically to advanced members of the 4th kingdom, our own, in the goal of preparing humanity for the new stage of consciousness that will emerge in the Aquarian Age.[14]

Contained within this great body of knowledge are ancient esoteric teachings from the East, concerning invisible aspects of life, which have been updated for modern scientific minds of the West.[15] Unraveling many of the great enigmas that had frustrated scientists and philosophers for centuries, these teachings served to illustrate the adage that a problem cannot be solved on its own level. The requisite insights to long-standing human dilemmas literally came from a higher dimension—from enlightened Beings who collectively embody "the expression of the accumulated wisdom of the ages."[16]

Prime among the mysteries unlocked by the wisdom teachings was the "Cartesian impasse." The solution to the mind-body conundrum was contained in the first transmission of higher knowledge, received between 1875 and 1890 by Helena Petrovna Blavatsky (1831–1891)—the Russian-born mystic, author, and co-founder of the Theosophical Society.[17] It was explained in *The Secret Doctrine*, which draws heavily upon esoteric science from the East, that spirit and matter—mind and body—are *not* two different substances as they appear to our physical senses. They are one substance, emanating from one source of life, but vibrating at vastly different frequencies. At the lowest frequency, this energy-substance appears as dense matter; at the highest frequency it is pure spirit. Spirit is matter at its highest vibration; matter is spirit at its lowest vibration.

When Blavatsky's writings first appeared, most scientists still believed that the atom was the basic building block of matter and was, as such, indivisible. She asserted that not only was the atom divisible, as physicists later discovered, but infinitely so. This reality underlies the Eastern view of the essentially illusory nature of matter—the notion that matter only *appears* to be solid and permanent. The ancient sages realized that "forms of matter are whirl-pools in a busy stream" and that "the world is *maya*, an illusion," as noted by Freddy Silva, a writer in the field of energy research.[18] Silva describes the phenomenon this way:

> Should the spin of an object exceed that which is de-tectable by the eye, it becomes both intangible and in-visible. Alternatively, if its spin rate slows down, the object appears to "physicalize." In fact, substitute the words "spin," "vibration," or "frequency" for "spirit" and we come ever closer to understanding the nature of the Universe.[19]

The fact that matter and energy *are* of the same substance was demonstrated by the 20th century world of physics. This reality is encapsulated in the mathematical equation that profoundly changed our world: $E=mc^2$. Formulated by Albert Einstein (1879–1955), this equation posited that particles of matter—moving at high enough velocities (i.e., the speed of light squared)—are convertible into energy. It says, in essence, that energy and mass are interchangeable. The ultimate proof of this equation was the explosion of the atomic bomb at the close of World War II, a tragic irony for Einstein, who was by nature a pacifist.

Einstein was also a mystic. He apprehended the oneness of the cosmos in the way of all true mystics, writing, "The mystical is the most beautiful emotion we can experience," and "the power of all true art and science."[20] He also spoke of the "oneness of all knowl-edge," a phrase that evokes the substance of *The Secret Doctrine*, whose subtitle is: *The Synthesis of Science, Religion and Philosophy*. As it turned out, Einstein was deeply familiar with the esoteric knowledge revealed by modern theosophy. According to a niece of his, who knew him well, he always kept a copy of *The Secret Doctrine* on his desk.[21]

The literal meaning of theosophy is *divine wisdom*. The goal of the theosophical movement that grew up around Blavatsky and her writings was to demonstrate to the scientific West, the Eastern con-

cept of the oneness of life lying behind all its diverse expressions—
from the spiritual oneness of human beings to the essential unity
of truth shared by religion, philosophy, and science. To Blavatsky,
theosophy was "neither a religion, a science, nor a philosophy, but a
definite body of teaching [that] endeavors to synthesize these three
ways of looking at life."[22] Its aim was to foster human brotherhood
by exposing "the actual basis of religion and scientific proofs of the
existence and permanence of the higher Self."[23]

This higher Self is, in essence, the divine soul of Plato. But
Theosophy vastly amplified our understanding of the soul and its
evolutionary unfoldment. It showed that evolution is intrinsic to *all*
of life in our universe—that it occurs not only within the realm of
physical form among organisms like bipedal primates, as scientists
had discovered, but also within the realm of consciousness. Souls
evolve just as physical bodies do. In fact, according to the wisdom
teachings, the very purpose of human existence is the evolution of
the soul—the perfecting of the aspect of ourselves that partakes of
divinity.

The wisdom teachings explain that evolution occurs in cycles
covering vast stretches of time—great "turnings of the wheel of
time"—and that different cycles serve different evolutionary purposes. Buried in the distant past of our species were long epochs
during which the evolution of the outer form was predominant.
Other cycles, such as the one we are now entering, are primarily
directed at the evolution of the consciousness *within* the form. The
divine purpose for the coming age is to awaken the human soul to
its spiritual origin and destiny. In order to further prepare humanity for this awakening, the Guides of the Race[24] transmitted a second set of wisdom teachings, between the years 1919 and 1949.

These teachings, conveyed through British-born Alice A.
Bailey (1880–1949), focus on the transition from our current point
of evolution—in which the rational mind or intellect has been con-
ceived as the pinnacle of human development—to an era in which
the divine soul of humanity will become conscious of itself. In the
writings of Alice Bailey[25] it is said that as the coming age unfolds,

the human soul, "a divinity" for Plato, will fulfill its long dormant potential. It will be the soul and not the mind—more precisely the soul *utilizing* the mind—that will come to influence the course of human events.

Countless philosophical enigmas swirling around the soul for centuries were explained in the Bailey books. For example, one of the questions that had preoccupied Descartes was the *locus* of the soul-body interaction. He had speculated that they joined at the pineal gland in the brain, and was later proven correct, *in part*: the soul is anchored at a subtle energy center *adjacent* to the pineal gland, according to the Tibetan master, the source of most of the Bailey books. The fact that our physical bodies are vitalized by subtle energy bodies—a basic tenet of Eastern medicine—was *the* crucial "missing link" for Westerners wrestling with the mind-body dilemma.[26] These subtle bodies have seven major centers, or *chakras*. The soul is anchored at *two* centers in the energy body: the crown chakra, next to the pineal gland, and the heart chakra.

Still another mystery solved by the esoteric wisdom of the East was one that had puzzled William James, who asked: How do "religious geniuses" come to be? What creates these "best fruits of religion" that are "the best things that history has to show"? In the Bailey books we learn that such individuals are old souls reaching the end of the long cycle of human evolution. After countless incarnations, having assimilated the gamut of human experience, the soul awakens to its true nature and approaches the Path of Return.[27] By treading this path, and conquering the physical nature, the soul evolves into a living expression of divinity on earth. What actually transforms such individuals is the light of their own souls, which in turn attracts the transforming light of spiritual guides and teachers.

Also supplied by these modern esoteric teachings was the missing element in Plato's quest for an ideal society. On the level of the individual, Plato understood the mechanism by which the divinity latent within the human soul is gradually revealed. He was familiar with the laws of karma and reincarnation by which the consciousness of the individual evolves. At the end of *The Republic*, in a section entitled "The Immortality of the Soul and the Rewards of Goodness," he recounts the Myth of Er—an allegory depicting how the soul's actions in one lifetime determine its experience in subsequent lives. But he may have been less clear about the mechanism responsible for the evolution of society as a whole.

Plato advocated two primary measures for creating the ideal society: adopting the highest moral laws, and producing the best systems of education. In the light of the wisdom teachings, however, it becomes evident that creating an ideal society will depend upon the evolutionary leap in consciousness that humanity is only now approaching. It awaits the time when *a critical mass* of individuals willingly embraces such Platonic ideals as Truth and Goodness. The worldview undergirding all human societies, based on the *apparent* separation of physical forms, will have to be replaced by a realization that all forms are unified by a single indwelling Spirit. When that occurs, the good of the individual will be seen as inextricably linked to the good of the whole—the key to any ideal community or society.

The wisdom teachings hold out great promise for the coming world era. Although the evolution of consciousness proceeds one soul at a time—by means of the spiritual awakening of each individual—the process as a whole is being accelerated as Earth moves through space into new fields of cosmic energy. For some time now, the energies of the constellation Aquarius and other cosmic rays have been stimulating human sensitivity to more subtle dimensions of life. The effects of these energies can be seen in the fact that millions of individuals around the globe are awakening, perceiving that we are more than *Homo sapiens,* and searching for higher truth.

This collective search will increasingly bring to light the fact that human beings are essentially spiritual beings existing in physical bodies. During our periodic sojourns on earth, these bodies (along with our emotions and minds) provide the means by which we gain life experience. The fruit of this experience emerges near the journey's end, as we awaken to the fact that we are actually Souls, infused with a spark of divinity. Over the course of lifetimes, the sacred fire of our individual nature is gradually forged into a unique expression of the Good, the True, and the Beautiful. In the coming age, as these divine sparks blend and fuse in the light of true understanding, the higher purpose of the human kingdom will be fulfilled.

Though we remain unconscious of who we are for eons of time, human souls are actually pilgrims on a journey toward the light. The spiritual journey proceeds in stages, each of which has a specific goal. The goal of the first stage is to "Know thyself," an adage harking back to the ancient Greek philosophers and the Oracle at Delphi. Alice Bailey expands upon this timeworn precept, pointing toward the stage that now awaits humanity:

> "Know thyself" is the first great injunction and long is the process of attaining that knowledge. "Know the Self" comes next and when that is achieved, man knows not only himself but all selves.[28]

When humanity comes to know the Self, and to realize the oneness of all Selves, we will have learned to make peace, not war, and to protect, not destroy, the environment that sustains the lives of all creatures on Earth. When that time finally comes, our planet will be recognized, in the words of physicist Gary Zukav, as "the home that we as immortal souls have chosen for our learning [that] terribly needs care and healing." Zukav adds, "As the human species awakens to itself as a collection of immortal souls learning together, care for the environment and the earth will become a matter of the heart." [29]

NOTES

1   The Age of Reason, characterized by a belief in the power of reason, was born with the European Enlightenment of the 17th and 18th centuries.

2   Anderson, Fulton H. Introduction to Plato's *Symposium*, 7.

3   Plato, *The Timaeus*, 73.

4   *Ibid.*, xxi.

5   Plato, *The Republic*, 14.
6   Plato, *The Timaeus*, 73.
7   Burnham, Douglas, and James Fieser, "René Descartes (1596-1650)," *Internet Encyclopedia of Philosophy* (accessed November 15, 2004).
8   *Ibid.*
9   Later in his life, on the eve of formulating the lectures that became *The Varieties of Religious Experience*, James had a mystical encounter that strengthened his intuitive understanding of the soul's reality.
10 James, *The Varieties of Religious Experience*, 57.
11 *Ibid.*, 37.
12 Ross Robertson, "Synchronicity Goes to Hollywood," *What is Enlightenment?* magazine, Nov.-Feb. 2004-5, 73.
13 See Chapter 9 for an explanation of the evolutionary process that forms Masters of Wisdom.
14 In addition to H. P. Blavatsky and Alice A. Bailey, whose works are cited here, other significant purveyors of esoteric knowledge of the late 19th and early 20th centuries include Helena Roerich, Rudolf Steiner, Annie Besant, and Anna Bonus Kingsford.
15 Esoteric knowledge is further defined in Chapter 2.
16 Bailey, *The Externalisation of the Hierarchy*, 701.
17 H. P. Blavatsky was a seminal figure in the history of modern esoteric thought. Although aspects of her legacy were controversial, our approach has been to honor truths conveyed by individuals in this stream of thought, without necessarily endorsing all their activities.
18 Silva, *Secrets in the Fields*, 266.
19 *Ibid.*
20 Frank, *Einstein*, 284.
21 Head and Cranston, *Reincarnation*, 513. Further evidence of this appears at the following website: http://users.aol.com/uniwldarts/uniworld.artisans.guild/einstein.html#anchor213593.
22 *Ibid.*, 488.
23 *Ibid.*, 493 (quotation from H. P. Blavatsky, reprinted in an article from *Theosophy and the Theosophical Movement*, 1890).
24 See Glossary.
25 Five volumes were written by Alice Bailey herself; the rest were transmitted by the Tibetan Master, Djwhal Khul.
26 Teachings on the interrelationships of soul, mind, and body (based on ancient Eastern texts) were also made available by other figures in the broad theosophical movement and by British Orientalists who began translating Eastern texts into English in the 19th century.
27 See Glossary.
28 Bailey, *A Treatise on Cosmic Fire*, 1237.
29 Cousineau, *Soul*, 172.

CHAPTER TWO

THE HIGHER SELF

The Soul has two eyes.
One looks at time passing,
The other sends forth its gaze into eternity.

~*Angelus Silesius*

THE "SELF" IS ONE of many names for the Soul that are used almost interchangeably in esoteric literature. The practice of capitalizing the first letter is a symbolic way of acknowledging the divine aspect of human nature. The intent is to differentiate the inner or higher Self from the outer or lower self—the persona or personality. Ancient Vedic texts made the distinction between Self and *not-self*—between the part of us that is real and immortal, and the part that is unreal and transitory.

Understanding the Self requires a profoundly new way of perceiving reality. To begin with, it calls for a fundamental reorientation to space and time. With all the wonders of the Space Age, and of the Information Age, the content of most of our lives still revolves around the present moment. The immense technological breakthroughs of recent times have not, in themselves, expanded human consciousness regarding our place in the larger scheme of things. In fact, the instant availability of news and the personalization of information appear to have had the reverse effect. Surveys show a marked decline in the average attention span and a sharply narrowed range of individual interests.

To comprehend the nature of the soul, as described in the Ageless Wisdom, we have to shift gears and move in the opposite direction. So vast is the scheme of the soul's evolutionary journey through time and space that our minds tend to shut down on first exposure. Our normal frame of reference is simply inadequate to assimilate the immensity of scale. The soul's journey cannot be measured in centuries or even millennia, but rather in *yugas* and *kalpas*.[1] And while the human soul unfolds in the visible, concrete world when in physical incarnation,[2] the spiritual Self also unfolds in higher, more subtle dimensions of reality inaccessible to the physical senses.

Science and technology have contributed immensely toward expanding human awareness of cosmic evolution. The astonishing pictures taken by the Hubbell Space Telescope reveal stars dying and being born billions of years ago, within galaxies whose dimensions are measured in hundreds of thousands of *light-years*. While most of us still struggle to fathom the "simple" fact that we learned as children, that our planet is part of the Milky Way Galaxy, the reality of Earth's place in the scheme of things is infinitely more complex. We inhabit one of eight recognized planets revolving around our Sun,[3] which is one star out of several *billions* of stars in the Milky Way, which is one of *billions* of galaxies in our universe.

If the vastness of space staggers the imagination, the vastness of time can prove equally elusive to the concrete mind. Our star, the Sun, has been evolving for over four billion years. Scientists estimate that life on our particular planet has taken many hundreds of millions of years to evolve into its present state, with its infinite number and variety of existing species. In the continually unfolding story of life on Earth, our own species—which comprises the 4th kingdom in nature according to esoteric science[4]—is a fairly new phenomenon.

Set against the backdrop of hundreds of millions of years, the emergence of the human kingdom is relatively recent—whether we accept the shorter timetable of exoteric science or the far longer one presented by esoteric teachings.[5] In these teachings, it is said that human evolution began twenty-one million years ago, when a germ of divine mind was implanted in bodies belonging to the most advanced representatives of the animal kingdom of the time. That seed of divine consciousness set us apart from the animal kingdom, and set us off on an unfathomably long evolutionary journey to discover our true identity as spiritual beings in physical forms.

Today, twenty-one million years later, the journey's end still remains out of our range of sight. Yet as countless individuals around the globe have begun to realize, we are on the brink of a great leap forward in consciousness.[6] To aid humanity in approaching this new stage of evolution, the Masters of Wisdom began updating ancient teachings over a century ago and transmitting them through disciples living in the West. The esoteric knowledge they conveyed about our origin and destiny was intended to lay the groundwork for the next two thousand-year cycle, or age, during which it is predicted that the soul of humanity will achieve a degree of awareness previously unknown.

As the word "esoteric" implies, the body of truth constituting the Ageless Wisdom has been largely hidden or veiled throughout most of recorded history. It was kept alive during humanity's darkest ages by a "golden thread" of knowledge secretly passed on from one isolated seeker to another. For many reasons, this knowledge was generally feared and often associated in the public mind with strange and dubious practices. But the word esoteric—from the Greek root "eso"—simply means "inner or inward, hidden from view."

Esoteric knowledge concerns the inner or subjective aspect of life, as opposed to that which is outer, objective, and *exoteric*. The wisdom teachings deal with invisible energies and forces emanating from subtler realms that vitalize and organize the outer, physical forms of our concrete, material world. If this sounds mystifying, consider the fact that our world is permeated by invisible forces such as electricity, magnetism, and gravity, which most of us barely comprehend. To the non-scientific mind, the nature of electricity remains an impenetrable mystery, albeit one upon which our daily existence has become totally dependent.

To understand the reality of the soul, in an esoteric sense, even more is required of us than expanding our perceptions of time and space. We also have to learn to think in terms of energies and forces that our physical senses cannot perceive. The soul, which has been described as a "vortex of force,"[7] is said to exist on the invisible plane of universal mind. Conscious on its own plane, it is a subjective force that guides the objective, outer life of the persona or personality on the physical plane. The soul serves this guiding function throughout the journey of human incarnation, long before the outer personality becomes aware of its existence.

The invisible world of the soul is governed by two interrelated esoteric principles. Both principles have been demonstrated by exoteric or physical science during the past century, to varying degrees. The first is: *all is energy.* Proven initially by Einstein's formula, $E=mc^2$, this notion has been progressively brought home to us by ongoing discoveries in quantum physics. On the sub-atomic level of life, all that exists is a churning sea of energies. What appears as dense physical matter is actually an illusion. It is largely space, containing sub-atomic particles vibrating at different frequencies. Paul Brunton, the British writer and mystic observed:

> Nineteenth century science pedestalled the theory that life is a product of matter. Twentieth century science... is watching matter dissolve into electrons...a mere collection of electrified particles, which elude sight and sense! The step from this state into the matterless world beyond is not such a far one—intellectually.[8]

The second esoteric principle is: *thought directs energy,* or as more commonly stated, *energy follows thought.* Quantum physics, which deals with the invisible universe, has moved toward demonstrating this principle by showing that the presence of the observer in a scientific experiment affects the appearance of what is observed.[9] At the sub-atomic level, energy exists as wave-particles, with the potential to become either one. The effect of the observer is to turn that potential into either a wave or a particle (a separate *quantum* or packet of energy). When observation ceases, or when consciousness is withdrawn, undefined wave-particles reappear.

Esoteric science offers an explanation for this phenomenon, based on the mind's capacity to influence energetic substance. The human mind is able to direct energy by forming thoughts. Thought-*forms*, like all forms, carry energy waves or vibrations—vibrations powerful enough to be registered by our subtle senses. Biologist Rupert Sheldrake has demonstrated, for example, that most people know when someone is staring at them.[10] In sub-atomic energy experiments, it could well be that the focused vibrations of observers' thought-forms serve to momentarily "freeze" wave-particles into separate forms, as if a snapshot had been taken. When the observation ends, i.e., when the focus of thought is directed elsewhere, the *appearance* of separate forms again gives way to formlessness.

The impact of thought on *visible* substance has been strikingly demonstrated in experiments with water pioneered by the Japanese scientist, Masaru Emoto.[11] When water is frozen, ice crystals form patterns that reflect surrounding thought vibrations. Even without the physical presence of a "thinker," words pasted on bottles of water appear to have remarkable power. Words such as "hate" and "war" produce jagged-edged, malformed crystal patterns, whereas "love" and "peace" produce crystals of awe-inspiring symmetry and beauty. Given the fact that our bodies are largely composed of water, these experiments suggest that our thoughts leave powerful imprints upon our *own* physical substance, as well as upon other people and life forms around us.

The capacity for thought, for thinking about ideas, is what distinguishes the human kingdom from the other visible kingdoms of nature. All other kingdoms possess consciousness or sentiency in some degree, but only ours has the potential for developed thought and self-conscious awareness. We alone have minds that can process the torrent of vibrations flooding in from our environment and decide where to direct our thoughts. The human mind is like a radio dial that can tune in to different stations. Wherever we direct our thoughts, energy follows in the form of words and actions.

When the soul awakens, we consciously turn the metaphorical dial to stations of a higher frequency.

Throughout most of our very long history as an evolving species, human thought has focused on the material plane of existence. We have been preoccupied with gathering food, finding shelter, reproducing our species, and other aspects of survival. Only in recent millennia did members of our species, beyond an exceptional few, begin to think about things beyond self-preservation. And only in recent years have large numbers of people begun to consciously direct their thoughts to more subtle realms of existence. Satiated with material comforts and alarmed by the state of our world, individuals everywhere have begun to search for spiritual truth—to focus their thoughts on higher planes of reality.

This widening search for truth reflects the fact that the human soul is awakening, as foreseen by the Masters of Wisdom. This awakening, however incipient, represents a ripening of the seed of divine mind implanted in early humankind. It is the fruit of countless cycles of incarnation extending over the course of millions of years. During that time, the incarnating "unit of consciousness" has been virtually fused with the outer persona, directing its attention to life in the material world. Now, as we approach the latter stages of the path of human evolution, countless individual souls are registering the existence of higher dimensions of life.

The soul is sometimes called "the Thinker." It is the part of us that learns to navigate the higher mental plane—the dimension of abstract mind that can function totally apart from the physical world of the senses. Thinking, as we know, is also the source of human creativity. The human being is endowed with the potential to "think things through into manifestation," or to create with the mind—to clothe subtle thought-forms with denser substance and bring them into the physical world. It is as creative beings that we are "made in the image of God." Yet only now are we discovering the *higher* purpose of our capacity for creative thought—a discovery that sets the stage for the next phase of human evolution.

In the coming age, we are told, human beings will become *co-*

creators on Earth with Higher Forces. Over the course of the next 2,000 years, as the soul of humanity further emerges, members of the 4th or human kingdom will develop the ability to work in co-operation with members of the 5th or spiritual kingdom. Advanced souls, consciously treading the spiritual path, will learn to receive thought impressions from the inner planes conveying aspects of divine will or purpose. By apprehending "ideas held in the Mind of God" and bringing them into manifestation, these souls will cooperate in creating a new, spiritual civilization.

To grasp the notion of "the Mind of God," and the significance of what lies ahead, we need a working understanding of what God is—and of the relationship between God and human beings. God clearly did not die, as was widely predicted in the last century, but neither did God survive the modern era in a form comprehensible to minds shaped by the scientific worldview. Modern science annihilated ancient concepts of deity by replacing *beliefs* about our world—based on biblical precepts and religious doctrines—with proven facts. Left unanswered by science, however, are all the ultimate questions, ranging from the nature of the force that created our universe and the intelligence behind its visible order, to the purpose and meaning of human life. Conceding the lack of answers, a recent scientific film about the cosmos began with the statement, "We live in a mystery. It's called the universe."[12]

Interestingly, a number of contemporary scientists who were once atheists or agnostics became convinced of the existence of a Higher Order through their own research findings.[13] This is especially evident among those engaged in probing life on the scale of the unfathomably vast and the imperceptibly small—the outer edges of our visible universe and the invisible world of subatomic particles. Their recognition of the inherent intelligence of life appears to have undermined the prevailing scientific view of the universe as a great machine, composed of separable parts, with no intrinsic consciousness. Referring to this unraveling worldview, the English physicist Sir James Jeans observed, "The Universe begins to look more like a great thought, than a great machine."[14]

But if the universe is a great thought, there must, then, exist a Great Thinker. The discoveries of many modern scientists have led them back to the fundamental question about *the nature* of the creative intelligence behind our visible universe. An answer to this question that makes sense of our world, though it may sound at first like a paradox, is presented in the wisdom teachings. God is defined as "the One, the All and the many"—a single entity with infinite expressions. As described by the Tibetan master in the books of Alice Bailey, this entity is an all-encompassing *Life* that contains lesser lives, both visible and invisible, existing at vastly different levels of consciousness.

Conceptually, the picture that emerges is that of *conscious lives* within *ever more conscious Lives*, or *gods* within *Gods*—a plural notion of deity that harks back to the ancients' usage of "the gods." At the outermost edges of our imagining, on a scale nearly inconceivable to human beings, there is a deity only briefly alluded to in the teachings. It is an immense cosmic presence expressing through seven different solar systems, of which our solar system is one. The name used to describe this Life, in whose infinite folds we exist, is "The One About Whom Naught Can Be Said." This cosmic Being is, simply put, beyond our grasp.

At the level of our own solar system, we begin to have glimmerings of understanding. The technical name of the deity that governs the systemic life of our Sun is the solar "logos," a word used in Greek philosophy to designate the "rational principal that governs and develops the universe."[15] In esoteric teachings, the solar Logos is the life-giving Intelligence that ensouls and brings into manifestation the planets, or planetary Lives, within its orbit. The solar Logos is the conscious entity behind the organized life of our solar system. Likewise, our earth is ensouled by a conscious entity—a *planetary* Logos—whose life contains all the kingdoms of nature.

Countless names and poetic metaphors have been used by the world's religions to evoke the essence of the Divine Being that has been called the God of our universe. The ancient Hindu sages who composed the *Bhagavad-Gita* alternately called this entity "the

Great Spirit," "the Oversoul," "Mighty Lord," "Self everlasting." Shri Krishna describes the breadth of this Being's consciousness in a few sublimely chosen words: "Having pervaded the entire universe with a fragment of myself, I remain."

The human soul's relationship to the God of our universe has been depicted in countless ways across the ages. A mystical perception of the soul's connection to the furthermost reaches of our cosmos was left to us by Fyodor Dostoyevsky, in the words of a fictional holy Elder:

> In his rapture he wept even for the stars that shone on him from the abyss [of space]... It was as if threads from all those innumerable worlds of God came together in his soul.[16]

Closer to home, the soul's relationship to the lord of our more immediate world, the planetary Logos, is depicted symbolically in one of the names given to God in the Judeo-Christian bible: "The One in Whom we live and move and have our being." According to the Tibetan master, a fundamental esoteric truth about life on Earth is expressed in this name.

> [It is the] basis of the relation which exists between the unit soul, functioning in the human body, and God. It determines also...the relation between soul and *soul*. We live in an ocean of energies, and all these energies are closely interrelated and constitute the one synthetic energy body of our planet.[17]

God is the name given to the conscious Life of Earth in the wisdom teachings. The Tibetan master refers to our planetary Logos as the "One Life" and the "sum total of organized lives." The nature of this Life is dual: it consists both of consciousness and physical form, as do all the lesser lives within it. Forms are composed of matter from the earth's outer substance; human souls are "fragments" of the Oversoul. Being made of the same spiritual substance, the soul is intrinsically aware of its relationship to the Oversoul and the One Life—an awareness that exists on the soul's plane before it is registered by the concrete mind. Both in spirit and in matter, the human being is, metaphorically, a cell in the body of God.

Our ability to perceive the life of our planet as a single body, to actually *see* it as one seamless whole, was the gift of science and technology to the dawning of a new age. The astronauts who took photos of Earth from outer space often sounded like mystics upon returning home.[18] Awed by the fragile beauty of our spinning blue orb, they were equally struck by the absence of borders between nations—by the wholeness of our living planet. Many returned with the inner conviction that Earth is ensouled by a divine being, an Intelligence that gives it order and coherence.

In attempting to grasp the nature of this divine Being, and our relationship to it, humanity has traditionally looked to religion and theology. In the West, where the Judeo-Christian tradition holds sway, God has been understood to have three primary attributes: omniscience, omnipresence, and omnipotence. Interestingly, the wisdom teachings likewise portray divine consciousness as having three major attributes, and there are some parallels. The triple nature of the Lord of our world is: illumined mind or *light*, radiant heart or *love*, and directed will or *purpose*. In this schema, the third attribute—divine will or purpose—has particular relevance for the coming stage of human evolution.

The teachings tell us that God, in whose life we exist, has a definite purpose. Life on Earth is evolving in accord with an evolutionary plan that is held in the "Mind of God," the consciousness of the One Life. Moreover, the human soul has the potential to apprehend the next evolutionary goal in the divine Plan and to cooperate in its attainment. As we progress from self-consciousness toward its higher octave, Self-consciousness, we gain the ability to discern the outlines of divine intent. At present, for the first time since the emergence of the human race, a significant number of spiritual seekers are becoming aware of participating in a greater Life whose purpose we are capable of knowing.

Beyond simply perceiving this purpose, humanity has a unique role to play in its fulfillment, a role that reflects our place in the scheme of planetary life. We are poised to become mediators in a great chain of being—between the three lower kingdoms in nature (mineral, vegetable, and animal) and the next higher one, the spiritual kingdom. Our ultimate purpose is to infuse the physical world of form with Spirit, by embodying spiritual awareness. When the soul awakens and we begin to *live* as souls, aware of our inherent relationship to all lives, we will create a collective bridge in consciousness between higher and lower kingdoms—a process that will be increasingly stimulated as our planet moves into the radiatory orb of the constellation Aquarius.

Before looking ahead to the future, however, it may be useful to take stock of where we are now in the evolutionary scheme and from whence we have come. In the course of our long journey of unfoldment, covering many millions of years, we have been cycling into incarnation in the goal of evolving consciousness. At certain points along this evolutionary trajectory, the expansion of consciousness has been accelerated by the planetary Logos—the intelligent, animating force of our world. This acceleration coincides with periods of great transformation within the life of our planet. We are now living through such a time, and *all* kingdoms within the One Life are simultaneously being affected.

There exists a vast spectrum of consciousness or sentiency—*responsiveness* to vibrations—within the Life of our planet. At one end of the spectrum lies embryonic awareness; at the other lies the pure light of the Mind of God. The human kingdom stands somewhere in the middle. Long before the appearance of the first human beings, the planetary Logos brought into manifestation three successive kingdoms—mineral, vegetable, and animal. Over time, each kingdom developed unique outer forms endowed with a unique aspect of sentiency. Each successive kingdom inherited the level of sentiency attained by the previous one, and manifested a more developed potential for responsiveness.

The mineral kingdom, the first to exist on our planet, represents the most embryonic level of sentiency. Its responsiveness operates on an invisible, molecular level, but the results are widely observable. The vibratory response of minerals to their diverse environments is stunningly visible in the massive array of mineral formations embedded in the earth's crust and on the floor of the sea. In recent decades, experiments with crystals and precious gems have demonstrated their capacity to respond to the human energy field.

The second kingdom to come into manifestation was the plant or vegetable kingdom. Its more advanced level of sentiency is seen in the responsiveness of plants to the varied aspects of their environment: climate, soil composition, moisture, and light. Heliotropism, the turning of flowers and plants towards the sun, is one of the more dramatic demonstrations of the awareness of this kingdom. Recent experiments have shown the acute sensitivity of plants to human vibrations and to music. Certain kinds of music have proven to enhance their life, while others cause them to wither and die. Italian wine-makers discovered that grapes thrive in a delicate balance of soil, sun, *and* classical music; those grown without the music were smaller and insect-infested.[19]

The third kingdom, the animals, manifested a whole new level of awareness on our planet: embryonic or *instinctual mind*. Working through five sense organs and a nervous system much like our own, though more sensitive in many respects, the animal mind brought a vastly enhanced responsiveness to environmental signals, which emerged along with autonomous movement. Previously unimaginable capacities of the animal mind have recently been discovered in areas such as language communications, rudimentary reasoning, and memory, in addition to a range of emotions similar to ours— from gratitude and empathy to depression and mourning.[20]

With the appearance of human beings, the fourth kingdom in nature, the preceding kingdoms' capacities for sentiency reached a point of culmination and an entirely new potential came into manifestation: *developed mind*. The very designation of our kingdom comes from the Sanskrit word for mind: *manas*. From an evolutionary perspective, mind is a higher "sense." Higher than the five physical senses, it is a new sense that incorporates the other five senses into one, plus it has a higher dimension. The spark of divine mind that infused the embryonic mind of animals and brought our kingdom into existence, also endowed us with the capacity to register the higher vibrations of abstract thought and thus respond to the world of ideas.

In addition, the developed mind, this higher "sense," harbors the latent human capacity to respond to the next higher kingdom, the spiritual kingdom, the plane on which the Guides of the Race exist.[21] This capacity begins to develop when the soul awakens. Prior to that time, for an exceedingly long span of evolution, the human mind is focused upon the outer world of form and thus upon the *self*. The perception of having a physical form that is separate from other physical forms is what gives rise to *self*-awareness. With the development of self-awareness comes a sense of individuality, and also the capacity for autonomous thought—the basis of free will.

Almost from the start, human beings have had *the potential* to think freely. We were endowed with the freedom to direct our thoughts towards any plane of consciousness, higher or lower. However, to reach the point in evolution where we are able to consciously exercise that freedom has taken eons of time. The journey of the human family from animal-man to our present stage of incipient spiritual unfoldment has involved a cycle as long as certain of the greater ice ages. Until now, this largely dormant human potential has been manifested by only the rarest of souls, those recognized by others as sages and seers.

To appreciate the distance humanity has traveled as a species, it is illuminating to consider the initial struggle to utilize the new, higher "sense" of mind. In the earliest stages of our existence, the physical brains of animal-men were unable to register the finer vibrations emanating from the spark of mind. Still dependent entirely on the five lower senses, lacking the capacity for even rudimentary thought, human existence remained largely instinctual. It is said to have taken three million years to develop the initial mind-brain connection, making it possible for the more refined substance of mind to impress the denser substance of the human brain—the recording agent of the mind.[22]

From that early stage until now, human evolution has proceeded through epochs of experience referred to in the wisdom teachings as "root races." Myths and legends about the ancient lands of Lemuria and Atlantis reflect sequential stages of development during which different human attributes unfolded. First came the body, including the brain; next the emotional nature; and finally the mind. These three dimensions—physical, emotional, and mental—constitute what the teachings refer to as the human personality. The individual personality, or outer persona, serves as a mask of the immortal Self, the soul, until the individual "unit of consciousness" evolves to the point of awakening to its true nature.

As individual units of consciousness, we find ourselves at many different stages on the path of evolution, reflective of past experience. As members of the human race, however, we incorporate into our beings the cyclic evolution of the root races through which humanity as a whole has passed in its development of sentiency or consciousness. Our physical bodies respond to basic instincts; our emotional "bodies" respond to feelings and desires; and our minds allow us to respond to life through thought—by thinking, first about the visible dimensions of existence, and later about abstract ideas and spiritual realities.

Most human beings, according to the wisdom teachings, are still in the process of developing the mind—learning how to think. The more mentally advanced among us are self-aware, thinking, and autonomous personalities. Those who become leaders within our ranks, whether for good or for ill, have attained the harmonious integration of the three aspects of personality—bringing the body, emotions, and mind into a smoothly functioning unit. The strong sense of individual selfhood exhibited by leaders grows out of a faculty of mind that has been sufficiently developed to control emotional reactions and physical instincts. But even this level of individual attainment, the fruit of lifetimes of experience, will be transcended as humanity evolves.

In the coming stage of evolution, discussed later in this book, the true Self will emerge into the foreground of consciousness. The awareness of the soul, which recognizes its spiritual unity with all souls, will replace the consciousness of the separative persona, identified with the world of outer appearances. The personality is in many ways like an actor on the stage of life, as Shakespeare famously observed: "All the world is but a stage. And all the men and women merely players." The individual remains unaware of merely playing a role, however, before the soul emerges into conscious awareness. Until that time, the soul waits patiently behind the scenes, directing its outer "actors" through lifetimes of experience in the world of form.

The momentousness of the soul's awakening, in the scheme of human evolution, can be glimpsed through the measurement of time. While it took three million years for the human brain to fully register the subtle forces of the mind, it has taken eighteen million years for the human mind to *begin* to register the soul. During most of that great expanse of time, the lower aspect of mind has been perfecting itself as an instrument of physical perception. The development of the higher, or abstract mind—necessary for the soul's direct perceptions of spiritual reality—is a far more recent phenomenon.

The lower mind, also called the concrete mind, is geared to the concrete, physical world in which forms appear to be separate. It processes stimuli received through the five physical senses of sight, smell, taste, touch, and hearing. As this aspect of mind evolves, it learns to analyze sensory perceptions by separating, measuring, contrasting, and comparing not only physical forms, but also thought-forms. Knowledge at this level advances by means of logic, through inductive and deductive reasoning. The highest manifestations of the concrete mind have born fruit in the realm of science, whose advanced instruments have discovered forms ranging from infinitely small subatomic particles to galaxies at the outer reaches of our universe.

The higher or abstract dimension of mind begins to develop as subtle realms become important to the individual. It confers the ability to engage in pure thought about subjects ranging from mathematics to archetypes, such as Plato's ideal "forms" of goodness, truth, and beauty. With the capacity to register ideas by means of intuition, it allows us to apprehend a realm of existence that is separate from physical reality. The higher mind also enables us to recognize the consciousness existing *within* particular forms—from human beings to architectural structures. This aspect of mind is what searches for the inner *meaning* of events and circumstances, looking for their hidden causes and significance. Seeing wholes rather than parts, it perceives the subtle connections between elements that may appear, outwardly, to be separate.

According to the Tibetan master, the higher abstract mind is "the custodian of ideas [and]...the conveyor of illumination to the lower mind, *once that lower mind is en rapport with the soul.*"[23] Subtle realities gleaned by the higher mind are transmitted by the soul to the lower mind, which imprints them upon the brain and brings them into conscious awareness. Perceptions of the invisible realms of existence, unknowable to the outer senses, are conveyed by the soul to the concrete mind for the purpose of making the individual conscious of those perceptions on the plane of everyday living. The soul, able to "see" in two directions, is the mediator between the two aspects of mind.

The two aspects of mind reflect the duality of the soul's nature: spirit *and* matter. Prior to its evolutionary cycle, the soul engages in a long cycle of *involution* in matter, one that is marked by conflict. While destined to blend spirit and matter by journey's end, it must first endure a prolonged struggle between the two—a struggle reaching back to the mists of time when the higher vibration of divine mind merged with the lower vibration of physical form. The spiritual aspect of the soul recalls its spiritual origins, even while involved in matter, and by its very nature yearns to free itself from the limitations of form. The material aspect, consistent with its own nature, becomes identified with its body, attached to its possessions, and mired in the transitory glamours and illusions of the material plane.

In the end it is the soul, "The Thinker," which inevitably prevails. By means of the higher mind, the soul finds its way from the not-self to the true Self; from the illusion of separation to the reality of the One Life. As attention is increasingly directed toward higher realities and the light of the soul grows in intensity, the Thinker is led to the Path of Return. Through meditation and contemplation, the soul learns to quiet the mind and withdraw the lower senses from the outer world. Turning its gaze toward the inner worlds, it becomes receptive to subtle impressions. Gradually, over time, the soul on the Path builds a bridge in consciousness between the outer and inner worlds, the lower and higher aspects of mind, and the higher and lower kingdoms.

The fact that countless individuals around the globe have found their way to the Path of Return marks a major turning-point in the evolution of humanity as a whole. Behind this great turning towards spiritual realities lies an esoteric cause, consonant with the Plan held in the Mind of God. The wisdom teachings tell us that subtle forces have begun to stream into our planet from other parts of the solar system and beyond. Their effect is to heighten the vibratory frequency of the human mechanism. While it has only recently begun, this effect will, over time, increasingly stimulate human sensitivity to higher and more subtle vibrations.

One stream of subtle forces affecting the earth is emanating from the constellation Aquarius, a fact that forms the basis of the idea that our planet is entering a new age. The notion of moving out of one age and into another involves a set of complex astronomical facts related to the tilt of the earth's axis. As Earth rotates around the sun, it tilts like a spinning top, with its north pole slowly tracing a circle around the belt of stars that ring our solar system.[24] As the axis point moves, so does the point at which the earth's celestial equator intersects the belt of zodiacal constellations surrounding our solar system.

It takes nearly 26,000 years for that point of intersection to make its way around the entire zodiac, a period known as the "Great Year." The crossing point remains in each sign for over 2,000 years. The so-called age "we are in" is determined by the sign in which that crossing takes place at the spring equinox, the first day of spring.[25] At present, we are in transition between the constellations Pisces and Aquarius, and thus between the Piscean and Aquarian ages. Each year, as Earth's axis shifts slightly counterclockwise, we move further into the orb of Aquarian energies, as those who are sensitive to subtle forces are aware. With every passing year, as Earth is increasingly exposed to Aquarian energies, it can be expected that growing numbers of souls will respond to these newer vibrations.

To understand the nature of these new energies, we leave the field of astronomy and enter the field of astrology. Astronomy tells us about the movements of planets and stars, while astrology tells us about the effects of those movements upon living beings. For thousands of years, astrologers have observed the subtle effects of planetary rays and their findings have produced a body of insight into human reactions to the energies of planets and constellations. These insights relate primarily to the personality level, but a new understanding of the effects of subtle cosmic rays upon the *soul*, called esoteric astrology, has also become available.[26]

These two dimensions of astrology offer complementary insights into the nature of the Aquarian Age. It is foreseen, for example, that spirituality will increasingly move into the foreground of life as the new age approaches, and with it, a sense of universality. Preoccupations with differences of race, religion, nationality, gender, and other aspects of the persona will give way to an awareness of the life *within* the form—the universal spirit dwelling within the human soul. Early manifestations of Aquarius, seen in humanitarian relief efforts and in movements for human rights around the world, will evolve into a widespread awareness of being part of the human race and a concern for the welfare of all. The growing perception of humanity as a single entity will in turn engender greater justice, compassion, cooperation, and sharing of resources.

The astrological glyph for Aquarius (♒), widely interpreted as a symbol of electrical waves, is associated with instant knowing—knowing that occurs with electric speed. On the physical level, this has become manifest with the instant transfer of data around the globe through electronic communications networks that have linked much of the human race. Scientists are now exploring computerized thought transfer—the transfer of thought waves directly to computers, from the mind to the screen, bypassing the keyboard. This advance foreshadows the next stage of human evolution predicted in the wisdom teachings: the transfer of thought waves from mind to mind, telepathically, according to laws of esoteric science.[27]

As the new age unfolds, the higher intuition—also called spiritual perception or direct knowing—will become paramount. Human beings will transcend the confines of the concrete mind and gain access—via the soul and higher mind—to higher planes of reality. "Intuitives" have existed through the ages, individuals gifted with flashes of intuition or sparks of insight registered as bolts of lightning from "out of the blue." In the Aquarian Age, the wisdom teachings tell us, the soul will develop steadier contact with the plane of intuition, the source of such flashes of insight. Occasional sparks of mental electricity will turn into streams of subtle energy linking higher and lower planes of being. This will occur naturally, as the soul awakens and learns to see in two directions.

NOTES

1   The current cycle, called the Kali Yuga, is 432,000 years long. See Bailey, *A Treatise on Cosmic Fire*, footnote, 39.
2   See Glossary entry for Soul.
3   There were nine planets in our solar system until August 2006, when Pluto was reclassified as a "dwarf planet."
4   According to biological science, humans belong to the 3rd or animal kingdom.
5   In particular, the books of Alice A. Bailey.
6   This statement is based on the outpouring of books, magazines, websites, films and other activities related to the emergence of a higher stage of consciousness, particularly since the 1990s. The reader is referred to Chapter 7.
7   Bailey, *Discipleship in the New Age*, Vol. 2, 193.
8   Brunton, *The Secret Path*, 26.

9   Observation by laboratory instruments appears to have a similar effect.

10 See www.Sheldrake.org and Rupert Sheldrake, *The Sense of Being Stared At*, Three Rivers Press, 2004.

11 Dr. Masaru Emoto, author of *Messages from Water, The Secret Life of Water* and other books, initiated ground-breaking studies on the effects of consciousness on water.

12 *Beyond the Solar System*. York Films, England. The Science Channel, September 13, 2005.

13 They range from geneticists to biologists, physicists, astrophysicists, and even astronauts.

14 Reagan, *The Hand of God*, 141.

15 Random House Webster's College Dictionary.

16 Dostoyevsky, *The Brothers Karamazov*, 362.

17 Bailey, *Esoteric Psychology*, vol. 2, 184.

18 See *The Home Planet*, ed. Kevin W. Kelly, with photos from space and commentaries by American astronauts and Soviet Cosmonauts.

19 ABC Evening News, September 27, 2005. For an in-depth study of this subject, see *The Secret Life of Plants* by Peter Tompkins and Christopher Bird.

20 *When Animals Talk*, Animal Planet, June 12, 2005.

21 See Glossary for Guides of the Race.

22 Bailey, *A Treatise on White Magic*, 440.

23 Bailey, *Education in the New Age*, 5. (Authors' italics)

24 The current pole star is Polaris.

25 The movement of this crossing point counter-clockwise around the zodiac is known as the "precession of the equinoxes."

26 *Soul-Centered Astrology* by Alan Oken and *Esoteric Astrology* by Alice A. Bailey are two such sources.

27 See *Telepathy and the Etheric Vehicle* by Alice A. Bailey.

CHAPTER THREE

AWAKENING

Lead us from darkness to light,
from the unreal to the real,
from death to immortality.

~An ancient prayer

THIS PRAYER, SAID TO be the oldest prayer known to mankind, finds special resonance with all who awaken spiritually. Piercing the illusions of the world of form, seekers find themselves in a foreign realm, in need of guidance on the path from the unreal to the real. What awaits them is a journey through stages of consciousness leading from the transient reality of the limited mortal self to the eternal reality of the Self that knows it is part of the One Life.

Like a dreamer awakening from a long sleep, the soul, as it nears the end of the path of human evolution,[1] breaks through the veil of illusion and penetrates the spiritual plane of reality. Until that time, the individual perceives life through the lens of separateness, experiencing isolation from other people, from nature, from the world, and from the spiritual Source. With awakening comes the unalterable awareness of being *part* of all that is, an atom in the ebb and flow of a divinely ordered universe.

Awakening experiences are as varied as the individuals who have left records of them. The more dramatic ones, involving awe-inspiring visions of light and perceptions of divine presences, are those that have traditionally been labeled "mystical." Yet break-throughs to the realm of Spirit commonly involve phenomena that are less sensational, if no less convincing: recurring awareness of an inner voice, repeated messages delivered by varied external sources, "coincidences" that cannot have been mere happenstance. Whatever form such experiences take, they serve to shatter the notion of who we are, derived from outer appearances, and propel the seeker further in the direction of what is Real.

While the use of a capital "R" denotes the existence of a higher dimension of reality, it is not intended to negate what we conceive of as ordinary reality. The notion that everything on this material plane is illusory, derived from Eastern teachings, has generated considerable confusion for many spiritual seekers. H.P. Blavatsky explains:

> Everything is relative in this Universe, everything is an illusion. But the experience of any plane is an actuality for the percipient being, whose consciousness is on that plane.[2]

Huston Smith echoes this point in his classic work, *The Religions of Man*.[3] He notes that in Hindu philosophy the words "maya" and "illusion" are frequently used in relation to our concrete world of form. This world, which we experience through our physical senses, is distinguished from the world that appears to a person who advances to "a state of super-consciousness." From this higher state, the world of form appears to be illusory. But as Smith writes, "This the Hindu would deny, pointing out that as long as it appears real and demanding to us, we must accept it as such."[4]

It is only at the end of a long cycle of lifetimes, when the soul in incarnation rubs up against the limits of the finite self—the personality—that awakening to a higher reality occurs. With the realization that there is more to life than meets the outer eye, an inner doorway opens, allowing the soul's reality to begin to impress itself upon the mind of the seeker. A glimpse of the soul's realm, however ephemeral, is often sufficient to turn a curious explorer of spiritual phenomena into a serious seeker of truth. That glimpse gives rise to the urge to reenter that state of consciousness and to discover, ultimately, how to remain in it.

Attempts to describe the experience of spiritual awakening present a curious dilemma. Ancient texts from the East say more about *how* to achieve it than what it is, experientially. The updated wisdom teachings, likewise, say little about the mystical experience itself, except that it is pivotal in the soul's journey: the portal to the spiritual path. Descriptions left by saints and sages of the past, as well as more contemporary accounts, are almost always qualified by the adjective "ineffable"—impossible to put into words. The language of the concrete mind has universally been deemed inadequate to the task.

The language of poetry, however, has helped to fill the gap. Illumined poets have portrayed various aspects of the mystical experience by means of metaphor. On the initial disorientation of awakening, for example, Walt Whitman (1819–1892) wrote: "I cannot be awake, for nothing looks to me as it did before, or else I am awake for the first time, and all before has been a mean sleep."[5] In Whitman's imagery we find both the altered state of awareness created by the experience and the dawning sense of duality that results—the realization that we are both self *and* Self. This duality is ultimately resolved into a higher state of unity, as the path unfolds, but for a long while the seeker's experience alternates between planes of consciousness. William Wordsworth (1770–1850) observed:

> We are laid asleep
> In body, and become a living soul.
> While with an eye made quiet by the power
> Of harmony, and the deep power of joy,
> We see into the life of things.[6]

The path to enlightenment was first charted by knowers of the East thousands of years ago. But it was in the West, only a little over a century ago, that the first study of spiritual awakening was conducted. Until the late 19th century, written accounts of such experiences were extremely rare and lay scattered around the globe. The project of collecting and analyzing them was undertaken by Richard Maurice Bucke, M.D. (1837–1902)—a psychiatrist, director of mental institutions, professor, president of both the British and American psychological associations, and an ardent seeker of spiritual truth.

Bucke had had a mystical encounter at age 36 that changed his life. At the time, such experiences were poorly understood in the West and were often diagnosed as a form of mental illness. But as a result of both his professional training and his personal search for enlightenment, Bucke recognized his experience for what it was and set out to investigate the phenomenon. The result was his landmark study, *Cosmic Consciousness*, which drew upon all known accounts of poets and writers, seers and sages, from different epochs and regions of the globe.

By cosmic consciousness, Bucke meant the state of consciousness transcending normal sensory perception, in which one is aware of being part of the larger cosmos. In the course of his inquiry, he combed through all available world literature, secular and religious, to identify individuals who had shown evidence of contact with a higher plane of reality, as demonstrated by their written and spoken words. All told, he found just under fifty examples. They ranged from the Buddha, Christ, and Mohammed—whose illuminations had resulted in the founding of world religions—to individuals at earlier stages of awakening.

Bucke's study was groundbreaking on several scores. It revealed the universality of higher consciousness, across time and geographical space, and showed that it was by no means an anomaly. It also uncovered common traits in the lives of individuals who had experienced this expanded state of awareness, such as high ethical and moral standards and high intelligence. Although most of the records he located were brief and fragmentary, he was able to weave together common threads in order to create a fuller picture.

What Bucke discovered led him to conclude that while the state of higher consciousness remained exceptional, it was a natural stage of growth. From an evolutionary perspective, he saw it as the inevitable next stage for humanity. Though the number of cases he had discovered was quite small, given that his search reached as far back as the time of the Buddha, he noted that the number had increased proportionately with the passage of time. That increase convinced him that just as humanity had made an evolutionary leap from instinctual consciousness to the present stage of individual or self-consciousness, so would we ultimately make the leap to cosmic consciousness—the realm of the "intuitional mind."

During the century between Bucke's time and our own, his intuition has been confirmed in many ways: increasing accounts of mystical experiences,[7] the growing body of spiritual seekers around the world, an expanding interest in the field of higher conscious-ness, and the spread of esoteric wisdom concerning the next stage of human evolution. But at the time that *Cosmic Consciousness* was published, one year before *The Varieties of Religious Experience* by William James, it broke completely new ground. James called Bucke a "benefactor to us all" for bringing "this kind of consciousness 'home'…in a way so definite and inescapable that it will be impos-sible henceforward to overlook it or ignore it."[8]

To this day, the works of Bucke and James remain touchstones for students of consciousness. James, a pragmatist, was fascinated by the phenomenon of mystical experience, convinced that it was capable of transforming a life for the good. In the course of his own inquiries, he had discovered characteristics that were common to all accounts of mystical experience and he set forth "marks" of those experiences he considered to be genuine. Two of the marks he deemed most significant were "ineffability" and "noetic quality."

People who had had a mystical encounter, James observed, in-variably reported an inability to convey the substance of it in words. The ineffability of the experience meant that it could not be "trans-ferred" to others; it had to be directly experienced. Yet often the noetic aspect, the knowledge yielded by the experience, *could* be communicated in words. Moreover, James noted, the quality of this knowledge—acquired by direct intuitive understanding—was au-thoritative. He called it "insight into the depths of truth unplumbed by the discursive intellect... illuminations, revelations, full of significance and importance."[9]

Interestingly, Bucke's account of his own mystical experience illustrates the noetic quality that James highlighted. Bucke was riding home one evening in a reflective mood, after a discussion of poetry with friends, when suddenly he had a sensation of being "wrapped around as it were by a flame-colored cloud." At first he associated the flame with a physical fire, but soon realized that it was a symbol of the light within. He wrote that the experience lasted "not more than a few moments" but left him with an exultant feeling and a set of unshakeable convictions. Referring to himself in the third person, he stated:

> He saw and knew that the Cosmos is not dead matter but a living Presence, that the soul of man is immortal, that the universe is so built and ordered that without any peradventure all things work together for the good of each and all, and that the foundation principle of the world is what we call love.[10]

Mystical encounters, shaped as they are by the individual's unique life experience and degree of soul awareness, differ in significant ways. But James observed that there are certain elements that commonly recur in accounts of awakening: an ecstatic sense of well-being; a divine presence characterized by love; sudden insight into the essence of all existence; an identification with the living cosmos. Many of these universal elements, seen in Bucke's account, are also evident in the diverse accounts that follow:

> In one quarter of an hour I saw and knew more than if I had been many years together at a university. For I saw and knew the being of all things...the descent and origin of the world and of all creatures through the divine wisdom. I knew and saw in myself all the three worlds.[11]
>
> ~*Jacob Boehme, 16ᵗʰ century German mystic*

Does there not exist...an inner illumination, of which what we call light in the outer world is the partial expression and manifestation, by which we can ultimately see things as they are, beholding all creation...by a cosmical intuition and presence, identifying ourselves with what we see? [12]

   ~Edward Carpenter, 19th century British scholar and poet

All melted into a luminescent sea... The entire cosmos, gently luminous, like a city seen afar at night, glimmered within the infinitude of my being.[13]

   ~Yogananda, 20th century Indian spiritual teacher

Gradually I noticed the room was becoming brighter... I found everything was exuding light... When I looked at the flowers on the stand, they had a luminous aura... I pulled my hand from under the sheet, finding it nearly translucent, and giving off a soft light. Here was my answer on the Oneness of All.[14]

   ~20th century American woman (called "Donna")

I perceived everything to be somehow part of me. As I sat on the peak of the mountain looking out at the landscape falling away from me in all directions... I experienced the entire universe looking out on itself through my eyes.[15]

   ~Protagonist of the novel, The Celestine Prophecy

   The phenomenal worldwide success of The Celestine Prophecy appears to validate, as well as any other single factor, Bucke's intuition about the growth of cosmic consciousness. Many millions of readers have been drawn to this parable of the spiritual quest—the tale of a collective awakening to spiritual forces and of an increasingly conscious relationship with them, as humanity stands on the threshold of a higher stage of evolution. Though the novel's readers may be at an earlier stage of awareness than the "cases" studied by Bucke, they are part of the gathering wave of souls around the globe who have embarked on a quest to discover what is real.

Foreseeing this current cycle of awakening, the "Guides of the Race," members of the spiritual kingdom, made available to humanity the kind of knowledge that would be needed at this time. The wisdom teachings were intended to help individuals, becoming aware of a higher dimension of consciousness, to find their way to the path of spiritual evolution, thus paving the way for the evolution of humanity as a whole in the Aquarian Age.

In these teachings, we find an explanation of the true import of the mystical experience. Previously, mystical encounters were viewed as rare and isolated occurrences without much significance to the world, apart from their intrinsic value to the individual. Even William James, fascinated though he was by the power of such experiences to transform an individual's life, had failed to see their practical relevance to the larger society. The wisdom teachings have shed light on the wider significance of individual spiritual awakenings by placing them in the context of human evolution.

In the evolutionary journey of an individual soul, the mystical experience of awakening is portrayed as a "second birth." It marks the soul's birth into the world of Spirit, just as the "first birth" involves entry into the world of form. Just as a newborn infant instinctively opens its physical eyes, there comes a time in the evolutionary journey when the maturing soul opens its "spiritual eyes." What follows is an expansion of consciousness that is called an "initiation." The literal meaning of the Latin root of the word initiation is "to go into." Awakening, according to the Tibetan master, is "the first step into the spiritual kingdom."

In the Aquarian Age, it is predicted that a collective new birth will occur within the human kingdom. The opening of many spiritual eyes will have major consequences for our world, as the collective awakening of humanity will bring about a new consensual reality. There is already a growing recognition of the unity of life on our planet. When this awareness is amplified by spiritual experience, it will have the power to transform many lives, leading in time to the transformation of human societies and cultures.

While a critical mass of human beings appear destined to reach the stage of awakening, there are nevertheless preconditions.[16] In contrast to awakening from the physical state of sleep, a natural reflex requiring no unusual effort, awakening from the "unreal" state of consciousness requires dedication, sacrifice, and active engagement in the quest for truth. Spiritual awakening is often depicted as "sudden," but is, in fact, always preceded by an intense struggle to "penetrate the veil of illusion." It marks the culmination of a persistent search to discover what lies behind the world of appearances.

Describing the years prior to his own awakening to "the cosmic sense," Richard Bucke observed: "Life for some years was one passionate note of interrogation, an unappeasable hunger for enlightenment on the basic problems."[17] He noticed a similar caste of mind among those he studied, describing it as "ardent, earnest and aspiring." In the case of Gautama the Buddha, six years of meditation under "the tree of knowledge" had preceded the hour of his enlightenment. For Mohammed, it was long periods of solitude, prayer, and fasting in a desert cave that led to the moment when he "heard a voice calling upon him [and] a flood of light broke upon him."[18]

One of the most detailed accounts of a prolonged interrogation into the fundamental questions of life was left to us by Leo Tolstoy (1828–1910). Tolstoy's *Confession*, containing the story of his own journey "from darkness to light and from death to immortality," can easily be read as an allegory of modern man in search of truth.[19] He was someone who had prided himself on being a man of reason, and who had viewed the rational mind as the sole arbiter of reality. Only after having completely exhausted the resources of that level of mind, however, did the light of Spirit break through for him.

What had initially sparked his quest for truth was a pervasive feeling of illegitimacy. Like other Russian writers of his ilk and his era, Tolstoy had been viewed as a "high-priest" of culture. He and others like him were seen as having a vocation "to teach mankind." For a period of time, that notion had given meaning to his life. But it gradually dawned on him that he understood nothing about the most fundamental questions of life, such as the very reason for being alive. With that realization, he concluded that he had nothing of any significance to teach anyone else.

Tolstoy's malaise, wrought by the "questions in his soul," first surfaced while he was writing *War and Peace* and *Anna Karenina*. During fifteen years of intense concentration on those celebrated works, deemed "insignificant" by him in his *Confession*, he had struggled to keep his soul's questions at bay. But they later reemerged with even greater insistence. He began suffering from bouts of despair, severe enough to cause him to contemplate suicide, "at a time," he wrote, "when all around me I had what is considered complete good fortune"—fame, wealth, and a much beloved family.

Yet his entire life appeared to be pointless as the reality of death loomed before him. "One can only live," he wrote, "while one is intoxicated with life; as soon as one is sober it is impossible." At age 49, one particular question had brought him to the verge of suicide: "Is there any meaning in my life that the inevitable death awaiting me does not destroy?" In search of the answer, he delved into every branch of knowledge concerned with human experience, starting with science, which claimed it could explain everything about life. After methodically examining the whole gamut of sciences, from pure mathematics to metaphysics, he realized that none of them had even addressed the most basic questions. Philosophy had at least *posed* the questions, but offered no satisfactory answers.

Having reached the limits of rational thought, something that he called "a consciousness of life" began to work inside of him. This consciousness revealed the error of his quest: He had been looking to sources of knowledge that were *finite* in search of meaning that is *infinite*—meaning that transcends the world of time and space. That

led him to the realm of faith, which dealt with the relationship between the finite and the infinite. He had personally eschewed faith
because of its "denial of reason," but conjectured that for people of
faith, life would be tenable. When he queried theologians, however,
he discovered that they obscured the question of life's meaning.
And despite their claims to faith, he observed that they feared loss,
suffering, and death as much as unbelievers did.

Ultimately, it was in the lives of simple peasants that Tolstoy
discovered genuine meaning. What gave real value to their lives, in
his view, was that they served a purpose—their labors were *needed*
by others. Moreover, their faith was demonstrably real: they were
able to face sorrow and death with equanimity. He realized that it
was only "the life of our circle, the rich and learned," which had
lost all meaning for him, not life itself. Throwing off the trappings
of wealth and the pretenses of the upper class, he discovered meaning in working to improve the lives of Russian serfs, for whom he
felt genuine love, and in efforts to promote social justice.

Having found a purpose that satisfied his soul, Tolstoy's quest
then turned in a new direction. It became a one-pointed search for
God, a quest to *know* God, increasingly propelled from the heart.

> That search for God was not reasoning, but a feeling,
> because that search proceeded not from the course of
> my thoughts—it was even directly contrary to them—
> but proceeded from the heart. It was a feeling of fear,
> orphanage, isolation in a strange land, and a hope of
> help from someone.[20]

On the basis of logic, he had concluded that there had to be
a "Cause of causes," a being commonly referred to as God. But
he wanted to know "how to think of God," how to relate to this
Being, and he felt an intense yearning to experience God's presence.
During his years of searching, and listening to the voice within,
he had experienced alternating tides of emotion: moments of ecstatic joy, when he sensed the Presence of God, followed by bouts
of despair. And then, finally, through the inner voice, he heard an
answer that served to make his existence bearable:

'To know God and to live is one and the same thing. God is life. Live seeking God, and then you will not live without God.' And more than ever before, all within me and around me lit up, and the light did not again abandon me. And I was saved from suicide.[21]

Tolstoy's *Confession*, written a century ago, retains a remarkable degree of relevance for contemporary Western seekers. It would seem to speak to everyone whose orientation to life has been shaped by modern science, and who has thus overvalued the mind as *the* instrument of perception and undervalued the heart. In the wisdom teachings, we find that the rational mind is essential to the spiritual quest, but at certain stages along the way it can become a hindrance. This truth is reflected in the saying, "The mind is slayer of the real," an enigmatic phrase with the ring of a Zen koan.

The meaning of these words lies in the esoteric fact that the rational or concrete mind, geared to the world of form, functions by separating and dividing, analyzing and categorizing. At the level of the concrete mind, it is not possible to perceive "the Real"—the invisible web of life that sustains and connects all manifestations of the visible universe. Higher reality can only be perceived through higher modes of consciousness—through the soul illumined by the higher mind and intuition, and the heart, "the seat of the soul."[22] Just as the concrete mind divides, the heart unites, and the soul *recognizes* the inherent unity of life.

One of the clearest statements of the soul's recognition of oneness at the second birth was left to us by the theosophist, human rights crusader, and writer, Annie Besant (1847–1933):

> It is then that he realizes for the first time *in himself* the outpouring of the divine Love, and experiences that marvelous change which makes him feel himself to be one with all that lives.[23]

In the West, the mystical quest for union has traditionally been defined as a search for God. Today, in more contemporary terms reflecting the influence of the East, it is often framed as a search for universal consciousness or oneness. In either case, what propels the seeker toward union with the Universe, or God, is the heart. When mind alone is activated, it is possible to accumulate knowledge *about* the quest—from books or from teachers—without fully involving oneself in it. When the heart is engaged, however, the quest leads inexorably to the path of transformation.

"To tread the path," wrote Alice Bailey, "we must become the path." Jalaluddin Rumi (1207–1273), the Sufi mystic and poet, similarly evoked the essence of the path and its goal. He wrote that "a true seeker of God" not only delights in reflections of God, such as the rays of the Sun, but learns "to *become* the Sun itself."[24] In a poem entitled "Say I am You," Rumi conveys the classical mystical sense of "the real"—the heart's perception of oneness.

I am
dust particles in the sunlight,
I am the round sun…

I am morning mist,
and the breathing of evening…

Both candle and the moth
crazy around it.

Rose and the nightingale
lost in the fragrance.

I am all orders of being,
the circling galaxy,
the evolutionary intelligence,
the lift and the falling away.

What is and what isn't
You who know Jalaluddin,
You the One in all,

say who I am.
Say I am you.[25]

There is a Buddhist adage that the path to enlightenment begins when "the mind drops into the heart." The Ageless Wisdom
echoes this idea: when the heart and mind are one, or when we
learn to "think in the heart," we are ready to step onto the path of
spiritual evolution. It begins with the opening of the heart, as the
heart is where we first encounter the presence of divinity. From
that point onward, however, treading the Path of Return to God
requires the mind as well as the heart, for this path is governed by
spiritual laws that require mental cognition.

One of these laws takes effect as the seeker becomes fully engaged in the process of active "interrogation"—the quest for life's
deeper meaning that precedes awakening. This is the law of action and reaction: "Ask and it shall be given you; seek and ye shall
find; knock and it shall be opened unto you," as Christ instructed.
This law is activated at the point when the resources of the mind
have been thoroughly exhausted, as Tolstoy experienced, and the
seeker, having nowhere else to turn, appeals earnestly for higher
guidance. With the response that invariably comes—whether in
the inner silence of the heart or through guidance appearing in the
outer world—a subjective relationship with the realm of Spirit is
established.

This law forms the basis of *The Celestine Prophecy,* a story
about living life as a quest—holding questions in the forefront of
one's mind and anticipating that answers will appear in the natural course of events. The spiritual learning process, common to
all paths, involves an increasingly subtle attunement to life in the
awareness that anything or anyone could be the bearer of an answer—a person, a book, even something as seemingly insignificant
as a street sign. All situations become potential sources of guidance
as one learns to decode their symbolic meaning. In the posing of
questions and the listening for answers, the seeker sets in motion
a "conversation" with the cosmos, a symbolic dialogue familiar to

indigenous peoples everywhere, through which spiritual guidance initially comes.

The most ancient and universal form of human appeal to the spiritual world is what we call prayer. Before the age of science, prayer was so integral to human living that it was seen as a basic instinct. Interestingly, the spiritual quest involves a similar dynamic as the seeker looks for answers leading to the light of truth. By asking for guidance from the inner realms—whether through meditation, a modality such as journal-writing, or simple prayer—a spiritual law is set in motion. What activates this law is the expectation of a response—"the hope for help from someone" in Tolstoy's words; faith, defined by the Christian apostle Paul as "the substance of things hoped for, the evidence of things unseen."

Spiritual living begins with the establishment of a dialogue between the objective and subjective realms. Thoughts directed to the realm of Spirit carry vibrations that evoke responses from Beings on the inner planes whose task it is to guide awakening souls. Responses come in an infinite variety of guises, uniquely tailored to the consciousness of the individual. When the seeker learns to correctly discern their source, and their validity, an interaction between the human and spiritual realms is initiated and the spiritual eyes are opened.

In the human evolutionary journey, spiritual awakening is an inevitability. The second birth is said to be "as inescapable as birth into the human family." It is seen as a formative stage in the developmental process of spiritual growth "from gestation until, in 'the fullness of time'... the soul begins to manifest on earth."[26] Since every soul will eventually arrive at this stage, it could rightly be viewed as a natural development. And yet, the struggle to reach this stage is experienced as anything *but* natural.

In actuality, the path upon which the seeker of truth embarks goes against the grain of ordinary human living in the most essential ways. He or she feels impelled to turn away from the world of material values, goals, and ambitions—the only world that is known until then—having no idea where the journey will lead or what it will demand in terms of personal loss or sacrifice. Nevertheless, the seeker is driven to discover the purpose of existence and the meaning of life. Without such understanding life becomes, to quote Tolstoy, "impossible."

For those who persist, the awakening experience comes as a "reward." Ultimately the quest bears fruit in a living encounter with that which has been sought, bringing *proof* of the higher reality. The great German mystic, Meister Eckhart (1260–1327), described it as "the birth of God in the soul." The encounter may consist of a momentary illumination, or repeated glimpses of inner light and love, or a more continuous extra-dimensional experience. The scale of the experience appears to be determined, like any true reward, by the degree of spiritual striving.

In many cases of spiritual awakening, ardent striving has been going on for lifetimes, and thus the mystical encounter represents the fruit of previous attainment. An unknown poet of an earlier time, one of the "cases" discovered by Bucke, left an account of illumination that clearly had its origins in lifetimes past. His soul's awakening was both a recapitulation of the past and an opportunity to enter further into the subtle realms of awareness. It reads, in part:

> So mused a traveler on the earthly plane
> Being in himself a type of all mankind.
> For aspirations dim at first possessed
> Him only, rising vaguely in his dreams,
> Till in ripe years his early musings changed
> To inspiration and the light of the soul.
> Then vision came, and in the light he saw
> What he had hoped now openly revealed;
> And much besides—the inmost soul of things,
> And "beauty" as the crown of life itself,
> Ineffable, transcending mortal form...

A spiritual Being, the feminine personification of beauty and love, becomes the poet's inner guide. After offering him rarified perceptions of the inner realms, she affirms:

"Thou long hast thought upon life's mystery,
Its vast, eternally recurring rounds,
Of rest and rebirth and activity,
And sought therein the passage of the soul
From light to dark, from dark to light again.
Come then with me, and we will see in part
The latter in its human phase unveiled."
So saying, with her presence she endowed
Him with new senses, faculties and powers,
That far surpassed the limits of the old.[27]

NOTES

1   The path of human evolution, also called the "path of human living," involves immersion in the material world of glamour and illusion, created by personal desires and ambitions.

2   Blavatsky, *The Secret Doctrine*, vol. 1, 295-6.

3   This book was republished in a second edition entitled *The World's Religions*.

4   Smith, *The Religions of Man*, 82.

5   Bucke, *Cosmic Consciousness*, 296.

6   Wordsworth, William, "Poetical Works," quoted in Bucke, *Cosmic Consciousness*, 286.

7   See especially *Venture Inward*, the magazine of the Association for Research and Enlightenment.

8   Acklom, George Moreby, foreword to *Cosmic Consciousness*, by Bucke.

9   James, *The Varieties of Religious Experience*, 329.

10   Bucke, *Cosmic Consciousness*, 10.

11   James, *The Varieties of Religious Experience*, 355-6.

12   Carpenter, Edward, "Civilization," quoted in Bucke, *Cosmic Consciousness*, 241.

13   Ullman, *Mystics, Masters, Saints and Sages*, 117.

14   Don Jeffrey, "Sharing Mystical Experiences," *Venture Inward*, May-June 2004, 14-15.

15   Redfield, *The Celestine Prophecy*, 98.

16   These requirements are identified in Chapter 5.

17   Bucke, *Cosmic Consciousness*, 9.

18   Irving, Washington, "Life of Mohammed," quoted in Bucke, *Cosmic Consciousness*, 126.

19 Tolstoy, "A Confession," *The Portable Tolstoy.*

20 *Ibid.,* 713.

21 *Ibid.,* 716.

22 The heart is actually one "seat of the soul;" the other is the pineal gland in the head.

23 Besant, *Esoteric Christianity*, 98-99.

24 Ullman, *Mystics, Masters, Saints and Sages*, 26.

25 *Ibid.,* 24-25.

26 Bailey, *From Bethlehem to Calvary*, 43.

27 Bucke, *Cosmic Consciousness*, 63-64.

CHAPTER FOUR

REBIRTH

The body is merely a garment.
Go seek the wearer, not the cloak.

~Rumi

ACCORDING TO ANCIENT LEGEND, the Buddha was deep in meditation on the night of his Great Awakening—the climax of a six-year quest. His meditation consisted of three "watches" or phases. First, he reflected upon his former existences; then, upon the chain of causation through which evil brings suffering and good brings a higher state of being in future existences; and finally, upon ignorance and desire, the cause of all pain.[1] With dawn came the illumination that formed the core of a new religion: that the cause of human suffering is selfish desire for things of a material and transitory nature, and that this cause can be eradicated.

All awakening souls follow in the footsteps of the Buddha, however dimly at first. In the early stages of soul awareness, the seeker may have faint glimmerings of the reality of previous existences or even flickering impressions of a past life or two. Such recollections, milestones on the spiritual journey, are still light-years from the Buddha's "power to call to mind various temporary states in days gone by; such as one birth, two births, three, four, five, ten, twenty...a hundred, a thousand or a hundred thousand births...in all their modes and all their details."[2]

What really matters, however, regarding recollections of the past, is the expanded sense of time that occurs with spiritual awakening. The soul's perception of being part of the larger universe produces not only a vastly enhanced sense of space, but also of time. Prior to awakening, we cannot see beyond the confines of a single lifespan. With a glimpse of the timeless realm of spirit, we begin to perceive the continuity of life. There is a dawning realization that other lifetimes have preceded this one, and that the seeds of current struggles are buried in the distant (largely unknowable) past.

With this realization, the seeker begins to grasp the principles of reincarnation[3] and karma, two of the oldest and most widespread religious beliefs in the history of humankind. In the Ageless Wisdom, these principles are seen as laws: the Law of Rebirth and the Law of Cause and Effect. They operate under the Law of Evolution, and together govern our progressive development. Though we remain ignorant of spiritual laws throughout the longest span of human evolution, they determine the entire journey of the soul—from its spiritual origin to "a descent into matter [and] an ascent through the medium of constant incarnations in form until those forms are perfect expressions of the indwelling spiritual consciousness."[4]

Belief in reincarnation and karma has been traced back as far as 10,000 BCE to Persia, Egypt, and India.[5] In India, and in much of the East, this belief has remained part of the fabric of life, although it is often misconstrued or ignored, as are most religious precepts the world over. In recent decades, acceptance of karma and reincarnation has been growing in the West. Many would be surprised to learn, however, that these beliefs were once central to Western civilization. In ancient times, adherents included Greeks, Jews, and Christians.

For reasons not easily ascertained, but now believed to have had as much to do with the politics of imperial Rome as with religion, the Church anathematized writings about the soul's rebirth in the 6th century, along with anyone who subscribed to the belief.[6] Since that time, Christians have been taught to regard reincarnation as a pagan superstition. Nevertheless from Plato's era to our own, many seekers in the West have found that discovering the principle of rebirth is like receiving the gift of sight: suddenly a light goes on and keys to some of the great mysteries of life present themselves.

Prior to that moment, it appears to the objective observer— perceiving life through the physical senses—that we live in a world where injustice, inequity, and moral anarchy reign supreme. The human being in search of truth innately rebels against the contradictory notion that God is benevolent and omnipotent, yet permits unbearable suffering and unspeakable evil. Intuitively we feel, though we cannot perceive it with the outer senses, that there *must* be a moral order parallel to the visible order of the natural world. In the workings of reincarnation and karma, we discover this higher order.

The simple principle of these complementary laws is that we reap what we sow—for good and for ill—*over time*. The law of karma is the evolutionary mechanism by which wrong is transmuted into right, injustice into justice—in accord with the higher purpose of aligning human will with divine will, a state often described as "perfection." Such a goal is obviously not achieved in the space of one lifetime, but gradually, over the course of "a thousand or a hundred thousand births." Untold life experiences are required to balance the scales of karma and transmute self-will into divine will, thereby turning the incarnate soul into an instrument of divine purpose.

In the West, these spiritual laws were effectively buried for well over a millennium. Thirteen centuries passed from the anathematizing of reincarnation—at the Second Council of Constantinople in 553[7]—to its reintroduction in the late 19th century, largely through the theosophical writings of H.P. Blavatsky, and through English translations of Eastern texts by British orientalists. Significantly, the notion gained even wider currency with the atrocities of the 20th century's First World War. Many thinkers, agonizing over the question of how a loving God could permit suffering on the unprecedented scale of that war, could not abide the conventional theological reply that "the ways of God are inscrutable." Among them was

British author and military historian, Owen Rutter (1889–1944), who wrote:

> Like most people who live in an ordered community, I wanted to feel that I was living in an ordered universe. Yet I could see no order, only chaos. With thousands of others, I was appalled by the human suffering throughout the world, by the unequal distribution of happiness, by what seemed to me the aimlessness of human life.[8]

Searching for the deeper meaning of life, Rutter found his way to the teaching of karma and reincarnation, which after years of study he came to accept as reality. In his book, *The Scales of Karma,* he describes the effect of this knowledge on his state of mind:

> I found a logical answer to every problem of human behavior, an explanation of every form of suffering which once had seemed unjust, of every reward which had seemed unmerited. I came to understand why I was here, what I was doing, where I was going.[9]

Rarely, if ever, are people convinced to believe something because other people do. For a belief to have the power to stir the soul, its inherent truth has to be grasped independently. Yet it seems worthy of note that among those who found truth in the principle of reincarnation, often despite the powerful opprobrium of religious forces, stand the towering figures of Western culture and philosophy. A short list of those best known from pre-modern times includes Pythagoras, Socrates, and Plato, among the ancient Greeks; Cicero, Virgil, and Ovid among the Romans; Plotinus, founder of Neo-Platonism in the 3rd century CE; and Dante Alighieri in the Middle Ages.

From the Renaissance onward, the list swells to include Leonardo da Vinci, Paracelsus, Giordano Bruno, Shakespeare, Spinoza, Leibniz, Voltaire, Benjamin Franklin, William Blake, Friedrich Schiller, Wordsworth, Balzac, Victor Hugo, Emerson, Thoreau, Whitman, Dickens, Browning, Wagner, Melville, Flaubert, Dostoyevsky, Tolstoy, Ibsen, Emily Dickenson, Louisa May Alcott,

Gauguin, G.B. Shaw, Arthur Conan Doyle, Mahler, Rudyard Kipling, Sibelius, W.B. Yeats, James Joyce, Mondrian, Robert Frost, Jack London, Herman Hesse, T.S. Eliot, Eugene O'Neill, Henry Miller, Pearl Buck, Aldous Huxley, Thomas Wolfe, and Norman Mailer. Also included are such pioneers of science and technology as Thomas Edison, Henry Ford, and Charles Lindbergh.[10]

Although the precepts of karma and reincarnation are generally associated with the East, they have deep roots in the Judeo-Christian heritage of the West. References to reincarnation and karma can be found in both early Jewish and early Christian teachings. The Jewish scholar Rabbi Moses Gaster noted that belief in the soul's rebirth had ancient origins in Judaism and was implicitly understood in the earliest writings. One illustration was a belief of the biblical Samaritans that a pre-existing soul "was given to Adam...which, through successive 'incarnations' in Seth, Noah, and Abraham, reached Moses."[11]

Moses, it appears, gave out more than one teaching on Mount Sinai. Scholars of Jewish mysticism maintain that Moses was not only the source of the Torah, the first five books of the Old Testament, but also of the Kabala, the esoteric tradition of Judaism. According to these scholars, the Torah was the *written* Law, intended by God for the people as a whole. The Kabala, unwritten and secretly transmitted by oral tradition for centuries, was intended for the select few deemed ready to approach God directly.[12] The Kabala was given to man "according to an early Rabbi, in order that...he might learn to understand the mystery of both the universe about him and the universe within him."[13]

Karma and reincarnation are woven into the fabric of the Kabala. The whole teaching is premised on the idea that God intended human beings to become perfect. To that end, He created a system of laws that the soul must learn to obey:

> Most souls being at present in a state of transmigra-tions[14] [from one human body to another], God requites a man now for what his soul merited in a bypast time in another body, by having broken some of the 613 pre-

cepts... Thus we have the rule: – No one is perfect unless he has thoroughly observed all the 613 precepts.[15]

Assuming that Moses was in fact the transmitter of the Kabala, his upbringing and education in Egypt would have duly prepared him for the task. Growing up in the court of the Pharaoh, he would have been schooled in reincarnation and karma, the basis of the ancient Egyptian religion as depicted in *The Book of the Dead,* also known as *The Book of Coming Forth into Life.* Dating back to at least the 5th millennium BCE but possibly earlier,[16] this book was widely known in Moses' time.[17] Moses is also believed to have received training in the ancient Egyptian Mysteries—secret ceremonies symbolically enacting the soul's journey from death to spiritual rebirth.

Scholars have deemed it likely that several streams of knowledge fed into the Kabala from both the near and far East. India has been identified by 19th century Hebrew scholar, Isaac Myer, as a likely source along with Central Asia, Persia, and Mesopotamia. Myer noted "several references to the wisdom of 'the Sons of the East' in the Hebrew Sacred Writings," and observed that "communication between the ancient nations of Asia" was far more extensive than had been generally known.[18]

In fact, so widely disseminated was the teaching of reincarnation in ancient times that its precise origins are difficult to trace. Herodotus, the ancient Greek historian, believed that the Egyptians were the first to propound the theory of rebirth.[19] Yet as Myer indicated, the notion could well have spread to Egypt from neighboring cultures or even from India, where some say it had an even longer lineage. The *Yoga Sutras* of Patanjali detail the workings of the laws of karma and reincarnation, leading to the soul's purification and illumination. According to certain Hindu scholars, Patanjali may have lived as far back as 10,000 BCE.[20]

Atlantis may actually have been the seedbed of this teaching. The island continent in the Atlantic Ocean is believed to have been destroyed by great volcanic eruptions and floods, the last of which occurred around the year 10,000 BCE. Plato, who wrote about both reincarnation and Atlantis, had access to esoteric knowledge about the lost continent as did, more recently, H.P. Blavatsky, Alice Bailey, and others. The golden age of Atlantis has been described as a time "when the gods walked with men"—a phrase that now appears to be more than merely allegorical. It is said that Masters of Wisdom existed in physical bodies then, as they will again in the Aquarian Age. The "sacred and secret doctrine" about the soul's evolution may well have been given out by them in Atlantis, spreading from there to all corners of the ancient world.[21]

While the doctrine of rebirth bears no proof of authorship, traces of it are found in two of the oldest books of the Old Testament, attributed to Moses. In Exodus (20:4-5) God speaks of "visiting the iniquity of the fathers upon the children unto the third and fourth generation." In Deuteronomy (24:16) it is written: "The fathers shall not be put to death for the children, neither shall the children be put to death for the fathers: every man shall be put to death for his own sin." This apparent contradiction is resolved, Owen Rutter points out, by the implicit understanding of the ancients: that souls who commit iniquities are reborn to face the consequences of their actions in subsequent generations.

As for karma, the Law of Cause and Effect, the Old Testament is replete with references. In the book of Proverbs, for example, the notion of sowing and reaping occurs repeatedly: "He who stretches out his hand against his neighbor shall not go unpunished; but the offspring of the righteous shall be delivered." (11:21) "God shall render to every man according to his works." (24:12) "He who closes his ears at the cry of the poor, he also shall cry to God, but shall not be heard." (21:13) "Do not oppress the poor because he is poor; neither afflict the needy in the gate. For the Lord will plead their cause and avenge the injustice which is done to them." (22:22-23)

Allusions to reincarnation have remained in the New Testament, as well, despite the apparent efforts of early Church authorities to expunge them. In the process of determining which texts would comprise the New Testament canon, a process that continued for over three centuries after Christ's death, many texts, portions of texts, and letters were deleted. By the year 367, when the canon was finally agreed upon, there was already substantial opposition to the doctrine of rebirth and in 553 the anathema was promulgated. Yet mysteriously, a number of references managed to evade the censors.[22]

Several of these references appear in dialogues between Jesus and his followers concerning the previous identities of John the Baptist and himself. The disciples wondered whether Jesus and John the Baptist were, in fact, the souls whose return had been predicted by the Old Testament prophets. One of the prophecies, which some see as further evidence of the *Jewish* belief in reincarnation, appears at the very end of the Old Testament in the Book of Malachi: "Behold, I will send you Elijah the prophet before the coming of the great and dreadful day of the Lord."

John the Baptist and Jesus were born five centuries later into an age of messianic fervor, a time when people were actively searching for signs of the fulfillment of prophecy. The identities of these two highly unusual figures caused widespread speculation. In one exchange with his disciples, Jesus asked them who the people thought he was. The belief in reincarnation is implicit in both the question and the disciples' answer, which included: Elijah, Jeremiah, "or one of the prophets." (Matthew 16:14)

Another question about the rebirth of the soul who had previously been Elijah was raised in the next chapter of Matthew's gospel. It arose as the three disciples closest to Jesus were descending from the Mount of Transfiguration, having been "greatly frightened" by what they had witnessed. On the mountaintop, when Jesus revealed his true Self to them, the disciples had heard the voice of God saying: "This is my beloved Son, with him I am pleased; hear him." Prior to that time, only Peter had recognized Jesus as the Messiah, the Christ.[23] Now, the other two did as well. But they wondered about the order of things, and they asked why the scribes had said that Elijah was to appear first, *before* the Lord, as in Malachi's prophecy. Jesus replied:

> Elijah will come first, so that everything might be ful-
> filled. But I say unto you, Elijah has already come, and

they did not know him, and they did to him whatever they pleased. Thus also the Son of man is bound to suffer from them. Then the disciples understood that what he had told them was about John the Baptist. (Matthew 17: 6-13)

Yet another reference to Malachi's prophecy of Elijah's return appears in the Gospel of Matthew (plus seven more references in the other three gospels). Speaking to the multitudes, Jesus reveals that John is:

...he, of whom it is written, Behold I send my messenger before your face to prepare the way before you... For all the prophets and the law prophesied until John. And if ye wish to accept it, he is Elijah who was to come. He that hath ears to hear, let him hear. (Matthew 11: 7, 10, 13-15)

Just as passages concerning the notion of reincarnation remained in the New Testament, so did the principle of karma. Perhaps the clearest reference to karma is contained in the question posed by the disciples about the man who had been born blind: "Who did sin, this man, or his parents, that he was born blind?" (John 9:1-2) The premise underlying the question is that blindness from birth represented a karmic debt from a previous existence. The disciples appeared to be asking *whose* debt it was—that of the man himself, or the parents whose lot it was to raise a blind child. Jesus answers that the cause was neither, "But that the works of God might be seen in him." Yet the premise of the question, indicating a belief in karma, is not refuted.

There are countless expressions of the workings of karmic law in the teachings of Jesus: "Give, and it shall be given unto you... For with the measure that you measure, it will be measured to you." (Luke, 6:38) "Whatever you wish men to do for you, do likewise also for them; for this is the law and the prophets." (Matthew, 7:12) And from Paul, the main exponent of the teachings: "Do not be deceived; God is not mocked; for whatever a man sows, that shall he also reap." (Galatians, 6:7) Owen Rutter comments, "Here is the whole teaching of the Law," adding, "The corollary...is equally true: 'Whatsoever a man reapeth, that hath he also sown.'"[24]

According to esoteric sources, Jesus—like Moses—was raised in an environment where karma and reincarnation were held as basic truths.[25] Joseph and Mary are believed to have been Essenes, members of the pious and ascetic Jewish sect described by the ancient historian Josephus as a "closely knit brotherhood with similarities to the Pythagoreans." At the time of Jesus' birth, the Essenes—whose communities flourished on the shores of the Dead Sea and elsewhere in Palestine from the 2nd century BCE through much of the 1st century CE—were preparing for the arrival of the Messiah. Manly P. Hall (1901–1990), a leading esoteric scholar of the 20th century, states that Jesus was raised by the Essenes and later initiated into their Mysteries.[26]

Exoteric knowledge about the Essenes comes from two sources: the Dead Sea Scrolls found in 1947 at Qumran, near the site of an ancient Essene community; and also accounts of writers from that time. Roman naturalist Pliny the Elder (23–79 CE) was so impressed by the Essenes' way of life that he called them "wonderful besides all others in the world." [27] Philo of Alexandria (c. 20 BCE–60 CE), citing the Essenes' definition of righteousness as "love of God, love of virtue, and love of mankind," observed: "Their love of man is proved by their benevolence and equality, and their having all things in common." Their life was "so highly to be prized," wrote Philo, "that not only commoners but also great kings look upon them with admiration and amazement."[28]

While there is no concrete evidence linking Jesus himself to the Essenes, scholars of the Dead Sea Scrolls speculate that John the Baptist was likely familiar with the Essenes' teachings, and that Jesus was initially a follower of John. Given New Testament depictions of the closeness of their mothers at the time of their births, and given their intertwined destinies, it would not be surprising to learn that both had emerged from the same community of "pious ones."

Of the several contemporaneous accounts of the Essenes' beliefs that have survived, the most extensive are those of Jewish historian

Flavius Josephus (c. 37–100 CE). In *The Jewish War*, Josephus, who writes unselfconsciously of his own belief that souls are reborn into conditions reflecting past-life actions,[29] also discusses the Essenes' beliefs. Commenting that "their course of life [is] better than other men," he notes that "they teach the immortality of the soul and esteem that the rewards of righteousness are to be earnestly striven for."[30] Their doctrine held, in part, that:

> ...bodies are corruptible, and that the matter they are made of is not permanent; but that the souls are immortal...and that they come out of the most subtle air and are united to their bodies as to prisons, into which they are drawn by a certain natural enticement; but that when they are set free from the bonds of flesh, they then, as released from a long bondage, rejoice and mount upward.[31]

The Essenes were known to have been among the most educated Jews of their time. Their doctrines on the soul reflected a commingling of the influences that pervaded ancient Palestine—ranging from the Kabala, which the Essenes held in high esteem, to Pythagoras (c. 570–490 BCE), the first of the Greeks to have articulated the doctrine of rebirth, to Buddhist teachings disseminated by monks traveling throughout the Middle East prior to the birth of Christ.[32] Although the word "reincarnation" does not appear in historical records, Essenes were known to have believed in the "pre-existence" of souls, as did many early Christians, and they described themselves as "people who live for a thousand generations" and as "an eternal people," terms highly suggestive of the soul's journey through innumerable lifetimes.[33]

If Jesus *was* educated by the Essenes and initiated into their sacred mysteries, he surely would have taught his disciples about the soul's evolution through rebirth.[34] There is evidence that for several centuries following his death, this belief was widely upheld by Christians. Among its strongest proponents were eminent Church fathers who had studied at the celebrated school of Neo-Platonism in Alexandria, where Plato's teachings were revived in the third century CE. Origen, whose writings on reincarnation were later banned, had studied there with Plotinus (205–270), who has been called "the fountainhead of the higher Christian mysticism."[35]

The writings of Plotinus reflect what many highly educated people believed about the life of the soul in the formative period of Christian theology. The following excerpt foreshadows the classic insight of Shakespeare—that "all the world is but a stage":

> For on earth, in all the succession of life, it is not the Soul within but the Shadow outside of the authentic man, that grieves and complains and acts out the plot on this world stage which men have dotted with stages of their own constructing... Every man...makes his way...to the place, good or bad, that suits him, and takes the position he has made his own. There he talks and acts, in blasphemy and crime or in all goodness: for the actors bring to this play what they were before it was ever staged... But these actors, Souls, hold a peculiar dignity; they act in a vaster place than any stage; the Author has made them masters of all this world.[36]

By the 4th century, the doctrine of reincarnation had been expunged from the New Testament canon but was kept alive by the Gnostics, a mystical Christian sect. Their teaching revolved around the search for *gnosis*, the Greek word for knowledge, by which they meant direct knowledge or intuitive perception of divine truth. Some scholars suggest that the original Gnostic teaching may have been derived from Jesus, who taught it to his close disciples, who then passed it on to others deemed worthy. The notion that Jesus had a secret teaching for his disciples is alluded to in the Gospel of Mark: "And Jesus said to them, To you is given to know the mystery of the kingdom of God, but to outsiders everything has to be explained by parables." (4:11) "Without parables he did not speak to them; but to his disciples, among themselves, he explained everything." (4:34)

Central to the Gnostic beliefs was the idea that a spark of Divine Spirit existed within every person. Christ, for them, was a title signifying that Jesus was a full embodiment of that Spirit.[37] They saw the purpose of Christ's incarnation, as he himself had taught, to be a demonstration of divinity. The words "no one cometh unto the Father but by me" were understood by Gnostics to mean "but by following the living example of the Christ." The key to understanding those words was contained in their secret doctrine: Through the workings of karma and reincarnation over lifetimes, the human soul ultimately reveals what the Apostle Paul called "Christ in you, the hope of glory."

The belief in the soul's evolution through rebirth did not die an easy death within Christendom. Internal struggles continued for centuries, taking different forms. With the official anathema, the doctrine was effectively suppressed *within* the Church, but not entirely among people who saw themselves as followers of Christ's inner teachings. In fact, some historians argue that much of the wrath that fueled the Inquisition of the 14th century was directed at such Gnostic heresies as reincarnation, and at Gnostic sects like the Cathars (whom others referred to as "the good men" and "the perfect ones"), which flourished during the Middle Ages and kept the forbidden teachings alive.

But why, one might well ask? Why was official Christianity so violently opposed to the principle of rebirth, while Eastern religions have taught it openly for millennia? It is also absent from standard Jewish teachings, though contained in a body of literature based on the Kabala that is now accessible to all who seek it. Likewise, it is now readily available in esoteric Christian texts. Still, within Catholic, Eastern Orthodox, and other mainstream Christian churches, the notion of the soul's rebirth continues to arouse fierce opposition. Why?

A possible explanation was offered by Joseph Head and S.L. Cranston, compilers and editors of *Reincarnation: The Phoenix Fire Mystery*, the most exhaustive study ever conducted on this subject. With regard to the actions of the "Defenders of the Faith," the

Inquisitors who sought to annihilate Christians who believed in re-birth, Head and Cranston conjecture that the explanation revolves around the issue of authority. "The believer in this teaching tends to hold himself responsible for his own progress and salvation," they wrote. "Such a person has no need of priests and little regard for...redemption conferred by institutional authority."[38]

In fact, according to the Ageless Wisdom, the readiness to ac-cept responsibility for one's own "progress and salvation" is the mark of an awakening soul. When an individual approaches the end of the path of human evolution and embarks upon the Path of Return to God, he or she comes under the authority of his or her own soul, leaving behind the need for outer authorities. A pivotal phase of this Path is called the Path of Discipleship, a stage charac-terized by the soul's willingness to take charge of its own spiritual growth through various self-disciplines.

The fact that in the past, only a rare few within any popula-tion reached that stage of spiritual maturity, might explain why both Moses and Jesus may have given one set of teachings "for the multitudes" and another for those prepared to assimilate truths concerning the life of the soul. Likewise, it would account for the fact that all major religions of East and West contain an inner core of esoteric teachings which share the premise that the soul evolves over lifetimes—through the workings of the laws of cause and ef-fect—and that there comes a point in the grand arc of the soul's journey when this truth is recognized. Grasping this truth involves a recognition, in the words of H.P. Blavatsky, of "the kinship of man's spirit with the Universal Soul—God."[39]

In the past, those few souls deemed ready for such teachings were guided to the inner mysteries by a teacher, rabbi, guru, or master. Not only was it considered psychologically dangerous for individuals to approach divine wisdom on their own, without the guidance of someone more advanced, but access to the secret wis-dom was tightly controlled. This began to change in the late 19th century with the recognition by the Spiritual Hierarchy that grow-ing numbers of human beings would soon be "coming of age," ready to assume responsibility for their spiritual lives. The reintroduction of the Ageless Wisdom to the modern West, initially through Blavatsky's writings, was a response to that readiness.

A core principle of these teachings may further explain Church opposition to the doctrine of reincarnation: the principle that everything in existence is constantly evolving—our galaxy, our solar system, our planet, and all kingdoms of life. While physical science has discovered the laws governing the form side of evolution, esoteric science contains the laws that govern the evolution of the consciousness within the form. Under spiritual laws, units of consciousness advance from one kingdom of nature to the next. As the workings of these laws fulfill the purposes of Earth's evolution, it is predicted that *many* members of the human kingdom will achieve Christ-like perfection and enter the spiritual kingdom.[40] For those who perceive Christ as the *only* son of God, this is blasphemy.

Paradoxically, one of the foremost proponents of reincarnation in the West *did* see this notion as blasphemy upon first encountering it. Edgar Cayce (1877–1945), the American clairvoyant known as "the sleeping prophet," began his life as a devout, evangelical Christian. Initially, he recoiled at the notion of rebirth when it turned up in a psychic reading that he gave while in a trance. Until then, information that he had transmitted in trance state had pertained largely to physical healing. But the credibility and efficacy of that information, with its cures for medical conditions deemed hopeless by physicians, had opened Cayce's mind. Over time, he came to see reincarnation and karma as the mechanism of human evolution. And like the Gnostics, he saw Christ as "the pattern"— not the *only* Son of God, but the exemplar for those seeking the way of return to God.

Cayce, about whom numerous volumes have been written, made a remarkable contribution to humanity's understanding of the workings of spiritual laws. Prior to the readings given by him, reincarnation was merely a concept for many people, particularly in the West. It was a theory that remained unproven, albeit one that had found resonance in many of the greatest minds. As a result of Cayce's past-life readings, and investigations into the effects of these readings upon the individuals who received them, reincarnation has emerged from the realm of theory into the realm of practical usefulness.

Cayce's legacy is all the more extraordinary in light of the facts of his early life. Growing up on a farm in rural Kentucky, he had aspired to become a preacher, but with only a ninth grade education was unable to reach that goal. He later became a Sunday school teacher, rereading the Bible once a year, while working as a bookstore clerk and insurance agent. Then suddenly, he lost his voice. At age twenty-one, an incurable case of laryngitis left him unable to speak for an entire year. When it became clear that medical doctors were stymied by his malady, Cayce sought help elsewhere. He consulted a hypnotist who put him into a trance and asked him to diagnose the cause of his own condition and prescribe the cure. He did so, and thus began a lifetime of healing.

Cayce's advice was sought in over 30,000 documented cases, 25,000 of which involved physical healing.[41] People from all over the United States, and later from around the world, sought readings from him to cure conditions beyond the reach of orthodox medicine. One dramatic case, involving a young girl from Alabama, demonstrated the nature of the medical insight accessible to him while in trance. The girl appeared to have suddenly, inexplicably, become "mentally ill," to the degree that she was institutionalized. In trance, Cayce saw that the girl's wisdom tooth had become impacted, affecting a nerve in her brain. With the removal of the tooth, her emotional health was immediately restored.

As Cayce's readings unfolded, the notion emerged that suffering in this life was often rooted in the past. With the unique ability to "read" the Akashic Record—the etheric imprint on the "skein of time and space" of all that has ever occurred—he was able to identify the causes of present suffering in previous incarnations. In one reading, it was explained that the "Book of Life" is the portion of the Akashic Record pertaining to an individual soul's history. It was further explained that this "book" could only be "opened when self has attuned to the infinite, and may be read by those attuning to that consciousness."[42]

This meant, in effect, that past-life readings were to be given only to individuals who had become spiritually mature enough to derive benefit from them. A systematic study of 2,500 of these readings, and their effects upon the individuals who received them, was undertaken in the 1940s by Gina Cerminara, a psychologist and author of *Many Mansions: The Edgar Cayce Story on Reincarnation*. Through her research, Dr. Cerminara identified a variety of different forms in which karmic liabilities from the past turned up in the present. She termed one group of cases "symbolic karma," as the affliction appeared to symbolically mirror behavior from the past.

One particularly well-documented case involved a boy whose problem was chronic bed-wetting. Neither psychiatrists nor other specialists had known how to alleviate the condition. When the boy was eleven, his father obtained a life reading from Cayce. It stated that in a previous life, during the witchcraft trials in Salem, Massachusetts, the boy had been a minister who had engaged in punishing "witches" by ducking them in a pond. The remedy offered did not address the physical condition, but rather the subconscious guilt carried over from the past.

It was recommended that the parents use positive suggestion every night as the boy was falling asleep, by repeating: "You are good and kind" and "You are going to help everyone with whom you come into contact."[43] His mother, a lawyer, reported that the nine-year cycle of bed-wetting was broken on the first night; the condition was completely cured within several months. Evidently, the idea that the boy's guilt could be expiated through kindness to others was registered subconsciously. Once highly introverted, he became well-adjusted and well-liked, exhibiting an unusual degree of tolerance toward others.

In Cayce's readings, the ultimate purpose of life is seen to be the achievement of spiritual perfection—defined as the embodiment of love, or Christ consciousness, expressed through service to others. The earth is viewed as a schoolhouse in which souls incarnate to learn from past mistakes, passing through the full range of human conditions while advancing toward oneness with all and with God, the "First Cause." The Sanskrit word "karma" means "act" or "action." By karmic law, action produces reaction in subsequent lives. Cayce saw the law's purpose as fostering an awareness of past wrongs and an acceptance of responsibility for them—two keys to spiritual evolution.

Another kind of proof of reincarnation emerged in the 20th century from an entirely different angle. Dr. Ian Stevenson (1918–2007), a psychiatrist on the faculty of the University of Virginia for many years, undertook a long-term study of children who had detailed memories of past lives. These children, living largely in Eastern countries like India and Sri Lanka, but also in other cultures around the world where reincarnation is accepted, numbered in the thousands. In his landmark book, *Twenty Cases Suggestive of Reincarnation,* Stevenson noted that it is common for a small percentage of children in such cultures to remember past lives. His contribution was to investigate and document these cases with rigorous, Western-style, scientific methods.

Though he used the word "suggestive" in his book's title, indicating that his research lacks the scientific verifiability of a laboratory experiment, Stevenson's cases are so air-tight that no other explanation seems plausible. For example, it is common for these children to begin speaking spontaneously of past lives as soon as they can talk—between eighteen months and three years of age[44]—reciting the child's previous name, the names of relatives in the previous life, the place of the child in the previous family's constellation, incidents that occurred in the previous life, and the circumstances of death. In many of the cases documented by Stevenson, previous family members and neighbors were still alive and living in close enough proximity for him to verify the information presented by the child.

Some of the most convincing cases involved young children who spoke languages or sang songs of foreign cultures with which they had had no contact whatsoever in this life. In many instances the children had birth marks at sites on their bodies where they had been wounded in a previous life, or had wounded someone else. Among the most astonishing cases are those involving children with fresh memories of having been a parent, who pleaded with their current parents to arrange a visit with the previous family. During these visits, the child behaved toward past-life family members not as a child, but as the previous parent had. Equally astonishing is that previous family members, once they were convinced of the soul's identity, responded to the soul in the parental role it had previously played. In some instances, restored past-life relationships were then sustained *along with* present ones.

Other forms of "proof" of rebirth are easier to discern. For example, according to the wisdom teachings, children called "prodigies" are actually souls demonstrating gifts and abilities that were developed in previous lives. The phenomenon of Mozart, who composed his first symphony at age four, was recently echoed in the life of a New York boy who began composing at four and whose symphonies were being performed by major orchestras when he was fifteen.[45] Another boy, able to add and subtract at eighteen months old and recite world history at age eight, graduated from college at thirteen while pursuing three advanced degrees, each in the goal of serving humanity.[46]

In the days of ancient Rome, Cicero (106–43 BCE) recorded his observations of the signs of reincarnation in children. After citing "the ancients" who believed in rebirth, including Pythagoras and Socrates, "the wisest of men," Cicero wrote:

> It is again a strong proof of men knowing most things before birth, that when mere children they grasp innumerable facts with such speed as to show that they are not then taking them in for the first time, but remembering and recalling them.[47]

There is a logic to the theory of rebirth that makes sense of otherwise inexplicable differences between human beings. Science cannot explain, on the basis of genetics and environment alone, why there are both serial killers and saints among us. Nor can it

account for the extreme differences that exist between siblings—
why one is a prodigy and another an ordinary student; why one
is a materialist and another is drawn to spirituality. Even among
twins, there are marked differences in interests and capacities that
can only be explained if we allow for the possibility that their souls
have had different "histories."

Often the question arises as to why, if we have lived before,
most of us have no memory of previous lives. The answer seems
to lie in the very workings of the laws of conscious evolution. The
fact that awareness of past lives is connected to spiritual awakening
suggests that a degree of wisdom is necessary before such memories can serve a useful spiritual purpose. Plato hinted at this in
his "Myth of Er," which portrays what occurs after death in "the
other world," as souls choose their next life and prepare for rebirth.
Before returning, all souls had to drink from the river Lethe, the
Forgetful River, "but those who had no wisdom to save them drank
more than the measure."

For incarnate souls who awaken to their true spiritual nature,
the memory of having lived before gradually seeps into conscious
awareness, although details of previous existences may not be re-
called. In presenting his arguments in support of reincarnation,
Sir Arthur Conan Doyle (1859–1930), the British writer, mentioned
"vague recognitions and memories which are occasionally too definite to be easily explained as atavistic impressions." In answer to
"the natural question 'Why, then, do we not remember such existences?'" he wrote:

> We may point out that such remembrance would
> enormously complicate our present life, and that such
> existences may well form a cycle which is all clear to
> us when we come to the end of it, when perhaps we
> may see a whole rosary of lives threaded upon one
> personality.[48]

In the final analysis, the truth of reincarnation either finds
resonance in the soul or it does not. Where resonance *is* found,
it becomes a "fact of life" as opposed to mere belief. The Ageless

Wisdom presents rebirth as a law, which operates in conjunction with the law of karma to assure that our souls return to Earth in human form until the scales of justice have been balanced and spiritual perfection has become manifest. In *A Study of Karma*, theosophist Annie Besant defined it as a law of causation, "eternal, changeless, invariable, inviolable; law which can never be broken, existing in the nature of things."[49] It is, she observed, "as much part of natural law as the laws of electricity." [50]

Describing the workings of this law, Alice Bailey wrote:

> It is the soul in all forms which reincarnates, choosing and building suitable physical, emotional and mental vehicles through which to learn the next needed lessons... Under the Law of Rebirth, man slowly develops mind, then mind begins to control the feeling, emotional nature, and finally reveals the soul and its nature and environment to man. At that point in his development, the man begins to tread the Path of Return, and orients himself gradually (after many lives) to the Kingdom of God.[51]

Reorientation from the human kingdom to the Kingdom of God, the spiritual kingdom, involves a process of refinement. As the laws of cause and effect work out, and the dross of the personality is purified, the soul on the Path attunes to higher vibrations. By distilling wisdom from life experiences in the human kingdom, the soul builds increasingly more refined personality "vehicles." Eventually, as this reorientation proceeds, the incarnate soul attains conscious resonance with the spiritual kingdom.

A long-time student and teacher of the Ageless Wisdom described the process poetically:

> Through all of our lives we gain in quality. As we raise our vibration, so are the higher qualities (virtues) built into the causal body—the body of the Soul. Our personal lives can be compared to the process of sculpture. We start out like a block of rough granite, with the Soul

as the Sculptor gradually removing all that is not needed and slowly shaping that rough block into something
that is eventually quite beautiful to behold.[52]

NOTES

1   Macquarrie, *Mediators Between Human and Divine*, 54.

2   From the Akankheyya-Sutta, quoted in Bucke, *Cosmic Consciousness*, 86.

3   Reincarnation refers to the cyclic rebirth of the human soul in *human* forms. It does *not* refer to transmigration, a term generally understood to connote belief in the migration of souls between the human and lower kingdoms.

4   Bailey, *Esoteric Healing*, 402.

5   Many contemporary scholars contend that these beliefs first appeared in India during the first millennium BCE with the Upanishads and the rise of Hinduism; others say they may have appeared as early as 10,000 BCE. See citation in endnote 20.

6   *The Catholic Encyclopedia* offers a revised account of the Fifth Ecumenical Council held at Constantinople in 553, explaining that technically the Church itself may not have promulgated the anathemas (specifically against Origen) as was long believed. Since Roman emperors then controlled the Church, the motive behind the anathemas may have been political.

7   The anathemas in question were made against Origen (c.185–254 CE) and his teachings. Although the word "reincarnation" does not appear in the controversy-laden anathemas, "pre-existence" does appear and was presumed by many, well into the modern age, to have the same meaning. Origen was a highly esteemed Greek theologian and Platonist, as well as an early Church teacher. When read in the light of Platonism, the wording of the anathemas against him points clearly to a belief in the soul's rebirth.

8   Rutter, *The Scales of Karma*, 10.

9   *Ibid*, 12.

10 The reader is referred to Head and Cranston, eds., *Reincarnation: The Phoenix Fire Mystery* for an exhaustive account of this belief through human history and for quotations from countless individuals, including those cited.

11 From the *Encyclopedia of Religion and Ethics*, quoted in *Reincarnation*, 126.

12 The first records of the Kabala were made in the 1st century CE; the first books were published in the Middle Ages. Still it remained largely an oral tradition, as it was recommended that seekers (all of whom were male until very recent times) be initiated by a personal guide.

13 Hall, *The Secret Teachings of All Ages*, CXIII.

14 The word "transmigrations" as used here implies the principle of reincarnation.

15 Quoted in Head and Cranston, *Reincarnation*, 130.

16 Rutter, *The Scales of Karma*, 67.

17 *The Encyclopedia Britannica* estimates that Moses lived around 1400 BCE.

18 Quoted in Head and Cranston, *Reincarnation*, 129.

19 Rutter, *The Scales of Karma*, 67.

20 Bailey, *The Light of the Soul*, xiii.

21 Hall, *The Secret Teachings of All Ages*, XXXIV-V.

22 It should be pointed out that orthodox Christian scholars offer other interpretations of these passages.

23 The word "messiah" is Hebrew for "anointed," which in Greek is "Christos."

24 Rutter, *The Scales of Karma*, 134.

25 These sources include esoteric scholars such as Head and Cranston, and Manly Hall; esoteric teachers such as H.P. Blavatsky and Annie Besant; and the extraordinary psychic Edgar Cayce. Most hold that Jesus was born into the Essene community, some that he was an initiate of their Mysteries.

26 Hall, *The Secret Teachings of All Ages*, CLXXIX. It should be mentioned that some of Hall's knowledge, gleaned intuitively, has aroused controversy.

27 These and the following quotes from Philo and Josephus appear at www.thenazareneway.com/classical_authors_on_the_essenes.html (accessed May 5, 2007).

28 These quotes from Philo appear in several different texts at the above-mentioned website.

29 Quoted in Head and Cranston, *Reincarnation*, 124-5.

30 Hall, *The Secret Teachings of All Ages*, CLXXVIII.

31 Quoted from Head and Cranston, *Reincarnation*, 125.

32 Head and Cranston, *Reincarnation*, 125.

33 To enter the Essenes' inner circles took years of probationary training. Those qualified for initiation into their mystery teachings swore oaths not to divulge what they learned on pain of death. Thus the secret teachings of the Essenes may never be discovered by traditional scholars.

34 Academic scholars of the Dead Sea Scrolls argue that they contain no specific mention of reincarnation, but only "pre-existence" of the soul.

Yet, as recently as the 18th and 19th centuries, learned individuals used "pre-existence" to mean reincarnation.

35 Head and Cranston, *Reincarnation*, 230.

36 Quoted from Head and Cranston, *Reincarnation*, 231.

37 Head and Cranston, *Reincarnation*, 155.

38 *Ibid,* 164.

39 Blavatsky, *Isis Unveiled,* vol. 1, 6.

40 According to the Apostle John, Christ said, "He who believes in me shall do the works which I do; and even greater than these things shall he do." (John 14:12).

41 Cerminara, *Many Mansions,* 13.

42 Todeschi, *Edgar Cayce on the Akashic Records*, xviii-xix.

43 Cerminara, *Many Mansions,* 54.

44 Stevenson found that such memories generally fade by age 6 or 7.

45 CBS, "60 Minutes," November 28, 2004. This boy's name is Jay Greenberg.

46 CBS, "Sunday Morning," February 6, 2005. This boy's name is Gregg Smith.

47 Quoted in Head and Cranston, *Reincarnation*, 222.

48 *Ibid,* 350-1.

49 Besant, *A Study in Karma*, 2-3.

50 *Ibid,* 4.

51 Bailey, *The Reappearance of the Christ*, 118-119.

52 Malvin Artley, e-mail letter to esoteric students, May 2005.

THE PATH

Soul unfoldment is...but one of the great processes of nature.

~Alice A. Bailey

A TELLING SIGN OF our times is the ubiquitous notion of "the path." Like a quiet river that suddenly swelled and overflowed its banks, the idea of the inner spiritual path—long submerged in the West— has been flooding our cultural landscape. In recent decades, the publishing industry has been saturated with book titles featuring words like "path," "journey," and "odyssey."

And yet, as with any idea whose popularity precedes genuine understanding, the truth about the inner path has remained largely veiled. An advertisement for a spiritual book club in 2006 serves to illustrate how popularity can often subvert true meaning. In this ad, the spiritual journey is portrayed as a travel adventure to a far-off land. Books, magazines, and even cruises for the like-minded are highlighted, with a sales pitch geared to making the journey more pleasant, comfortable, and enjoyable.

In actuality, the spiritual path is never pleasant or comfortable, though joy is surely among its ultimate rewards. Unlike a cruise, which picks us up and drops us off at the same place with our personalities intact, the spiritual path transfigures the very nature of our being. By treading the path we become an entirely different being from the personality with which we were identified at the start, undergoing a metamorphosis that is, by its nature, often painful.

One of the most enduring metaphors for the spiritual path is the transformation of the lowly caterpillar into a butterfly. Out of its own substance, the ground-hugging grub weaves the medium for its metamorphosis—the chrysalis within which it evolves into a beautiful creature with wings. The human being undergoes an equally dramatic transformation, unfolding the path to liberation from within the depths of the soul and emerging, after great struggle, as an expression of divinity in the world.

What results from this inner struggle is a lattice of consciousness between two worlds—the human and the divine. This concept, foreign though it may seem to the modern scientific mind, lies at the heart of every major world religion. Within Hinduism, Judaism, Christianity, and Islam there is an inner path that leads the awakening soul into the crucible of reorientation, purification, and illumination, culminating in union with God. In Buddhist sects with no concept of a personal God, the goal is parallel.[1] Nirvana, the ultimate state of Buddhist consciousness, literally means "extinction" (of the boundaries of the personal self), allowing for absorption into the boundless Absolute.

Such elevated states are not easily understood or readily embraced, yet they represent the true purpose of the spiritual path. The fact that this purpose is often obscured appears linked to a phenomenon unique to our times: the emergence of spirituality into "the world." Earlier in human history, the individual who pursued the path to God was obliged to leave the world—to renounce worldly possessions, sever personal ties, and enter a cloister or hermitage. The goal of the spiritual path was deemed so antithetical to worldly values as to be impossible of achievement outside the protective insulation of monasteries, forests, or caves.

In this time of transition to a spiritual age, it appears that the *idea* of the path has entered the world largely divorced from traditional religious settings, where the ultimate goal of divine union *was* well understood. With the confluence of Eastern and Western traditions, contemporary spiritual seekers are often attracted to certain practices of a particular religious path, often learning them in isolation from the deeper transformative processes. Adding to the current lack of clarity is the dearth of genuine role models for seekers who are living in the world while pursuing the path.

Until fairly recently, individuals who chose to follow the path to God did so not only away from the material world, but also within the confines of the religion of their birth. This ancient practice initially came under challenge only a little over a century ago, as a result of the first World Parliament of Religions held in Chicago in 1893. This seminal encounter between religious leaders of East and West had the effect of allowing diverse spiritual teachings to flow into the larger world—an evolutionary advance that may have served, if only temporarily, to untether many spiritual insights from the inner path of transformation.

The most outstanding individual at this historic event, by many accounts, was a striking, turbaned figure from the East— Swami Vivekananda (1863–1902), the closest disciple of the Hindu saint, Ramakrishna. Considered the most brilliant and charismatic speaker among the delegates, Vivekananda electrified the congress with passages from Hindu scriptures on the universality of religious truth, the convergence of all paths to God, and the brotherhood of humanity. He was showered with accolades by fellow delegates, Western journalists, and by distinguished Americans and Britons—many of whom later became his disciples. This singular individual contributed significantly to the wave of universal spirituality that has since spread around the globe.

The response of the World Parliament caused Vivekananda to realize that India had a gift to offer the world. Remaining in the West for several years thereafter, he established societies for the teaching of Vedanta—the Hindu philosophy of the inherent relationship between the individual Self (Atman) and the Absolute (Brahman). Upon returning to India, he mounted an intensive campaign to encourage his countrymen to "broadcast" the wisdom bound up in their religion, declaring: "The wonderful truths confined in our scriptures must be brought out from the books, the monasteries, and the forests and scattered over the land."[2]

Traditionally, monks in India, as elsewhere, had left the world in search of *personal* liberation, living in isolation and practicing severe self-disciplines to achieve divine realization. Vivekananda set out to create a new order of monastic life, exhorting his fellow monks to bring light *into* the world—to reflect the divinity inherent in the human soul through their teaching and their personal example. It became his mission, for the remainder of his short life, to "raise the condition of the masses through loving service and to spread the life-giving ideas of the Master [Ramakrishna] over the entire world."[3]

Whether directly or indirectly, Vivekananda may well have lit the spark that later led countless Hindu monks to the shores of the United States. By the 1960s and 70s, self-styled Indian gurus could be found in many major U.S. cities, often forming their own communities and teaching centers. Buddhist monks and teachers from many nations soon followed. Their collective presence left an indelible imprint upon the religious landscape of America in the latter half of the 20th century. While many churches were emptying out, young Americans were flocking to Hindu *ashrams*, Zen monasteries, and Tibetan Buddhist learning centers.

What attracted them, in the observation of Thomas Keating—a Catholic priest, monk, and abbot—was "a living experience of spirituality" that was absent from mainstream churches. Watching the rapid growth of Eastern spirituality in the U.S. during the mid-20th century, Father Keating realized that Catholic and other Christian churches were failing to satisfy the needs of individuals searching for an *inner* experience of God. Gurus from the East were teaching about the divinity of the human soul, in striking contrast to the doctrine of original sin, and they presented the notion of a *pathway* to divine union. For tens of thousands of Americans, meditation—fundamental to the spiritual path—was becoming a daily practice.

Father Keating's response was the creation of a program to bring the inner path of Christianity out of the cloisters and reintroduce it to modern laypeople. In *Open Mind Open Heart: The Contemplative Dimension of the Gospel,* he notes with levity: "The idea of laypeople pursuing the spiritual path is not something new. It just hasn't been popular in the past thousand years."[4] Citing the 3rd century Church father, Origen, who believed the place to practice Christian asceticism was within the world, the former abbot commented, "The essence of monastic life is not its structures but its interior practice, and the heart of interior practice is contemplative prayer."[5]

Contemplative prayer is described by Father Keating as a method of inner transformation that leads to union with God. In the silence of the heart, the womb of the mystical relationship with the divine, it is said that a "restructuring of consciousness" takes place that alters one's perception of reality. Over time, the practitioner is empowered "to perceive, relate and respond with increasing sensitivity to the divine presence in, through, and beyond everything that exists."[6] He sees this method of prayer as "the school through which we pass" to arrive at the contemplative *life*, an "abiding state of divine union in which one is moved both in prayer and in action by the Spirit."

Starting with a group of twelve colleagues in New York City in 1985, Father Keating set out to introduce this path to Christian seekers living ordinary lives in the world. To facilitate their entry into the inner silence—twice each day—he developed a technique called "centering prayer," a method of stilling the mind that he borrowed from Eastern meditation practices. By 2005, the centering prayer network had mushroomed to include 60,000 people in thirty countries committed to "an ever-deepening union with the living Christ and the practical caring for others that flows from that relationship."[7]

The rapid growth of movements such as Centering Prayer may well foreshadow a reawakening of the *inner* dimension of Christianity, still the dominant religion of the West. As the soul of the religion emerges, the focus can be expected to shift from doctrine and dogma to its inner core: the life of Christ. From an esoteric perspective, the major events of Christ's life symbolize the stages of the spiritual path encountered universally by every soul: birth, baptism, transfiguration, crucifixion, and resurrection. According to Richard Smoley, author of *Inner Christianity: A Guide to the Esoteric Tradition,* "The story of Christ is not only an account of an historical man but also a figurative representation of the path that each of us must follow to attain liberation."[8]

In the past, Christians who followed the inner path of liberation without Church sanction were often persecuted. The Gnostics, for example, who sought direct access to God, were viewed as subversive by the Church hierarchy and ultimately condemned as heretics. Their search for *gnosis,* defined by Smoley as "direct, intuitive knowing that surpasses ordinary reason and confers spiritual liberation,"[9] led them to perceptions and practices that often contradicted official Church doctrine. Though they believed they were following the path to God revealed by Christ to his closest disciples, the inner authority of their *gnosis* was seen as a threat to the outer authority of the Church.

With the eradication of the Gnostic gospels by the official church, esoteric knowledge about the inner path of Christianity went underground, where it was kept alive by small sects and passed along secretly for many centuries. The rediscovery of Gnostic texts in 1945 in Nag Hammadi, Egypt, has served to reignite Christian esotericism, and may also herald a development of more universal significance. According to the wisdom teachings, a hallmark of the Aquarian Age will be the inner authority of the soul. It is *gnosis*—the experience of direct, intuitive knowing—which confers this inner authority.

In the Ageless Wisdom, there are two essential pathways to the inner authority of the soul and the Kingdom of Spirit: mystical experience and esoteric knowledge. Traditionally, these two approaches have been seen as being poles apart. Typically, the mystic is viewed as heart-centered, propelled toward divine union by love, reliant on faith and prayer for inner growth, and drawn to Mystery. The esotericist, on the other hand, is seen as mind-oriented, impelled by the urge to understand "the Mind of God," and attracted to the concreteness of esoteric science with its laws, principles, and systems of knowledge about the cosmos.

In actual practice, however, mystical experience and esoteric knowledge are complementary rather than mutually exclusive. The Ageless Wisdom itself, a blend of East and West, encompasses both science *and* mystery, mind *and* heart.[10] Given the overwhelming influence of the mind since the dawn of the modern era, it is noteworthy that the "prerequisite" for actually stepping onto the spiritual path is experiencing the flow of love that accompanies the opening of the heart, upon awakening. As mentioned earlier, the soul's journey from the human into the spiritual kingdom begins in "the cave of the heart."[11]

From that point onward, however, once the heart opens and the seeker begins to experience that "feeling of oneness with all that lives," in the words of Annie Besant, esoteric knowledge becomes invaluable to spiritual progress. Contained in the wisdom teachings are conceptual "maps" of the world of spirit, a figurative "compass" for orienting to that world, and a set of requirements for entering progressively further into it.[12] The seeker discovers that the spiritual realm, like all realms of nature, is governed by laws. Knowledge of these laws can serve to accelerate conscious evolution. Adherence to these laws, over time, transforms mystical glimpses of spiritual reality into a higher *stage* of conscious awareness.

One of the names given to the Ageless Wisdom is the "science of the soul." But unlike physical science, this science, paradoxically, is riddled with mystery. It deals with subtle dimensions of reality that we cannot see or touch, as does quantum physics. But in contrast to quantum physics, which has instruments for registering subtle energies, the science of the soul essentially teaches seekers *themselves* to become instruments for registering spiritual energies. The means by which we develop the sensitivity to discern spiritual forces and energies is by treading the path of transformation.

From one angle, what transpires on this path can be explained with the vocabulary of science. Keeping in mind that spirit is matter at its highest rate of vibration and matter is spirit at its lowest rate, the soul on the Path of Return is actually learning to raise the vibrational frequency of its human mechanism to the point where it becomes resonant with the frequencies of the spiritual kingdom.

Achieving this resonance is what allows for the soul's conscious interaction with the next higher kingdom.

And yet, notwithstanding such rational explanations, the path of spiritual transformation is permeated by Mystery. The mystery of *all* mysteries, and the essence of the "secret doctrine" that has been buried through the ages, has to do with the true nature of the human soul—its origin and its destiny. The awesomeness of this intrinsic mystery is prefaced by the Tibetan master, Djwhal Khul, with these words:

> Humanity is the custodian of the hidden mystery, and the difficulty consists in the fact that that which man conceals from the world is also hidden from himself. He knows not the wonder of that which he preserves and nourishes.[13]

This primordial mystery, hidden even from ourselves until now, concerns the spiritual seed that our species has borne within it for millions of years. The divine spark of mind that gave birth to the human kingdom, endowing us with the faculty of thought, contained within it the germ of an even higher dimension of consciousness. It presented us with the latent capacity to grow *beyond* the limits of the mind, *beyond* the realm of thought, and thus to transcend the human kingdom itself. Our spiritual DNA contains the possibility for members of the human kingdom to evolve into members of the spiritual kingdom, in the footsteps of the Buddha and the Christ.

In principle, thinking people know this to be true. The idea itself is hardly a secret. Throughout history, religions have grown up around divinized human beings or "god-men"—those who have demonstrated the process of "transhumanizing a man into a god," in the words of Dante Alighieri. This concept is enshrined in a simple adage popular among Eastern Orthodox Christians: *God became man so that man could become God,* meaning that Christ incarnated as a human being to illustrate the path to divinity. In Russian Orthodoxy, the word for "saint" means "becoming like" (Christ). In Catholicism, the ritual of canonizing saints reflects the understanding that human beings are capable of transforming their nature. Still, the idea has remained shrouded in mystery.

One of the keys to unlocking this mystery, for Westerners, lies in the workings of reincarnation—the law of rebirth. In avatars, saints, and other illumined beings we witness the *fruit* of the process of spiritual evolution, a process that unfolds over "hundreds of thousands of lives," some Buddhists say. Only when we understand the soul's cyclical journey into incarnation, and the long periods of growth that precede its full flowering, does the gap between an ordinary person and a saint become comprehensible.

When one lifetime is seen as the totality of life, the attainments of sages and saints defy logical comprehension. As reincarnation is better understood, however, an explanation for the mystery appears. Human beings are said to be reincarnating lives "driven by the Law towards earthly manifestation in order to become fully conscious."[14] And it is predicted that in the coming age, the process of becoming fully conscious will be viewed as a natural part of human evolution. It will be understood that there is a *path* to higher consciousness which unfolds gradually, through lifetimes of experience. By lifting the veil of secrecy surrounding the evolution of consciousness, the Masters of Wisdom have sought to quicken humanity's spiritual unfoldment.

Before examining the substance of the spiritual path, it may be useful to take another brief look at our current place within the evolutionary scheme and how we arrived here, as outlined in the wisdom teachings. Eighteen million years ago, at the dawn of our species' evolution, the human individual was barely distinguishable from a higher animal. Faculties of mind—such as self-awareness, reasoning, and reflection—existed only as potentials, much as soul consciousness now exists largely as a potential. Advanced members of the animal kingdom stood at the portal to the human kingdom then, just as advanced human beings stand at the portal to the spiritual kingdom now.

We arrived at our present stage of advancement as a result of *both* creation *and* evolution. The human kingdom was created from the elements of two other kingdoms of life—one below us and one above us. It was the "touch" of Spirit upon animal substance that gave birth to the human race. By cosmic design, we were created part animal and part divine; part matter and part spirit. From the time of our birth as a race, it has been our ultimate destiny to serve as a bridge between these two kingdoms, and later to advance, by evolving in consciousness, into the spiritual kingdom.

In the Grand Design for humanity, it was intended that our consciousness evolve in two distinct stages. The goal of the first stage was individual autonomy, as exhibited by fully self-conscious members of the human kingdom. The next stage involves the transformation of *self*-conscious human beings into Self-conscious expressions of divinity, or members of the Kingdom of God. The problem for us, in attempting to grasp this higher destiny, is that throughout the duration of the first stage of our evolution, spanning millions of years, we have remained totally blind to the existence of a second stage. This was true for those lone individuals who developed ahead of the race, in times past, as it is true for the growing numbers of us who are now awakening.

What has eluded our comprehension, causing material living to seem meaningless to those who intuitively sense that there must be more, is the dual nature of the evolutionary journey. In the first stage, the path of *human* evolution, the individual "unit of consciousness" grows through experience in the material world, gradually developing an integrated persona. The goal of this stage is the coordination of body, emotions, and mind into a harmonious whole that can function effectively on the material plane. In the second stage, the path of *spiritual* evolution, this integrated personality learns to become subordinate to the Soul. The goal of the spiritual path is to transform the personality into an instrument of divine service.

Until the end of the first leg of this journey, the soul remains "behind the scenes," directing the unfoldment of consciousness from its own plane. As an individual spark of the divine Oversoul, the soul is pure energy existing in a formless, timeless dimension. For the purpose of evolving into an individual expression of divinity on Earth, a planet where consciousness evolves through the limitations of form, the soul projects itself progressively into the realm of tangible form. Its first form or body is subtle—an invisible orb of light hovering, as it were, above the realm of time and space. Cyclically, this orb of light projects an emanation of itself into the world of form, giving life and consciousness to a unique *personality* that appears for the span of a lifetime.

It is through these cyclic "appearances" in time and space, in repeated incarnations, that the soul progressively evolves consciousness. The process is guided from the inner planes via the soul's subtle body, esoterically known as the "causal body"—the body of causes. At the end of each incarnation, the personality's experiences are distilled into energy patterns and stored as *causes* whose effects will manifest in subsequent lifetimes. Two essential types of patterns are stored in the causal body: one type is related to the developing personality—the physical, emotional, and mental aspects of our nature; the other is related to soul consciousness, reflected in qualities such as wisdom, compassion, and self-sacrifice.

At the start of human evolution, the individual causal body is largely colorless and empty, containing only the instinctual patterns inherited from higher animals. Content is added with each human incarnation. The nascent personality, mired in matter, is unaware of the soul that projected it into form. The voice of conscience is barely audible to a self preoccupied with surviving and satisfying instinctual urges. The ego, perceiving itself as a separate physical entity, blindly pursues selfish motives and desires. The harm inevitably inflicted upon others is distilled into patterns that are entered into the soul's data bank (the causal body) to bear consequences in subsequent lifetimes.

The way out of blind human living arose with the development of mind—the last aspect of the threefold personality to emerge. Mind can be a double-edged sword, as it creates its own patterns—thought patterns that are often as harmful and resistant to change as physical or emotional ones. Yet it is mind—with its capacity to analyze, discriminate, and discern cause and effect—that holds the potential for breaking *all* patterns. Through suffering, born of karmic consequences, the developed individual gradually gleans the soul's intended lessons and musters the will to change. Like an alchemist in a laboratory, the soul in incarnation uses the mind as an instrument for transforming the base metals of human existence into the gold of spiritual being.

Drop by drop, this spiritual gold is extracted from the vortex of human experience and added to the causal body. As the soul's sheath begins to fill with light and vitality, a positive feedback loop is established. The growing radiance of the causal body is mirrored in improving conditions of successive incarnations. Karmic debts are gradually paid and as liabilities diminish, the accumulated assets are increasingly devoted to expressing truth, beauty, and goodness in the world.[15] Eventually, the resonance between the soul and its outer persona reaches the point where the persona finally awakens to the living reality of the soul.

Until the moment of awakening, reality—for the persona—is synonymous with the material plane. The soul in incarnation is identified with its physical body, emotions, and mind. Its own small world is the only world of any consequence. But as the light of the soul intensifies, the personality becomes more aware of the world beyond its own "ring-pass-not."[16] A growing sensitivity to the human condition begins to manifest in idealistic pursuits. The individual feels increasingly called to right the wrongs of the world—to mitigate injustice, inequality, oppression, cruelty, poverty, and all the other causes and conditions of human suffering.

The idealist is destined, however, to experience disillusionment. Some battles are won, but most are lost. Reforms are sometimes achieved and lives improved, but the underlying causes and conditions of human suffering have remained unchanged since the dawn of history. Through the wisdom teachings, it becomes clear that human suffering is the inevitable outgrowth of this *first stage* of human evolution—the separative stage where souls are identified with their individual forms, families, tribes, and nations, relentlessly pursuing selfish interests, regardless of the pain inflicted upon others.

An idealist, a person who has begun to identify with humanity as a whole, is ahead of the evolutionary curve and is thus fighting against the current tide of human civilization. Inevitably, such an individual faces a crisis of disillusionment—a painful shattering of illusions about the possibility of changing the material world to conform with one's ideals. With this shattering, there arises doubt about one's perceptions of reality. The "promise" of finding personal happiness in the material world, for oneself and for others, increasingly appears to be a mirage.

Disillusioned, the idealist begins to question everything about life—wondering, for example, why suffering is so universal and happiness so fleeting. He or she struggles to discern the meaning and purpose of life, beyond physical propagation, survival, and the pursuit of transitory pleasures. Satiated with material living, no longer seduced by its glamours, the soul has a compelling need to know what is true, real, and eternal. The perennial questions arise: Who am I really, apart from a physical body? Why am I alive? Does my life have any relevance in the larger scheme of things? As the quest for answers intensifies, a seeker of truth is born.

Though as yet unaware, the seeker is nearing that crucial turning point where the path of human evolution ends and the path of spiritual evolution begins. The individual divine spark, having descended into matter to evolve consciousness through experience, now perceives the illusoriness of the material realm. The soul is on the threshold of learning its true identity and stepping onto the path of light where it will discover, over time, its place in the divine plan. "The Journey Home," in the words of a Sufi teaching, "is the [way of] transformation that brings man out of his subjective dream state, so that he can fulfill his divine destiny."[17]

On this homeward journey, among the first limitations encountered are those of the mind. This is a curious paradox, as it is the mind that enables us to discern illusion from reality, and to pose the questions that ignite the search for higher truth. Yet the answers to those very questions lie beyond the capacities of mind alone. Paul Brunton (1898–1981), the British philosopher and mystic, observed: "Intellect, which is able to propound a multitude of enigmas concerning man, destiny and death, is unable to solve them."[18] In time the seeker discovers, as Tolstoy did,[19] that the answers lie outside of science, philosophy, theology, and all other fields of human theorizing. "When matter is exhausted," Balzac observed, "Spirit enters."[20]

"What you are searching for is what is searching," declared Saint Francis of Assisi (1181–1226), alluding to the soul, which holds the answers. Yet to arrive at the place where the soul can directly perceive spiritual truth, the seeker turns naturally to the wisdom of those who have preceded him or her on the Path. In the past, such wisdom was usually sought from the religion of one's birth. Today, as the spiritual quest becomes increasingly universal, it is common for Jews to turn to Buddhism for answers, Hindus to Christianity, Christians to Islam or Hinduism, while still others turn to the Ageless Wisdom, whose essence is universal.[21]

Regardless of the teachings or teachers one is drawn to, the path itself is unique to the individual. Each soul charts its own course toward the Light out of its own experiences, circumstances, relationships, and qualities. Rabbi Adin Steinsaltz (1937–), Jewish scholar and mystic, explains:

> All souls flow in and out of the same primal source, and all similarly aspire to reach out and grow and return to this source... [however] the way of every soul—for all it has in common with and resembles all the others—is unique unto itself and justifies its separate existence. Myriads of sparks reflect the primal light, every one of them with its own situation and set of circumstances.[22]

At the same time, while there are as many paths to God as there are seekers, the *nature* of the Path is universal. In describing the journey from "unreality to reality," or from material living to spiritual consciousness, illumined teachers of different persuasions generally concur on three fundamental stages: 1. *Awakening* to the inner realm of the soul or the plane of Spirit; 2. *Purification* of the lower self and its reorientation from the material plane to the spiritual; 3. *Illumination* of the purified persona by the light of Spirit.

Stage one, the experience of awakening, has been called the

seeker's reward. Having searched for truth in books and from teachers, and having learned to still the outer voices of the world in order to hear the inner voice, the light of the soul eventually breaks through. Mystically, the veil between matter and spirit is pierced, affording the seeker a glimpse of the greater Reality. "The infinite dawns upon him," Balzac observed, "and he catches a glimpse of his destiny."[23] In Whitman's words: "Bibles may convey and priests expound, but it is exclusively for the noiseless operation of one's isolated *Self* to...reach the divine levels."[24]

Awakening confers upon the soul in incarnation an awareness of the subtle world of spirit. The spark of divinity that is the soul, masked even to the individual self until this point, begins to consciously perceive that all is energy—another word for spirit. It dawns on the soul that behind the world of form is a pulsating sea of energy containing all that lives, visible and invisible. While the personality remains anchored on the material plane, the ground of being begins to shift. In the language of the Tibetan master, the seeker now becomes a spiritual "aspirant"—one who aspires to enter the spiritual kingdom. He writes:

> Man stands midway between heaven and earth, with his feet deep in the mud of material life and his head in heaven. In the majority of cases his eyes are closed, and he sees not the beauty of the heavenly vision, or they are open but fixed upon the mud and slime with which his feet are covered. But when his open eyes are lifted for a brief moment, and see the world of reality and of spiritual values, then the...life of the aspirant begins.[25]

Upon awakening, one glimpses the reality of the spiritual world. As the word "glimpse" signifies, the initial experience is usually brief. But despite its brevity, the experience is either powerful enough, or repeated often enough, to reorient the life and launch the aspirant onto the Path of Return. As worded in the ancient teachings, the Pilgrim now sets forth upon the Endless Way that leads to the Heart of God.[26] Many lifetimes are said to unfold between awakening and genuine illumination—the first and third stages of the journey into the spiritual kingdom. However, the longest span of the path by far, and the one involving the greatest struggle, occurs between stages one and two—*awakening* and *purification*.

The process of spiritual purification is portrayed as a battle-ground. A struggle for domination takes place between the lower self, the ego, accustomed to controlling the individual's life, and the awakening Self, the soul, which has higher aspirations. In the ancient terminology, a battle begins between the "Dweller on the Threshold," the illusory identity of the persona, and the "Angel of the Presence"—the divine "messenger" or soul.[27] The "dweller" is composed of all patterns of selfishness and separation that stand between the seeker and the true spiritual Self. It has been defined as "All that a man is, apart from the higher spiritual self."[28]

All that a man or woman is, up to this point, is an integrated personality—a well-functioning unit composed of mind, emotions, and body. A product of the world of form, the personality has an established sense of individuality with well-defined ego boundaries. But the call is now to enter a formless realm, a realm without boundaries. The aspirant on the threshold of the spiritual realm is thus required to dissolve "the sum total of the forces of the lower nature"[29] that have been cultivated over the course of lifetimes. Overcoming "the dweller" involves confronting what Jung termed "the shadow"—the negative, largely unconscious aspects of the persona—plus letting go of *everything* to which the individual self continues to cling.

And thus the battle ensues, as the center of gravity shifts from the self to the Self. The elation of the mystical vision, the first taste of the soul's reality, is soon followed by the emergence of the shadow, giving rise to what mystics often call "the dark night of the soul."[30] Having glimpsed Higher Reality, the aspirant is faced with all that imprisons him or her in form, creating a separation from that Reality. The struggle to overcome that separation lies at the heart of the purification process and explains its longevity. In the wisdom teachings, purification has little to do with morals and ethics, as basic character development precedes this stage of growth. The goal is rather to remove the dross of personality that prevents the soul from expressing its true, spiritual nature.

Setting out on the Path of Return, the aspirant quickly discovers that progress is hampered by habitual, often unconscious, attachments to the world of form. The central learning at this stage is that of *non*-attachment. Passing through the "fires of purification," one gradually learns to let go of the contents of each dimension of the persona: physical urges and appetites, emotional desires and attachments, mental ambitions. The goal is for the outer persona to become free of worldly ties, learning to become purely an instrument of the soul in the world.

Intrinsic to this stage of the path is the sense of duality, the experience of having two selves—one of spirit, one of matter. As the aspirant slowly crosses the bridge in consciousness from the form world of the outer senses to the formless world of the inner senses, he or she is identified partly with the material realm and partly with the spiritual realm, belonging fully to neither. This duality is resolved at a higher stage of unity, with the transformation of identity. The Latin root of the verb "identify" means "to make the same as." The great struggle involves turning a being once thought to be the same as matter, into a being that is the same as spirit.

The key methods for bringing about this transformation are those taught by the Buddha: detachment, dispassion, and discrimination. All involve the use of the mind. Progress on the path requires learning to discern the true from the false, the real from the illusory, while gaining mental detachment from the transitory world of form, and dispassion from the grip of emotions. The emotional "body" is purified and stabilized by the mind, which gradually gains control of its fluctuations and learns to establish a state of equilibrium. The mind, in its turn, comes under the sway of the soul, by which it is eventually illumined.

After lifetimes on the path of purification, the aspirant is finally tested to determine his or her readiness to enter further into the spiritual kingdom. In the book *From Bethlehem to Calvary*, Alice

Bailey portrays the seeker's obligatory trials in the light of the three temptations of Christ. The outcome of these trials determines three basic things: whether the incarnate soul remains capable of using spiritual power for selfish purposes, whether it still has any doubts about its identity as a divine being, and whether it can still be tempted by self-exaltation and worldly power. Once these tests have been passed, the light and love of the soul flood the personality, signaling the third stage of the path. The "soul-infused personality," now a conscious member of the spiritual kingdom, becomes an increasingly illumined instrument of divine purpose.

In many ways, the ageless wisdom teachings about the stages of the path parallel those of other spiritual and religious traditions. In one important respect, however, the teachings conveyed by Alice Bailey diverge markedly. They portray the spiritual kingdom, toward which souls consciously treading the path are moving, as a "center" of planetary life that is actively engaged in Earth's evolution. Within that center there exists a spiritual hierarchy of conscious lives, many of which are grouped into *ashrams* responsible for different aspects of human and planetary evolution. Each group works under the guidance of a Master of Wisdom, one who has mastered or perfected the goal of human evolution. And all of the masters and their ashrams serve under the guidance of the Christ, the "Master of Masters."

From the vantage point of Masters, the spiritual path is a training ground upon which aspirants are transformed into disciples. Souls nearing the end of the cycle of experience in the human kingdom enroll in this training voluntarily. Through meditation and other spiritual practices, each progressively builds an inner bridge between the visible and invisible worlds. It is a bridge of consciousness that first links the personality to the soul, and then links the soul to those who guide its unfoldment from the spiritual plane. As the orientation shifts from material to spiritual living, the aspirant attracts the guidance of inner plane teachers who help, over lifetimes, in the training of a full-fledged disciple of one of the masters within the spiritual hierarchy.

For the disciple, such inner plane relationships eventually become an integral part of treading the path. The Tibetan master describes the path as a "steady expansion of consciousness...with increasing sensitivity to the higher vibrations [which] works out first as sensitiveness to the inner voice...one of the most necessary faculties in a disciple." He then adds, "The Great Ones are looking for those who can rapidly obey the inner voice of their soul."[31] Once this responsiveness is steady and reliable, inner teachers and guides work to impress the disciple's mind, leading him or her toward greater illumination, and revealing the task which the disciple is destined to fulfill—in cooperation with the master's group—in service to the unfolding Plan of God.

NOTES

1 Some Mahayana and Tibetan Buddhists have personal Gods, but Hinayana sects do not.
2 Tejasananda, *A Short Life of Swami Vivekananda*, 71.
3 *Ibid.*, 76.
4 Keating, *Open Mind, Open Heart*, 28.
5 *Ibid.*, 29.
6 *Ibid.*, 4.
7 Quoted from a 2005 Contemplative Outreach brochure.
8 Smoley, *Inner Christianity*, 4.
9 *Ibid.*, 2.
10 The remainder of this chapter is based largely on the books of Alice A. Bailey, but also contains insights from the writings of H.P. Blavatsky, Annie Besant, and other esotericists.
11 Bailey, *The Light of the Soul*, 308.
12 This is a reference to stages of spiritual growth discussed later in this chapter and in Chapter 9.
13 Bailey, *Esoteric Psychology*, vol. 1, 312.
14 Bailey, *A Treatise on Cosmic Fire*, 745.
15 Traces of karma born of past actions remain until perfection is achieved at the close of the cycle of human evolution.
16 See Glossary.
17 From "The Eleven Principles of the Naqshbandi Path" published by the Golden Sufi Center.

18 Brunton, *The Secret Path*, 30.
19 See Chapter 3.
20 Quoted in Head and Cranston, *Reincarnation*, 305.
21 Jerry Adler, "Where We Stand on Faith," *Newsweek*, Aug. 29/Sept. 5, 2005, 48. This article reports that 20% of Americans claim to have left the faith of their childhood and adopted another faith or path.
22 Steinsaltz, *The Thirteen Petalled Rose*, 148.
23 Quoted in Bucke, *Cosmic Consciousness*, 213.
24 *Ibid.*, 229.
25 Bailey, *Esoteric Psychology*, vol. 1, 312.
26 These terms are from the Old Commentary, a metaphorical esoteric teaching of ancient origin.
27 The culmination of this battle occurs at the third initiation when the soul gains conscious control of the personality.
28 Bailey, *Glamour*, 91.
29 *Ibid.*, 90.
30 A more intense "dark night of the soul" occurs at still a later stage. See Chapter 9.
31 Bailey, *A Treatise on White Magic*, 353.

CHAPTER SIX

THE FRUITS OF SUFFERING

Call the world...'the vale of Soul-making'
Then you will find out the use of the world.

~*John Keats*

THE ENGLISH POET JOHN Keats (1795–1821) was only twenty-three years old when he wrote these words in a letter to his younger brother.[1] At the time, they were grieving the tragic loss of a family member, one of many losses in a prolonged wave of illness and death that engulfed their parents, two siblings, and the grandparents who raised them. In these few lines, steeped in suffering, Keats managed to distill the evolutionary purpose of human life on Earth: the revelation of the Soul—the spirit within the form.

From an esoteric vantage point, "Soul-making" is the harvest of human evolution. The visible flowering of spirit marks the soul's triumph in its long and often painful struggle through the vale of material living. Prior to that time, in the endless conflict between the opposite poles of our nature—matter and spirit—matter generally wins, resulting in the pain and sorrow of human living. When the soul breaks through to consciousness, suffering is transformed into something other than pain. It becomes a source of understanding, wisdom, and spiritual evolution.

Keats is one of many writers who have alluded to life on Earth as a schoolhouse for the edification of souls. This metaphor was also familiar to Louisa May Alcott (1832–1888), daughter of New England Transcendentalist Bronson Alcott, a kindred spirit of Emerson and Thoreau. In a letter to a friend she mused: "I think immortality is the passing of a soul through many lives or experiences, and such as are truly lived, used, and learned, help on to the next, each growing richer, happier and higher." She added, "This accounts for the genius and great virtue some show here. They have done well in many phases of this great school."[2]

Reflecting on her own soul's learning, Alcott wrote:

> I seem to remember former states and feel that in them I have learned some of the lessons... and in my next step I hope to leave behind many of the trials I have struggled to bear here and [which I] begin to find lightened as I go on.[3]

If the earth is, in fact, a vast schoolhouse for souls, then what, we may ask, are its intended lessons? The outlines of an answer can be discerned in the lives of individuals such as Keats and Alcott, who reached the higher grades and left a record of their reflections. Two things are prominent in their lives: first, both exhibited a profound sensitivity to the human condition, the level of sensitivity that breeds wisdom and compassion; and second, both of their biographies contain a good deal of suffering.

Suffering, in the wisdom teachings, has a clear objective. It is viewed as a prod to spiritual growth. The purpose of pain is to rouse us from the illusion of our separate, form-based, ego identities and awaken the true, spiritual being within—the soul, the part of us that recognizes our essential unity with all of life. The human constitution is such that when a person is in pain, unable to function normally, he or she is prompted to look more deeply at the inner side of life.

In the realm of suffering, human beings are said to have an advantage over other creatures. All life forms experience pain, to the extent that they are conscious, but of all the kingdoms of nature only the human kingdom is equipped to *learn* from suffering. We have been uniquely endowed to "reap the benefits of [suffering] in the realm of intellect."⁴ With a developed mind, and the capacity to step back from life and take the stance of the observer, it becomes possible for us to discern cause and effect—or action and reaction—and thus to work to eliminate harmful causes from within ourselves.

Toward the end of the path of human evolution, as the seeker awakens, suffering evokes the question "why?" In pursuit of an answer, the soul begins to turn a searchlight on possible underlying causes. Recently, with the frequent occurrence of large-scale human disasters, it is common to hear people ask: "Why is this happening to me?" Some pose the question rhetorically, not expecting a response; others pose it angrily, feeling victimized by a wrathful God or abandoned by a heartless government. Yet others wonder: "Why is this happening to *me* and not everyone?" Recognizing the inequality of circumstances, sensitive souls are prompted to ask themselves: "What might I have done to *cause* this?"

In the search for answers to this question, suffering begins to bear fruit in the realm of intellect. The individual who poses this question is preparing to leave behind the cycle of "blind" human experience and enter the soul's realm of causality. At this point in the journey, there is an opportunity to learn principles essential to spiritual growth—a form of learning that leads eventually to the transcendence of suffering. It dawns on us that we have committed wrongs in the past and thus bear responsibility for present circumstances. Sensing that behind the veil of material reality there exists a causal realm, where actions bear consequences, a light goes on when difficulties arise.

Suffering—the question of why human beings suffer—is central to all religions, though answers appear to differ substantially. In Eastern religions, as in esoteric teachings (including those of Jewish and Christian origin), suffering is understood to be the working out of the laws of cause and effect. Although few of us have past life impressions as clear as those of Louisa May Alcott, everyone can understand the principle: "as we sow, we shall reap" or, in the current vernacular, "what goes around comes around." Since the conditions of suffering are often not attributable to actions of the present lifetime, the idea that seeds of the present were sown in the past satisfies the rational mind's need for logic.

In the monotheistic faiths—Judaism, Christianity, and Islam—there is no such logical accounting. All three reject the concept of the soul's rebirth. Among Jews, the absence of a causal explanation for suffering has led to widespread atheism, particularly in the wake of the holocaust. Among many Christians, there is a struggle to reconcile a belief in a just and merciful God with the inequality of suffering. "The fact of suffering," wrote theologian John Stott, "undoubtedly constitutes the greatest single challenge to the Christian faith... Its distribution and degree appear to be entirely random and therefore unfair."[5] It is likely that many Muslims are similarly troubled, as the Koran holds that suffering is earned (by acting with evil intention), without accounting for the plight of innocents.

When it comes to providing an explanation for particular conditions of suffering, therefore, significant differences appear to exist among the world's religions and teachings. Yet if we step back and view the cause of suffering through a wider lens, a surprising degree of consensus emerges. Virtually all faith traditions and teachings point to a cause of human suffering that is even more fundamental than karma-producing actions: *separation* from God, Allah, Brahman, Supreme Reality, the One Life.

The state of separation from the divine is described variously as: rebellion, disobedience, alienation, isolation, disunion. Different aspects of the human psyche are emphasized by the scriptures and teachings of different cultures and epochs. In the West, the root cause of suffering, as reflected in the story of the Fall of Man in the Garden of Eden, is man's assertion of *his* will over God's will. In the East, the root cause is seen as the pursuit of selfish desire. Yet there is a shared perception, dating back thousands of years in both East and West, that the seeds of human suffering are sown in the consciousness of a self cut off from its Source.

Likewise, there is an essential sameness to the *purpose* of suffering in the world's sacred scriptures and texts: healing the breach between man and God, human being and Absolute Being, Atman and Brahman. And yet, this purpose is fulfilled at vastly different points along the spectrum of consciousness. Suffering is most commonly portrayed as a form of retribution for wrongdoing or a payment of debts. But at a higher stage of awareness, suffering has a purpose beyond redeeming past actions. It is seen as a means of *perfecting* the human being—a word understood in the West as aligning individual will with Divine Will, in the East as attaining selflessness, the precondition for merging with the One Self.

Retributive suffering is pervasive in the Old Testament. Starting in the *Book of Genesis*, those who obeyed God's will were showered with blessings while those who disobeyed were severely punished. Noah, the most righteous man of his generation, "a just man and innocent," was chosen by God to preserve "two of every living thing." About Noah it was written, "according to all that God commanded him, so did he." As a consequence, he and his family were abundantly blessed. All the rest of Adam and Eve's descendants, deemed wicked and corrupt, were destroyed by the Flood.

In the stories of Abraham and Job, by contrast, suffering is aimed at perfecting the individual. In these accounts, God demands more mere than obedience. He tests his most righteous creatures to see if they will remain faithful in the face of unspeakable suffering. Abraham, having already proven his worthiness to the degree that God had chosen him to be the father of all the nations, was asked to further demonstrate his steadfastness through a *willingness* to sacrifice his long-awaited, beloved son, Isaac. Of Job, the Lord said, "there is none like him in the earth, an innocent and upright man, one who reveres God, and turns away from evil." Yet God allowed Satan to afflict unmitigated suffering upon Job, that he might further prove his faithfulness.

The theme of God subjecting his most flawless creatures to suffering finds its apotheosis in the New Testament. As the "only begotten Son of God," Christ was born without sin. Yet it was his destiny to undergo a more extreme degree of perfecting, by totally surrendering his will to the will of the Father, though the outcome was to be his own crucifixion. Only later would he fully realize the divine purpose: that of "overcoming death"—the triumph of Spirit over matter that occurred with Christ's resurrection. "Because of...[the] suffering which he endured," wrote the Apostle Paul, "he learned obedience, and he grew to be perfect."[6]

Suffering as a means of perfecting, distinct from retribution, was also addressed by the Apostle Peter:

> What praise have they who endure suffering because of their faults? But when you do good and are made to suffer and you take it patiently, then your glory is greater with God. For to this purpose you were called, because Christ also died for us, leaving us an example, that we should follow in his steps.[7]

In Islam, it is taught that suffering is alleviated by submission to divine will. The word "Islam" literally means "submission" or "surrender" (to the will of Allah). Religious scholar Huston Smith suggests a broader meaning, however, which highlights the perfecting aspect. Pointing out that "Islam" is derived from *salam*, whose primary meaning is "peace" and whose secondary meaning is "surrender," Smith offers a fuller definition: "the perfect peace that comes when one's life is surrendered to God."[8]

"Muslim" is the adjective corresponding to the noun "Islam." In the Koran, a Muslim is one who submits himself to the Laws of Allah, who always acts justly and righteously as prescribed by Allah, and is a true believer "from the heart." Regular disciplines observed daily, monthly, annually, and once in a lifetime (a pilgrimage to Mecca) are intended to instill constant awareness of Allah and submission to his will. Suffering is overcome by *complete* surrender of self-will to Higher Will. The Muslim who achieves that state will find "peace, safety, security, and immunity from evils and afflictions of any kind from within or without."[9]

In Eastern religions, and in many esoteric teachings, the central cause of human suffering is seen as ignorance—*avidya*, "without knowing"—rather than rebelliousness. We suffer due to a lack of knowledge about who we really are. Acting out of ignorance, we contravene immutable spiritual laws. Behaving selfishly, we commit actions harmful to others, unaware that we will face the consequences in the future.[10] On the premise that suffering is the result of karma, or past action, teachers of the East tell us that we are responsible for our own suffering, as well as for finding the way to overcome it.

In the East, while the specific conditions of suffering are understood as karmic in origin, pain is also seen as intrinsic to human living, starting with birth. In Hinduism, the underlying cause of human pain is wrong identification. When confronting illness, loss, impermanence, aging, and death, we suffer primarily because we identify with our *finite* self rather than our true, infinite, eternal Self. At a certain stage in evolution, however, suffering itself impels the soul to search for a way to transcend it. The seeker, according to his or her nature, will gravitate toward one or another of the forms of yoga—one of the paths of knowledge and self-discipline leading to union with Absolute Being.[11]

Buddhism grew out of Hindu philosophy, yet the Buddha claimed to teach one thing only: "suffering and the end of suffering." His blinding insight had revealed to him the underlying cause of all suffering: *tanha*, usually translated as desire. A more precise definition of *tanha*, according to Huston Smith, is "dislocation"—the result of selfish desire or self-seeking at the expense of others. Acting instinctively, impulsively, and out of alignment with the natural order, one fails to recognize others as "fellow facets of the same Reality"[12] and thus creates karma. The Buddha's antidote was the Eightfold Path, a path of intentional living aimed at reaching the state of selflessness that leads to Nirvana—the extinction of the separate self in the ocean of Supreme Reality.

Universally, in all major world religions, the root cause of our unhappiness is living in a state of consciousness in which we are separate from God or Supreme Reality. In the New Testament, a sinner is one who is "cut off from the living God."[13] The wisdom teachings echo this idea, stating that the only *real* sin is the sin of separation, as all sins or errors spring from that single all-encompassing error. In the Hindu *Upanishads*, this separative state is likened to a single grain of sand so encrusted with debris that it is oblivious to the infinitude of grains of sand in which it is immersed.

Pain is viewed as a caustic agent for removing that encrustation. If allowed to seep into our consciousness, without being suppressed, suffering can serve to loosen the layers of debris that build up around the individual who has become thoroughly identified with the threefold personality existing in the world of form. The Tibetan master explains its salubrious effect: "Pain has always been the purifying agent, employed by the Lords of Destiny, to bring about liberation...it tends to focus humanity's attention upon the life aspect and not upon the form."[14]

Whether pain is experienced physically, emotionally, or spiritually, it has the effect of shifting one's gaze away from the outer world and turning it inward to "the life aspect"—the spirit, the part of our being that is independent of the phenomenal world. When suffering is acute, the conditioned reflexes and routines of daily living give way to a deeper, more reflective mode of consciousness that allows the Self to emerge into the foreground and with it, the aspect of mind that relates cause and effect in the light of truth. "The uses of pain are many," the Tibetan master states, "and they lead the human soul out of darkness into light, out of bondage into liberation..."[15]

Pain also works on the heart, the seat of the soul and the locus of genuine relatedness. Over eons of time on the path of human evolution, the persona becomes insulated by its own ring-pass-not—a self-created barrier protective of selfish desire, ambition, and will that gives rise to "hard-heartedness." Pain has a way of tearing down walls of separation that feed the illusion of self-sufficiency, thus "softening" and "opening" the heart. A heart tenderized by pain becomes more sensitive to the pain of others, and also to subtler, higher forces and energies that foster the transformation of consciousness.

Dr. Elisabeth Kübler Ross (1926–2004), psychiatrist and author of the groundbreaking book *On Death and Dying*, said this about the fruits of suffering:

The most beautiful people we have known are those who have known defeat, known suffering, known struggle, known loss, and have found their way out of the depths. These persons have an appreciation, a sensitivity and an understanding of life that fills them with compassion, gentleness, and a deep loving concern. Beautiful people do not just happen.[16]

Generally, the inner changes wrought by pain take place in the private recesses of one's soul. Poets and writers often share their reflections, but only rarely does personal transformation occur in the public eye, as it did in the case of Robert F. Kennedy (1925–1968). Prior to the assassination of his older brother, President John F. Kennedy, the younger Kennedy had often been portrayed as a ruthless political operative. His brother's death catalyzed a visible metamorphosis that was depicted in the film *RFK: A Story about Change and Suffering.* The film description reads: "JFK's death plunged him into unremitting pain and grief... In his suffering he began to empathize with impoverished Americans and others who were marginalized or disenfranchised."[17]

The transformation of Robert Kennedy took place over the course of an extended period of mourning. During that time, he turned repeatedly to the wisdom of the ancient Greeks for solace. On the occasion of another American tragedy a few years later, RFK publicly shared some of that wisdom. It was his destiny to break the news of the assassination of Martin Luther King, Jr., on April 4, 1968, to a largely African-American audience whom he was addressing during his short-lived campaign for the presidency. Pleading for love, wisdom, and compassion to prevail over hatred, division, and violence, Robert Kennedy quoted Aeschylus, his favorite poet:

Even in our sleep, pain which cannot forget falls drop by drop upon the heart, until, in our own despair, against our will, comes wisdom through the awful grace of God.

The kind of searing pain that alchemically produces spiritual light, by the grace of a greater Light, has been described as a "sacred wound" by psychologist Jean Houston. It is a wound so deep that "the psyche is opened up and new questions begin to be asked about who we are in our depths."[18] She, too, alludes to the wisdom of the ancient Greeks in describing the transformative power of pain:

> In the Greek tragedies, the gods force themselves into human consciousness at the time of pathos. It is only at this time of wounding that the protagonist grows into a larger sense of what life is all about and is able to act accordingly.[19]

It goes without saying that suffering, in and of itself, is not necessarily salutary. To produce a transformation in consciousness, the individual has to have reached the point in evolution where there is a readiness to relinquish old patterns of perception and awaken to a higher order of reality. When this occurs, the light of the soul begins to penetrate the personality's awareness. Over time, the tested individual gradually learns to shift identity from the lower self, limited by form, to the higher Self, which recognizes its oneness or fellowship with all Selves. The individual then begins to live for a higher purpose, expressed through service to others.

Examples of service born of "fellow feeling" have multiplied in recent times. In the U.S. alone, the suffering of individuals has led to countless efforts to mitigate the anguish of others. One of the more visible examples is Mothers Against Drunk Drivers (MADD), founded in 1980. By 2005, mothers of teenagers killed in drunk-driving accidents had formed 600 chapters, all in the goal of helping other mothers avoid the same fate. Another driving-related peril—"speed thrill" accidents—came to public attention in 2005. The father of a teenager killed in such an accident established a new foundation to expose this danger, with the help of his son's best friend—the driver of the car in which the deadly accident occurred.[20] The friend, suffering the excruciating pain of guilt, had decided to dedicate his life to saving other lives.

In the aftermath of September 11, 2001, the most public effort to prevent further suffering of that nature was The 9/11 Commission.

Initiated by mothers and wives whose husbands had left for work at the World Trade Center that morning and never returned, the commission's goal was to learn the truth about what had occurred to diminish the likelihood of future terrorist attacks. The four women, transformed into activists by their pain, persevered against tremendous odds (including the reluctance of the White House to release information), until they persuaded the U.S. Congress to establish the commission. What motivated them was preventing other American families from suffering as they had.

One of the spiritual "uses of pain" is the opportunity to take stock of one's life and make different choices. Under the right conditions, a crisis can become a propitious turning point on the path of life. Many lives were changed literally overnight by the destructive power of Hurricane Katrina, which devastated the Gulf Coast in the summer of 2005. In the immediate aftermath, a man from New Orleans wrote a revealing account of his experience that circulated on the Internet.[21] Though he had lost his home, his business, and "a city that I love so dearly," he had remained there to care for abandoned pets. "My heart feels more open than it ever has," he wrote.

"The universe will never fail to give us opportunities to evolve," the man reflected. "This is mine." Perceiving his crisis as a challenge to his preoccupation with his own "small microcosm of the universe," he began moving in a new direction within days. What loomed larger for him than his personal loss was the percentage of New Orleans residents living below the poverty level. "Until mankind addresses this deeper core issue," he wrote, "and until we correct this inequity worldwide, there will be many more 'cries for help.' I feel their pain, their fear, their feelings of loss and despair."

It has been said that every wound is also an opening. A breach in the outer wall of the persona allows the soul to touch and be touched by other souls in a way that can profoundly nurture and heal. People who endure terrible pain and sorrow often find solace in expressing compassion to others. The late actor Christopher Reeve, paralyzed for many years by spinal cord injury, spoke openly of this dynamic. When asked how he coped with his condition, mentally and spiritually, he replied that the best antidote to his recurring bouts of depression, beyond public and philanthropic work to find a cure for conditions like his own, was reaching out to others who were suffering as he was.

To have compassion literally means "to suffer with"—to identify with others to the point of feeling their pain. Compassion is a core value taught by many religions, but the best life teacher appears to be the *experience* of suffering. A genuinely compassionate person is one who has suffered in a way that leaves a mark upon the soul, sensitizing that soul to others to the extent that one is moved to help alleviate the suffering of others. Huston Smith wrote of the prophet Mohammed, who suffered deeply as a child: "His bereavements having made him sensitive to human suffering in every form, he was always ready to help others, especially the poor and the weak."[22]

When suffering has the effect of sensitizing the soul and shattering the illusion of separation, it serves the evolutionary purpose of our time. According to the wisdom teachings, the goal of the *present* stage of human evolution has been the fulfillment of individuality—the coordination of mind, emotions, and the physical "instrument" into a free, autonomous, and *independent* personality. The next evolutionary goal for humanity is the conscious recognition of our *interdependence*. The concept that all souls are "units of consciousness" in the one Oversoul, arrayed in a multiplicity of different forms, will become a widely accepted truth over the next 2,000 years, resulting eventually in an era of genuine peace.

Interestingly, it is said that joy will become the major catalyst to spiritual growth in the new age, as pain has been until now.[23] While pain serves to liberate the soul from its imprisonment in form by cracking open the outer shell of that form, joy is a quality of the liberated soul emerging into conscious expression. It flows from the awareness of being part of the One Life and contributing to that Life. The spark of divinity finding its way back to the Source, increasingly attuned to the spiritual world that interpenetrates our own, derives joy from serving as a "conduit" for divine ideas and energies to enter the material realm.

Joyfulness is plainly evident in such great souls as the Dalai Lama and the late Mother Teresa, embodiments of the consciousness that will emerge during the next stage of human evolution. In recent times, however, numbers of "ordinary people" have also shown signs of approaching this stage. One example of many is a Texas businessman who offered to use his private plane to ferry homeless people out of New Orleans after Hurricane Katrina, at the point when government officials were still immobilized. When a reporter asked him why he had done what he did, the man smiled radiantly and replied, "You can't imagine how much joy I feel."

At this time of accelerated evolution, the extent of human suffering tends to overwhelm and obscure such instances of joy in service to others. And yet, just as collective suffering seems to have become "the new normal" so, too, has the collective outpouring of compassionate giving. Since September 11, 2001, which has been called "the day that changed everything," the soul of humanity has emerged more palpably than ever before. The voluntary response by individuals to victims of disaster has been unprecedented in scale and in kind.

Strains of Aquarian consciousness have been heard from individuals everywhere whose lives were changed by their own spontaneous responses to the suffering of others. A former television reporter left a glamorous job to work for a relief agency saying, "I can see my own child in the faces of all the suffering children. I want to be able to look him in the eye knowing I've done my best to make the world a better place."[24] A Marine Corps General, describing himself as "broken-hearted" by the suffering he witnessed in Indonesia after the 2004 tsunami, said of the rescue effort he led: "I've been in the Marine Corps for thirty-four years. This is a new kind of service. This is the service I'm proudest of."[25]

Like fleecy clouds appearing on the horizon, expressions of soul consciousness have filled the airwaves during recent disasters, only to evaporate with the passage of time. As each crisis subsides, old patterns reassert themselves. Most people return to material preoccupations, losing sight of life beyond the bounds of personality. With each retreat to "normalcy," people speak almost longingly of how exhilarating it felt to be part of a community, how joyful it was "to connect on a human level" and to "remember that we are all part of the human family." Around the globe, people have noted how instinctive it is to transcend differences of race, religion, and ethnicity when tragedy strikes. The Prime Minister of Sri Lanka observed, "We are all brothers in misery."

The obvious question for humanity—for those concerned with creating a more peaceful, spiritually fulfilling existence—is how to bring about conditions of human unity *without* continual suffering. How do we establish the state of brotherhood, or solidarity, in which masks fall away and spirit responds to spirit, *without* the lash of pain? The soulfulness often noted in people from races, cultures, and nations with a history of oppression has been bought at a price of unconscionable suffering. What, we may wonder, is required for the human soul to remain in the foreground of awareness when such conditions are no longer present?

The answer to this question, from the wisdom teachings and from saints and sages of all times, seems to be one and the same: spiritual awakening and transformation. The particular path one follows appears not to matter, as reflected in a Sufi saying: "All paths lead to the same mountain top and those closest to the top are the first to recognize each other as brothers." When the dross of the persona is removed, the Soul stands revealed. The grain of sand, stripped of its layers of debris, recognizes its affinity with all other grains of sand on the ocean's shore.

Suffering, with its purifying fires, is the most powerful catalyst to spiritual growth at this present stage of human evolution. In one lifetime or another, it leads the soul to the Path of Return. Through the process of self-purification, karmic debts are paid. Incurring further debt is avoided through practices and disciplines such as those outlined in the Buddha's Eightfold Path: right knowledge, right livelihood, right aspiration, right speech, right behavior, right effort, right mindfulness, and right absorption.[26] By developing self-disciplines, practicing meditation, and learning about higher realities, the way eventually opens to the realm of Spirit.

In the end, the fruit of suffering produces the seed of possibility for transcending personal suffering, by treading the path of liberation. And yet this path entails its own form of suffering. It is the kind of suffering that accompanies any form of self-discipline—from dieting to exercising—in which immediate gratification is sacrificed for a goal of greater value. But the sacrifice required on the spiritual path is of a different scale. In the process of transformation, personal attachments are yielded in favor of the life of the soul. Self-satisfaction gives way to concern for the greater good. The lesser self, built up over eons of time, is placed on the altar of sacrifice to the One Self.

The scale of the challenge facing the spiritual seeker is framed in one of the enigmatic expressions of Christ: "It is easier for a camel to pass through the eye of a needle than for a rich man to enter the Kingdom of Heaven." While scholars have long debated the meaning of these words, if "a rich man" is understood as a person with a grandiose sense of self-importance, the meaning becomes clear. In the wisdom teachings, the price of entering the spiritual kingdom is transcending the ego. On the path of transformation, identification with the ego gives way to identification with the Life of God—by whatever name. Metamorphosis entails pain. Yet the pain that purifies, as the ancient Greeks taught, is the means by which "the gods force themselves into human consciousness."

Pope John Paul II, who suffered intensely throughout much of his life, often spoke of suffering as a "great Mystery." Alluding to its redemptive aspects, he said:

> It is in suffering that man shows himself to be far more capable of expressing the human values of the spirit, such as friendship, affection, love—all those qualities ...which in suffering and need are much more exalted and more profoundly comprehended.[27]

Speaking of the perfecting aspect of pain, he said:

> Physical or moral suffering... is a call, an invitation, a
> pressing exhortation to improve, to change our life, to
> be reborn, to convert. Nothing happens by chance. In
> every circumstance we must ask ourselves: "What does
> the Lord want from me? From my situation, from this
> forced inactivity, from the people I encounter—what
> is the message that will enable me to purify my feel-
> ings, raise my spirit, and hear the voice of truth and
> conscience?"[28]

In the wisdom teachings, the voice of truth and conscience is
the voice of the soul. That voice grows increasingly stronger as the
path of human evolution ends and the path of spiritual evolution
begins. Through meditation, study of higher truth, and service to
others, the soul emerges steadily into the foreground of life. Crises
become opportunities for the soul to reveal itself more definitively
and permanently. With each new degree of emergence, the soul
becomes more attuned, vibratorily, to the spiritual realm. In time,
impressions are received from the realm of "the gods" that guide
the soul toward its destined part in the divine plan.

As the new age dawns, cosmic energies are flowing into our
planet with the goal of advancing the process of spiritual transformation. The Plan for our time entails *collective* spiritual growth as
the basis of a new civilization. There are many signs that collective
suffering is serving this higher purpose. By loosening the grip of
material reality, it is freeing sensitive souls to take a different path
in life. And yet, while the tide of evolution is pulling us in the direction of spiritual reality, it is important to recall that the break-
through to Spirit occurs one soul at a time. The reorientation from
selfishness to selflessness, from the realm of matter to the realm of
spirit, lies entirely in the domain of individual free will.

NOTES

1 Keats to "the George Keatses," 21 April, 1819, in *The Complete Poems of John Keats*, 549.

2 Louisa May Alcott was the daughter of New England Transcendentalist, Bronson Alcott, an acquaintance of Emerson and Thoreau. She grew up in an environment where reincarnation was an accepted fact of life. Excerpts of her letter are quoted in Head and Cranston, *Reincarnation*, 338.

3 *Ibid.*

4 Bailey, *Esoteric Psychology*, vol. 1, 311.

5 John Stott, Christian minister and author, quoted from www.suffering. net.

6 Hebrews 5:8-9.

7 I Peter 3:20-21.

8 Smith, *The Religions of Man*, 217.

9 www.quaranicteachings.co.uk (accessed March 3, 2005).

10 In Buddhism, harm is done not only through words and deeds, but begins on the level of thought.

11 There are five main forms of yoga: hatha, jnana, bhakti, karma, and raja. However, hatha yoga, pertaining solely to disciplines of the physical body, does not have the same aim.

12 Christmas Humphreys quoted by Smith, *The Religions of Man*, 114.

13 Hebrews 3:12.

14 Bailey, *Externalisation of the Hierarchy*,116.

15 Bailey, *Discipleship in the New Age,* vol. 1, 677.

16 This quotation has been used with the kind permission of the Elisabeth Kübler Ross Foundation (www.ekrfoundation.org), and is cited from www.elisabethkublerross.com.

17 PBS, "The American Experience."

18 Jean Houston, "The Sacred Wound," excerpted from *The Search for the Beloved* in *Green Tara 1993*, 46.

19 *Ibid.*

20 The Brake For Brett Foundation.

21 This man identified himself simply as "Scott."

22 Smith, *The Religions of Man*, 219-20.

23 See, for example, Bailey, *Education in the New Age*, 120. This is an important concept in the books of Agni Yoga, an esoteric teaching known as "Living Ethics."

24 Margaret Larsen, interview by Keith Morrison in Banda Aceh, Indonesia, MSNBC, January 11, 2005.
25 CBS, "60 Minutes II," January 5, 2005.
26 See Smith, *The Religions of Man*, for an excellent description of each.
27 John Paul II, *The Private Prayers of Pope John Paul II*, 54.
28 *Ibid.*, 41.

CHAPTER SEVEN

SOUL AWARENESS

All are but parts of one stupendous whole
Whose body nature is, and God the soul.

~Alexander Pope

THERE ARE FEW INDIVIDUALS in the modern West, other than poets, who have written lucidly about the nature of the soul. One
who did so, informed by study as well as inner experience, was
Ralph Waldo Emerson (1803–1882), the American transcendentalist. Although Emerson was quick to acknowledge the "residuum"
of unresolved mysteries surrounding the soul, he had come to view
the world through the light of the soul. The oneness of human
beings was a basic truth for him, attributable to "that Unity, that
Over-Soul, within which every man's particular being is contained
and made one with all other[s]."[1]

Emerson drew a sharp distinction between the soul's awareness of reality and ordinary perceptions of life obtained through
the physical senses and the rational mind. "The soul's scale is one,"
he wrote, "the scale of the sense[s] and the [logical] understanding
is another." Calling the measurements of time and space "but inverse measures of the force of the soul," he lamented the influence
of science, which in his view had "in most men overpowered the
mind to that degree that the walls of time and space have come to
look real and insurmountable." He reflected:

> We live in succession, in division, in parts, in particles. Meantime within man is the soul of the whole; the wise silence; the universal beauty, to which every part and particle is equally related; the eternal ONE... We see the world piece by piece, as the sun, the moon, the animal, the tree; but the whole, of which these are the shining parts, is the soul.[2]

What enables the soul to grasp the whole, Emerson asserts, is its oneness with the invisible life force that vitalizes all the separate forms. By contrast, the unillumined concrete mind can perceive only the outer sheath of those forms. The lower mind, looking outward upon the world of time and space through the physical senses, sees only individual forms, including that of its own body, which appears to end with the contours of its skin. The soul, perceiving through a higher sense, looks inward to the world of spiritual reality and recognizes that its essential being, along with the inner being of all forms, is inseparable from the seamless web of Life in our universe.

Until fairly recently, the ability to penetrate the soul's realm was rare in the West. Though individuals like Emerson have always existed, they were so unique as to be considered outside the norm and thus unrepresentative of "human nature." Modern science, viewing the human being as a biological entity, has taken the stance that human nature is uniform, unchanging, and thus predictable. Scientists have operated on the assumption that virtually all members of our species, subjected to the same stimuli, would react in fundamentally the same way—given our common biological and emotional "equipment." Moreover, despite some obvious exceptions to the rule, it has been assumed that our biology was our destiny.

These assumptions are now beginning to be challenged. There is a growing awareness that despite the likeness of our outer forms, human consciousness exists on many different levels. This new awareness, along with mounting evidence that our future as a species rests upon the further evolution of our consciousness, has spawned a new field of inquiry broadly known as the "science of consciousness." Embracing aspects of science *and* spirituality, this new field has begun to heal the longstanding breach between these spheres. Subjects included under its umbrella range from studies of the physical brain, to efforts to probe the subtler, more spiritual dimensions of human awareness.

Emerging from research in this new field is a realization that deals a blow to the deterministic "human nature" school of thought. It is becoming apparent that members of our species exist along a wide spectrum of consciousness, and that the individual's place within this continuum is likely to be far more predictive of behavior than mere biology. Students of consciousness are discovering that people living under the illusion of separation will behave differently from those who have penetrated the veil of matter and have glimpsed the underlying unity of life.

Researchers are finding that consciousness expands in *stages*, and there is significant agreement about the substance of these stages.[3] In several theoretical models, individuals at the lower stage of consciousness identify largely with their own separate self (the physical form) and their clan; at the highest stage, they identify with the life of our cosmos. Between these poles, consciousness expands in ever-widening circles of inclusiveness: from one's own tribe, to the community of tribes that form a nation, to the human community as a whole, to the aggregate of life species on Earth, and to the larger universe of which Earth is a part. With the expansion of one's sphere of identity, some hypothesize, there is a corresponding development of moral responsibility and compassionate action.

Interest in the relationship between human behavior and stages of consciousness is a fairly new phenomenon. It was only a century ago that pioneering thinkers, such as Richard Maurice Bucke, first made the case that a higher level of consciousness could, in fact, be attained by human beings. More recently, with the emerging view that "the earth is a live planet rather than a planet with life upon it,"[4] and that human behavior is seriously threatening our living planet, the practical effects of higher consciousness have drawn the attention of serious researchers. Some have focused on the pivotal relationship between higher stages of awareness and ethical behavior—"caring for others enough to make their problems one's own."[5]

A useful overview of the staged unfoldment of human consciousness was presented by Bucke in his landmark study, *Cosmic Consciousness*. It begins with a portrayal of the evolutionary processes of life—starting with inorganic life—as "a series of gradual ascents, each divided from the next by an apparent leap over what seems to be a chasm."[6] At the juncture where humans enter this upward arc, after the animals, Bucke outlines three distinct stages of awareness. The first—*simple consciousness*— is shared by higher animals. This stage of awareness is largely limited to sensory impressions and embryonic forms of reasoning. While some humans remain at this stage, much of humanity has reached the second stage—*self consciousness*—the fruits of which have ripened into modern civilization.

According to Bucke, *self* consciousness came into being with the faculty of language, which provided words for our concepts and gave rise to the capacity for abstract reasoning. The self-conscious individual, aware of being "a distinct entity apart from all the rest of the universe," has the capacity to think. With thinking comes "knowing that we know," the ability to realize: "Yes, that thought I had about that matter is true; I know it is true, and I know that I know it is true."[7] This, Bucke says, is the essence of the human intellect, "from which spring judgment, reason, comparison, imagination, abstraction, reflection, generalization."[8]

The third stage—*cosmic consciousness*—requires "exceptionally developed intellectual and moral faculties." At this stage, the person "knows without learning," by means of pure intuition, while having a vastly expanded capacity to learn. "The prime characteristic of cosmic consciousness," writes Bucke, "is a consciousness of... the life and order of the universe."[9] With the opening of "the spiritual eyes," one perceives that the cosmos is "entirely spiritual and entirely alive...that the universe is God and God is the universe."[10]

This results in a dual consciousness, both human and spiritual, and in "direct unmistakable intercourse" between the individual human soul and the spiritual realm.

Despite the relatively small number of "cases" of cosmic consciousness that Bucke was able to document in the late 19th century, he apprehended it as an embryonic faculty that would slowly develop within humanity. He was convinced that "our descendants will sooner or later reach, as a race, the condition of cosmic consciousness, just as, long ago, our ancestors passed from simple to self consciousness."[11] When this occurs, he wrote, "Man will enter into his heritage and into his true work."[12]

By way of illustrating the gradual nature of *most* evolutionary changes, Bucke retraced the history of humanity's perception of color. Researchers discovered that between ten and twenty thousand years ago, our species recognized only one nondescript color. There followed a period when two colors were known—red and black. A third color, yellow, appeared in the Hindu Rig Veda, composed between 1500 and 1200 BCE. A millennium later, Aristotle still made reference to a "tricolored rainbow," suggesting that blue and green had not yet been discerned as distinctive colors, separate from black. Bucke indicates that humanity's enhanced color sense, along with a refined sense of fragrance and music, have all developed *since* the time of ancient Greece.

By contrast, we are now witnessing a speeding up of evolutionary processes. A portion of humanity is entering one of those periods described by Bucke as "an apparent leap over what seems to be a chasm" between levels of consciousness. Most of humanity—still at the stage of *self* consciousness—remains unaware that a new stage is rapidly unfolding within a segment of the world's population. This new stage is not yet "cosmic consciousness," according to the wisdom teachings, but an intermediary phase that bears directly on our transition to a new civilization.

In the Ageless Wisdom, a distinct stage of awareness precedes cosmic consciousness that is known as *soul consciousness* or *group consciousness*. This stage unfolds when *self* consciousness has been realized; it emerges when pure self-interest has been outgrown. The soul (consciousness itself) awakens from its long journey through the material realm and recognizes its inherent relationship with other living beings. Arising first in the heart, the essence of soul consciousness is inclusive love—a spiritual love that flows from the soul's perception of being part of the One Life.

Given the present state of our world, the notion that even a portion of humanity is approaching soul consciousness would appear, to many, as a mirage. Yet increasingly, this higher stage of awareness is being seen as an evolutionary imperative. Moreover, history reveals that darkness is often the womb of light. It was the ignorance and superstition of "the dark ages" that fueled the Renaissance and Enlightenment, setting us on course to become *thinking* beings. The current ignorance manifesting as greed and selfishness, threatening our own species as well as countless others, may become the necessary catalyst for our evolution into *loving* beings.

This new stage of human evolution was long ago foreseen by some of our greatest writers and philosophers. Having themselves experienced the soul's inclusive love, they intuited that all human beings had the same potential. One of these writers was Fyodor Dostoevsky (1821–1881). In *The Brothers Karamazov*, Dostoyevsky starkly portrays the problems of his own era while pointing toward a new time ahead. Speaking through a spiritual Elder, he attributes the isolation experienced in modern life (the root of cause of many crises) to the influence of science. By reducing reality to data gathered by the senses, he asserts, "the spiritual world, the higher part of man's being, is rejected altogether." When the spiritual world is rejected, says the Elder, human solidarity gives way to isolation, separation, and division.

The Elder foresaw, however, that the age of isolation would eventually exhaust itself. He envisioned the dawn of a new era of human unity, while realizing that the means of bringing that new era into manifestation rested with the individual. It was, he said, "a matter of the soul, a psychological matter." And he counseled his listeners, "In order to make the world over anew, people themselves must turn onto a different path psychically. Until one has indeed become the brother of all, there will be no brotherhood."[13]

Reflecting on his own age and the one to come, the Elder says:

> Everywhere now the human mind has begun laughably not to understand that a man's true security lies not in his own solitary effort [to acquire wealth], but in the general wholeness of humanity. But there must needs come a term to this horrible isolation, and everyone will all at once realize how unnaturally they have separated themselves from one another...and they will be astonished that they sat in darkness for so long, and did not see the light. Then the sign of the Son of Man will appear in the heavens... But until then... every once in awhile, if only individually, a man must suddenly set an example, and draw the soul from its isolation for an act of brotherly communion.[14]

Another prophet of spiritual evolution was Pierre Teilhard de Chardin (1881–1955), the French scientist and theologian. Having lived through the devastation of two world wars, Teilhard was acutely sensitive to the pain of isolation in which people "suffer and vegetate."[15] Yet he saw love as a superior force—the force of attraction that undergirds our universe and impels our evolution toward greater wholeness. For him, love was "the most universal, formidable and mysterious of cosmic energies" and "the very blood stream of spiritual evolution." He was convinced that the power of love would ultimately lead to an "Omega Point" at which all of life on Earth would converge into a unified whole.

Love is also seen as the single most powerful universal force in the Ageless Wisdom. It is the attractive, magnetic attribute of divinity, as real as the forces of magnetism and gravity that are measurable by science, and as powerful as the light and heat of the sun. Universal love is the coalescing force in the manifest world, the energy that binds the elements of a physical form—from the particles of an atom to the planets within a solar system—into a coherent whole. In the human being, it is the soul, whose essence is love, that endows the persona (at whatever stage of evolution) with coherence.

Until awakening occurs, the notion that love is an actual force in our universe, and the most essential quality in a human being, would appear far-fetched, at the very least. To those still living under the illusion of separation, in the grip of the concrete mind and unaware of any higher dimension of consciousness, such an assertion would likely sound like mystical hokum. And yet, in the words of the poet Rumi, the soul's "motion is inspired by love." Love is the force that ultimately causes the soul's awakening, by opening the heart.

The heart, in the view of the Tibetan master, is "the focal point through which the energy of love can flow...from the Heart of God...[into] the hearts of men."[16] The heart is pivotal in the Eastern system depicting the unfoldment of consciousness. The heart referred to here—the focal point through which the energy of love flows upon awakening—is not the physical organ, however, but a subtle energy *center* near that organ. It is through the subtle energy body of a human being that the life force flows into the physical body. This "vital body," the soul's instrument in the world, is the interface between the realms of spirit and matter.

In Eastern teachings, the vital energy body is the basis of another framework for understanding the unfoldment of human consciousness. Called "the golden web of life," the vital body consists of a vast and intricate network of energy channels that converge at seven main centers or crossing points, called *chakras*. Chakras are centers or vortices of energy, located along the spine and in the head, from which vital energy is distributed throughout the body. Each of the seven main chakras is related to a stage of consciousness.

In this ancient Eastern system, consciousness evolves with the activation of the centers (wheels of energy), from the lowest to the highest. The heart center—the middle of the seven centers—is the pivot between lower and higher stages. Prior to the activation of the heart center, the human soul (using the vital body as an instrument for experience in the world) is preoccupied with the separate life of its individual form, as yet unaware of its higher nature. Once the heart center opens and the energy of love begins to flow, the soul is drawn into conscious expression in the world—in service to other human souls and other creatures on our planet.

The place of a soul on the evolutionary path can be discerned by those who have developed etheric vision,[17] based on the degree to which the chakras are functioning. In the early stages of evolution, while the soul is involved in developing a sentient physical instrument, only the lower chakras are active. These are, in ascending order: the center at the base of the spine, which governs the "fight or flight" syndrome; the sacral center, which governs sexual and reproductive activity; and the solar plexus, the "instinctual brain," which "thinks" in terms of "me, my, and mine." The activation of these three chakras alone would constitute, in Bucke's schema, "simple consciousness."

The turning point in evolution comes with the activation of the chakras above the diaphragm: the heart center, which confers awareness of being part of a greater life; the throat center, which allows for individual self-expression and creativity; and the "center between the eyebrows" or *ajna* center—located near the pituitary gland—which brings about the integration of mind, emotions, and the vital energy body, preparing the persona to become an instrument for the soul.

Last to be activated is the "crown chakra," located in the head near the pineal gland. This is the ultimate "seat of the soul." As it opens, the soul's energies pour downward, illuminating the now coordinated and integrated personality. What occurs, in effect, is that the light of the soul from the crown center blends with the love of the soul in the heart center. When all seven centers are awakened, the human being becomes a fully conscious Soul—a spiritual being in a physical form dedicated to manifesting divine love, light, and purpose in the world.

At present, according to spiritual teachers with etheric vision, the heart center of humanity as a whole remains largely closed, although the exceptions are numerous and increasing. In "average humanity," the lower chakras are the most active, while two of the higher ones have begun to open: the throat center, the locus of self-expression, and the ajna center, the locus of personality coordination. In cases where these two centers become highly developed *before* the heart opens, we find powerful individuals capable of causing great harm. In cases where both the heart and crown chakras are *fully* active, we find those whom humanity has designated saints and sages.

One of the most hopeful developments in our time is that these two centers are starting to open within "advanced humanity."[18] In the segment of humanity on the evolutionary edge, there are many indications of the heart opening, the soul emerging, and the mind being impressed by higher intuition. Advances are particularly evident in three spheres of life, each of which serves to illustrate the evolutionary trend of our times: 1. the realm of humanitarian activity, where soul consciousness is now most visible in the world; 2. the field of collective consciousness, where higher awareness is now being studied; and 3. the emergence of "the new kids," a population of children who embody a higher stage of consciousness.

Humanitarian aid has become such an established fact of life around the world that it is now almost taken for granted. Organizations such as the Red Cross, the Salvation Army, and countless others have become so intricately woven into the fabric of modern life that when disaster strikes, it is now assumed that they will be there to provide immediate aid for the victims. Interestingly, however, this collective expression of the human soul is a new development, when seen against the backdrop of our species' long evolutionary unfoldment.

We are told that only 500 years ago, when Martin Luther and Copernicus were alive, just before the time of Shakespeare, human beings had no sense of obligation to help others, outside of their own immediate clan. The Tibetan master states: "The sense of responsibility for one's brother" reflected in the widespread philanthropic enterprise that currently exists "was totally unknown in the year 1500."[19] Giving alms to the poor was not uncommon, but there is a significant difference between an almsgiver and a humanitarian—"a person actively engaged in promoting human welfare and social reforms, as a philanthropist."[20]

It is striking to realize that a sensitivity to *human* suffering, flowing from a sense of spiritual brotherhood, first became manifest in the world—in the form of relief agencies—a relatively short time ago. The world's first humanitarian organization, the Red Cross, was founded in 1864 by a young Swiss businessman, Jean-Henri Dunant (1828–1910), who happened to witness the brutal slaughter that took place at the Battle of Solferino, Italy. That battle, which occurred on June 24, 1859, resulted in 40,000 casualties—Italian, French, and Austrian—within a matter of *hours*.

Struck by the terrible suffering of the wounded left on the battlefield, Dunant immediately organized a relief effort. Three years later, he published *A Memory of Solferino*, a pamphlet calling upon all nations to create voluntary relief societies. The intent was for nations to prevent and alleviate the suffering of *all* their people, without regard to race or creed. Dunant also proposed an agreement among nations that would guarantee the humane treatment of wounded soldiers, which evolved into the expanded protections of the Geneva Convention.

In the course of a century and a half, the impulse to alleviate human suffering has become increasingly universal. The founding purpose of Doctors Without Borders, for example, was to eliminate *all* barriers to delivering aid. Started by a small group of French doctors and journalists who were dismayed by the world's neglect of the 1971 famine in Biafra, Nigeria, the group has since attracted volunteer medical workers from nearly every region of the world and has served in seventy nations. For delivering emergency aid and bearing witness to *human* suffering—caused by war, epidemics, and disasters—it received the 1999 Nobel Peace Prize.

The United Nations itself was originally envisioned as a global expression of the soul of humanity, as its founding declarations attest. A half century after its inception, this impulse is still clearly evident in its humanitarian agencies. Yet for much of its history, the UN has been a battleground between the latent soul of humanity and its lower self. The governments of nation-states, motivated by selfish interests, have often voted *against* measures that would mitigate human suffering—from famine relief and debt relief, to guarantees of the rights of women and children, to calls to halt such crises as genocide and global warming.

The soul of humanity has, however, found a steady and reliable voice at the UN through the expanding global community of *non-governmental organizations* (NGOs)—non-profit agencies with humanitarian goals. These groups have grown both in number and influence since the UN's inception, totaling over 4,500 by 2006.[21] It was during the 1990s that they emerged as a solid "constituency of consciousness," in the words of long-time UN observer, Clovis Maksoud.[22] Former UN Secretary-General, Kofi Annan, observed in 1998 that the relationship between this constituency and the member states had been "transformed beyond all recognition since 1947."[23] According to a scholar quoted by Annan, the growth of NGOs was "as important a development to the latter part of the 20th century" as the rise of the nation-state had been in earlier centuries.[24]

With the spread of global electronic communications in the 1990s, the NGO community gained the capacity to mobilize public opinion worldwide. Emerging as an embryonic counterforce to the interests of nations and multinational corporations, on the eve of the new millennium, the members of several thousand NGOs threw their collective weight behind a global effort to end world poverty—"the worst form of violence" in the words of Mahatma Gandhi. NGOs were the major force behind the UN's campaign to alleviate the suffering of the poorest half of the human family by 2015, a program known as the Millennium Development Goals.

In the aura of optimism surrounding the new millennium, 189 nations agreed to support these goals in September of 2000. Only four years later, the wealthiest nations had already reneged on their commitments. The coordinator of the campaign, Eveline Herfkens, observed, "The world has the resources. We've never been richer. We know what to do."[25] Speaking to the NGO community in 2004, she expressed her fear that the campaign would fail without relentless pressure on national governments from NGOs, the force that had "extracted promises from reluctant governments" in the first place.

On that same occasion, another speaker addressed the need

for a "world consciousness" to replace the consciousness of the UN, which functions primarily "as a multilateral organization where nations are competing to get the best for their own interests." Jacques Attali, an economist, writer, and special advisor to a former French president,[26] remarked that the UN needed to shift "from national priorities to mankind priorities." Reflecting on the significance of the UN's "constituency of consciousness" he said, "It is only in a room like this one where we see people interested in issues without borders, without any national selfish interests."

The *actual* absence of borders between human beings—on the more subtle planes of existence—has recently become a subject of active investigation both formally and informally. In just over a decade, the study of collective consciousness, encompassing "collective intelligence" and "collective wisdom," has emerged as a serious field of scientific inquiry. Researchers have been demonstrating in scientific settings that human beings affect one another unceasingly—though invisibly *and* unconsciously—through energy fields that we co-create with our thoughts and intentions.

In less formal settings, students of collective consciousness have begun to probe the practical, beneficial uses of these subtle energy fields. In the 1990s, numerous groups formed spontaneously to explore how fields of energy (or consciousness) are created and how these energy fields can be utilized. Interestingly, a number of experiments have shown that when members of a group share a common intention to serve the greater good, they are able to access a higher dimension of consciousness. The success of these groups in finding creative solutions to problems and demonstrating expanded awareness has made them the subject of widening study.

A journalist who examined this phenomenon observed in 2004:

> A growing number of people are discovering through their own experience...that when individuals come together with a shared intention, in a conducive environment, something mysterious can come into being, with capacities and intelligences that far transcend those of the individuals involved.[27]

Collective consciousness has been defined by one researcher as "a mode of awareness that emerges at the first transpersonal stage of consciousness, when our identities expand beyond our egos." [28] Robert Kenny, in a paper entitled *What Can Science Tell Us About Collective Consciousness?*, has documented the recent explosion of interest in this higher stage of awareness. When he began his investigations in 1992, he found only one item related to the scientific research of consciousness in a search of the Internet. By 2003, he reported finding 64,000 such items.

In late 2005, a Google search on "science and consciousness," not limited to research studies, turned up over 19,000,000 items [29] including several hundred thousand websites. Interestingly, by 2008 the total number of items was noticeably smaller, but the field appeared to have become consolidated. A Google search in mid-2008 turned up numerous books, university courses, scientific journals and conferences, plus centers and institutes for the study of consciousness, supported by foundation grants.

One branch of this blossoming field of inquiry has called itself "collective wisdom," with the implicit understanding that consciousness has a higher dimension. A pioneering group in this new field, the Collective Wisdom Initiative, says the following in its Declaration of Intent:

> We believe there exists a field of collective consciousness—often seen and expressed through metaphor—that is real and influential, yet invisible. When we come into alignment with this field, there is a deeper understanding of our connection with others, with life, and with a source of collective wisdom. The work is on-going and dynamic. We are calling into awareness this field of collective consciousness and invite you to join us in building this discipline of collective wisdom, its study and practice. [30]

The surge of interest in this field is clearly a phenomenon of our times, yet studies of consciousness actually began well over a century ago. Research into parapsychological or *psi* phenomena was conducted throughout the 20th century, providing substantial evidence that consciousness extends beyond the boundaries of the physical brain.[31] The human capacity to perceive through non-physical senses, known as psychic ability, has been documented quite extensively. Starting in the 1930s, with the development of Kirlian photography, it also became possible to *see* the etheric body—the electro-magnetic human energy body that surrounds and extends beyond the physical form, and merges with the energy field that connects the energy bodies of all forms.

What is different now, however, is that current explorations of subtle energies are taking place in a climate of awareness that humanity is entering a new phase of evolution. It is being learned that subtle capacities, once believed to be present in an isolated few individuals, can be cultivated by many individuals and by groups—a significant advance in the unfoldment of human potential. There is also a growing awareness that we live in *fields* of consciousness—subtle energy fields that affect individuals' thoughts and emotions, and which are in turn affected by the thoughts and feelings of others, either negatively or positively. Significantly, the *force* of love—once an esoteric notion—is now being observed in the laboratory.

Several kinds of repeatable experiments have demonstrated the workings of consciousness beyond time and space. A common one, called "remote viewing," involves a sender, who is taken to an undisclosed location, plus a receiver, who remains in a laboratory. The sender attempts to telepathically transmit images of his or her surroundings to the receiver, the "remote viewer." Kenny reports that a large number of trials have shown that "remote viewers have been able to describe the transmitter's surroundings with a statistically significant degree of accuracy." He adds, "Intriguingly, pairs who had an emotional bond have obtained the strongest results."[32]

In experiments with "distance healing," transmitters of healing thoughts and intentions have demonstrated an ability to impact people in need of healing. Kenny reports that of 150 controlled studies, sixty-seven per cent showed that "individuals and groups can use intention, relaxation, enhanced concentration, visualization, and what is described as 'a request to a healing force greater than themselves' to heal others to a statistically significant degree."[33] Again, he notes that in cases where the senders and receivers of these thoughts and energies had an empathic rapport, the healing effects increased.

The telepathic communication described in these experiments, evidence of expanding soul consciousness, can be explained by a fundamental tenet of esoteric science: our subtle bodies are part of the subtle body of our planet (and universe). The etheric body of an individual soul, composed of intricate channels and centers of energy, flows into the etheric body of the *anima mundi* or world soul—a virtual ocean of energies connecting all living things. Traveling through the subtle energy body of our world, that which we refer to as "space,"[34] are vibrations of all grades—from the densest to the most subtle. Among the more subtle vibrations are thoughts. When thoughts are consciously imbued with the attractive-magnetic force of love, their transmission is significantly enhanced.

The attractive power of love has been experienced by many groups experimenting with synergy—the principle that the whole is greater than the sum of its parts. As with all manifestations of soul consciousness, the success of these groups depends upon the lowering of ego barriers. When this occurs, a group entity emerges—a group *soul* as referred to in the wisdom teachings. Participants in such groups report an enhanced sense of unity, plus access to higher dimensions of wisdom. Esoteric science explains that soul consciousness is both a cohesive energy and a magnetic force capable of attracting energies from the plane of intuition—the source of "love-wisdom."

A participant in one of these group experiments made the following observation:

> In the group, I experienced a kind of consciousness that was almost a singularity, like a dropping of personalities and a joining together where there was no sense of conflict... It became obvious that we weren't responding to individual personalities but were responding to something much deeper, much more real in each other

that was collective... And with that experience came a sense that there was just one body in the room.[35]

From another group experience, a participant reported:

When someone else spoke, it felt as if I was speaking. And when I did speak, it was almost egoless, like it wasn't really me. It was as if something larger than me was speaking through me... It was almost as if when someone would speak, something would become illuminated, something would be revealed, and that would open up something else to be revealed.[36]

Interestingly, the phenomenon of group synergy has recently emerged in the public arena of sports. The coach of the most successful team in American basketball history, Phil Jackson, has turned soul consciousness into a practical force, "call[ing] on the players' need to connect with something larger than themselves."[37] Jackson, author of *Sacred Hoops: Spiritual Lessons of a Hardwood Warrior*, speaks of "the energy that's unleashed when players put their egos aside and work toward a common goal," referring to "a powerful group intelligence [that] emerges that is greater than the coach's ideas or those of any individual on the team."[38] Describing the inner workings of group consciousness, he says:

When players are totally focused on the *team* goal, their efforts can create chain reactions. It's as if they become totally connected to one another, in sync with one another, like five fingers on one hand. When one finger moves, the rest of them all react to it.[39]

The flowering of group consciousness—or soul awareness—in many diverse arenas would seem to indicate that humanity *is*, collectively, approaching a higher stage of consciousness. Of all the forms of evidence now available, however, perhaps the most dramatic is the wave of "old souls" entering the world in the bodies of young children. The qualities exhibited by these children demonstrate irrefutably that their hearts are open and their souls are awakened. Among these qualities is a pronounced humanitarian impulse—an altruistic desire to make the world a better place—often expressed as early as ages four and five, along with an extreme sensitivity to subtle energies and higher planes of existence.

These remarkable children were first identified in 1971 by a California parapsychologist with etheric vision who claimed to see an aura—or light body—surrounding them that was the color of indigo.[40] In the 1980s, as their numbers grew, they were dubbed "the indigo kids" and later, "the new kids." They have been found in countries as diverse as China, Mexico, Russia, Japan, the Czech Republic, and the United States. In the first book about the indigo kids, published in 1999, the authors described the phenomenon as "perhaps the most exciting, albeit odd, change in basic human nature that has ever been observed and documented."[41] They have since been the subject of many books, articles, and a film.

These "new kids" appear to be endowed with both extraordinary intelligence and highly developed intuition. Gifted in both traditional and non-traditional ways, they tend to score high on I.Q. tests *and* to demonstrate such capacities as healing—through energy radiating from their hands—and telepathy. In a recent documentary, *The Indigo Evolution*, a nine-year-old girl, poet and artist from age four, was asked how she conveyed such astounding wisdom and beauty in her work. She replied that if she had a question, she closed her eyes and asked God for help. Alice Bailey offers an explanation: "A sense of God, an appreciation of the true and beautiful, and a contact with the mystical vision is at all times possible to those whose heart center is awake and functioning."[42]

The phenomenon of these children also has a problematic side, in the view of traditional institutions. A large number of "new kids" respond negatively to authority figures, particularly those whom they regard as inauthentic or unqualified for the roles they play. At school, they do not always show respect to adults simply because they are older, and often express impatience with classroom settings which to them feel repressive. As a consequence, many "indigo kids" are diagnosed as having behavior problems and are treated with drugs.[43]

Whether they are helped or hindered by their environment, however, it appears that many of these children have incarnated at this time for the purpose of helping others. They seem to have been born with an acute sensitivity to the suffering of other people and an impulse to serve humanity. From the angle of the soul's evolution, it could be surmised that their karmic obligations had been largely met in previous lifetimes, leaving them free to actively and creatively contribute to the emergence of a higher stage of consciousness on our planet.

In 2005, the journal *Kosmos* devoted an issue to the emerging planetary civilization. In this issue, several of these advanced souls were asked to explain what it means to be "a world citizen." One respondent, a college freshman, gave this reply:

> It is to be at one with the earth and all its members—
> the birds, the lions, the elephants, and the humans...
> [I]magine a world in which every member views them-
> selves as part of the same family. War, hate, and igno-
> rance get thrown out of the window. Why would you
> want to kill a member of your family?... [W]e are all in
> this together. Let us begin to understand each other,
> help each other and love our neighbors as ourselves.
> We have had enough of the blind, intolerant patriotism
> that sets us at odds with each other. [44]

A high school student responded:

> We are all part of the whole, part of something that is
> greater than any one person, or one country... We all
> share one environment... [I]t is important that we put
> aside our borders in order to unite in an effort to cre-
> ate an entire society of peace... Now, during this time
> of terrorism, disease and poverty, I see a light glowing
> from a watchtower over the world. It is a light powered
> by knowledge, understanding and love. I am, you are,
> we are, citizens of this brighter world. [45]

NOTES

1   Emerson, *The Best of Ralph Waldo Emerson*, 207.
2   *Ibid.*
3   The work of Ken Wilber is most widely known in this area, however his own work builds upon that of earlier pioneers such as Clare Graves, Jean Piaget, Sri Aurobindo, Jane Loevinger, Don Beck, and others.
4   Sahtouris, *Gaia*, 21.
5   Felix Adler (1851-1933), American educator and reformer, offered this definition of ethical behavior.
6   Bucke, *Cosmic Consciousness*, 19.
7   *Ibid.*, 2.
8   *Ibid.*, 24.
9   *Ibid.*, 3.
10 *Ibid.*, 17.
11 *Ibid.*, 3.
12 *Ibid.*, 213.
13 Dostoyevsky, *The Brothers Karamazov*, 303.
14 *Ibid.*, 303-04.
15 These phrases from Teilhard de Chardin, drawn from several sources, commonly appear in works about his philosophy.
16 Bailey, *The Rays and the Initiations*, 618.
17 See Glossary.
18 See Bailey, *Esoteric Healing* and *The Soul and Its Mechanism*.
19 Bailey, *A Treatise on White Magic*, 407.
20 From *Random House Webster's College Dictionary*.
21 UN General Assembly, *UN Foundation to Hold Forum on NGO Access to UN*, November 20, 2006.
22 Ida Urso, *Report of the 51st Annual Conference of the UN's Department of Public Information (DPI) and Affiliated NGOs*, September 1998, www.aquaac.org. (Clovis Maksoud was the Arab League's chief representative to the United Nations and United States, 1979-1990.)
23 *Ibid.*
24 Kofi Annan, "The Meaning of the International Community," *Address to the 52nd Annual UN DPI/NGO Conference*, September 15, 1999.
25 Ida Urso, *Report of the 57th Annual UN DPI/NGO Conference*, September 2004, www.aquaac.org.
26 *Ibid.*
27 Craig Hamilton, "Come Together: The Mystery of Collective Intelligence," *What is Enlightenment?* magazine, May-July 2004, 58.
28 Robert Kenny, "What Can Science Tell Us About Collective Consciousness?" 2004, www.collectivewisdominitiative.org/papers.

29 Separate searches turned up 13,200,000 items under "collective intelligence" and 6,810,000 under "collective consciousness."

30 This statement appeared on The Collective Wisdom Initiative website, last accessed July 17, 2008.

31 Both the Soviet and American governments, particularly the military branches, conducted extensive research in this field.

32 Robert Kenny, "The Science of Collective Consciousness," *What is Enlightenment?* magazine, no. 25, May-July 2004, 78.

33 *Ibid.*, 79.

34 Western physicists once universally accepted the ether as the medium through which all objects in our universe move, a notion later rejected but again finding acceptance. It is central to Eastern science.

35 Craig Hamilton, "Come Together: The Mystery of Collective Intelligence," *What is Enlightenment?* magazine, May-July 2004, 60.

36 *Ibid,* 62.

37 Ross Robertson, "The Soul of Teamwork," *What is Enlightenment? magazine,* May-July 2004, 67.

38 *Ibid.*

39 *Ibid.*

40 John Leland, "Are They Here to Save the World?" *The New York Times,* January 12, 2006.

41 Carroll, Lee and Jan Tober, *The Indigo Children,* xi.

42 Bailey, *The Soul and Its Mechanism,* 134.

43 They are commonly assessed as having attention deficit problems like ADHD and treated with Ritalin.

44 Matt Cooperrider, "Voices of Youth," *Kosmos,* no. 1, 2005, 22.

45 Chelsea Trengrove, "Voices of Youth," *Kosmos,* no. 1, 2005, 21.

CHAPTER EIGHT

THE SOUL'S RELIGION

Mankind comes to me along many roads,
And on whatever road a man approaches me,
on that do I welcome him,
For all roads are mine.

~The Bhagavad-Gita

FOR MOST OF RECORDED history, religion has served as the cornerstone of human civilization. Its primacy was challenged only recently, when modern minds began to suspect that God was a strictly human invention. Before the incursion of doubt, there was a general presumption that a person's fortunes depended on the will of higher forces. Our ancestors believed they were at the mercy of deities who could bestow wealth or poverty, health or sickness, life or death. Religious practices revolved around rituals of atonement and sacrifice designed to appease the gods and thus insure one's survival and well-being.

Until well into the Age of Enlightenment, God was widely feared as the bearer of affliction. Tragedies such as a woman's death in childbirth or the destruction of a home by fire were commonly attributed to the wrath of God. One of the first serious challenges to such beliefs came in 1752 with Benjamin Franklin's discovery that lightening could be safely conducted into the ground. Before that time, when a person was struck by lightning it was deemed an act of God. Later, when lightening rods were routinely installed on buildings and men began to believe they could conquer nature, such beliefs were disparaged as religious superstition.

In the West, starting with the Copernican revolution, the advances of modern science posed mounting challenges to religion. Successive discoveries about our physical universe cast increasing doubt on the veracity of ancient scriptures, contributing to the erosion of faith in religious doctrine. This process was accelerated by the two world wars of the 20th century.[1] The first world war, widely regarded as a senseless slaughter, had such a terrifying impact that people believed it must have been "the war to end all wars." In the war that followed, the scale of horror caused many to pose the ultimate questions: If a god *did* exist, and if this god was both omnipotent and benevolent, why had it failed to crush the forces of evil?

In the eyes of many thinking people, the two world wars had demonstrated convincingly that the "hand of God" had been withdrawn from history. In the second world war, when forces of evil had threatened to overtake the world, it appeared that human beings alone had been responsible for the triumph of the good. Human intelligence had prevailed on the battlefield; human ingenuity had dealt the final cataclysmic blow in the form of an atomic bomb. The awesome power unleashed by that bomb, the sheer magnitude of its destructive force, suggested that human beings had uncovered a potential rivaling the power of deity.

In the decades following that war, a wave of prosperity reinforced the illusion of man's omnipotence and further weakened the hold of traditional religion. Cushioned by comfort and security, many Americans had begun to question the relevance of God and religion to their lives by the 1950s. By the 60s, growing numbers of people were asking who and what God was, while clergy and theologians increasingly found themselves unable to offer satisfying answers. The religious uncertainty of that era was trumpeted on the cover of *Time* magazine in 1966 with the startling question: "Is God Dead?"[2]

With hindsight, what appears to have died in those years was the concept of God as "the elderly man with a flowing white beard out there in space." Growing doubts about the nature of the transcendent God of the West—the biblical Creator of the Old Testament—had served to loosen the grip of religious doctrine. And with the death of the anthropomorphic concept of God, there emerged a vacuum of belief in countless lives. And yet the quest for God had not ended, as many observers had mistakenly assumed. "Faith is not dying in the West," remarked a Catholic theologian at a 1976 conference on meditation, "it is merely moving inside."[3]

The spiritual practice for "moving inside," known as meditation, began to fill the religious vacuum for many Westerners in the 60s. It was taught largely by teachers from the East who introduced a new facet of divinity: God immanent—existing as a divine spark within the human soul. As the word "meditation" infiltrated our culture, it became synonymous with everything from relaxation techniques to methods for sharpening the mind. But the spiritual purpose of meditation, from ancient times, has always been to awaken that inner spark of divinity. In place of doctrines, scriptures, and rituals—performed by intermediaries between human beings and God—growing numbers of Westerners chose the inner path leading directly to the divinity within the human soul.

By the 1980s and 90s, the new wave of spirituality in the West had taken on the character of a quest for the Soul. The bestselling poet in America at the time was Rumi, who became known as "the poet of the soul."[4] Jalalu'ddin Rumi (1207–1273), a 13th century mystic of Persian origin, had become a spiritual teacher for innumerable 20th century American and European seekers. The son of a Sufi master, belonging to the mystical branch of Islam, Rumi himself was a master who had inspired the birth of a new Sufi Order. Yet like all awakened beings, his awareness transcended the boundaries of "man-made" religion. The universality of his message is captured in the following lines:

> We are all the same, all the same, longing
> To find our way back,
> Back to the one, back to the only one.[5]

While underscoring the sameness of the human soul, Rumi was not oblivious to differences between people in the sphere of religion. The differences that concerned him, however, were related to states of consciousness rather than creeds. "The ones who know the conventions are of one kind," he observed cryptically, "while those whose spirits and souls burn are another kind."⁶ It was the latter kind, those longing to find their way "back to the one," whom he saw as being the same—seekers awakening from the illusion of separation and aspiring to return to the Source, the Absolute, the one God.

Finding the way back is, in a very real sense, the inner religion of the Soul. One who treads the path of return is making a conscious decision to "bind (the self) back"—the literal meaning of the Latin word *religare*. Implied in the notion of binding *back* is a recognition that there once existed a bond between human beings and their Source, that it was severed, and that it is in need of restoration. The soul on the Path undergoes a self-initiated process of transformation in the goal of restoring that bond. Along the way, the essence of the original connection to Spirit—the spark of divinity within all souls—is progressively revealed.

Genuine mystics of all times have testified to the universal essence of the human soul. But it wasn't until seven centuries after Rumi that practitioners of different faiths first came together to *demonstrate* this truth. In 1968, an historic meeting took place between the Dalai Lama (a Tibetan Buddhist), and Thomas Merton, a Trappist (Catholic) monk who was familiar with Zen Buddhism. Their dialogue, enriched by their respective years of meditation and contemplation, brought to light a wide expanse of common ground. Having experienced the realm of the soul—also known as the Buddha nature—through their individual spiritual practices, they were able to see deeply into one another's faiths.

The meeting of these illumined souls broke new ground in the realm of religious dialogue between East and West. The spirit of their exchange, reflective of the Second Vatican Council's call for interreligious dialogue, served to catalyze the interfaith movement of the latter part of the 20th century. Simultaneously, however, another kind of interfaith impulse was germinating—one that was occurring within the confines of individual souls. Western mystics had begun to venture outside of the bounds of their own faiths to explore the spiritual wisdom of the East. In so doing, they unknowingly paved the way for a multitude of seekers who would later feel free to embrace teachings and practices of East and West, in their own quests for higher truth.

So unusual was this pluralistic form of spirituality that it was addressed by religious scholar Ursula King in her book, *Christian Mystics: The Spiritual Heart of the Christian Tradition.* Highlighting the newness of this trend, first noted in the 20th century, King profiled the lives of some of its pioneers. One early exemplar was French writer and social activist, Simone Weil (1909–1943). Born into an agnostic Jewish family, Weil felt intensely drawn to Catholicism and was transformed by mystical experiences of the presence of Christ. At the same time, she was deeply influenced by both Greek and Indian philosophy—particularly by the ancient Hindu scripture, the *Bhagavad-Gita,* the "Song of the Lord."

Another personification of this inclusive approach to spirituality was Henri le Saux (1910–1973), who became Swami Abhishiktananda. Le Saux was a French Benedictine monk for twenty years before going to India, where he and a colleague co-founded the first Catholic ashram. They did so with "the intention of identifying the Hindu quest of the Absolute with their own experience of God in Christ in the mystery of the Holy Trinity."[7] The swami felt that it was his calling to manifest his dedication to Christ "from within the depth of this Hindu spirituality, a calling lived out 'in the cave of the heart.'"[8]

Other mystics and visionaries of the 20th century sensed that our evolution as a species was intrinsically tied to a growing awareness of the *universality* of spiritual truth. Among them was scientist and theologian Pierre Teilhard de Chardin (1881–1955), who perceived the life of our planet as a "divine milieu" permeated by the presence of God. Teilhard saw our species evolving toward unity through our collective spiritual resources—wisdom flowing from *all* religious streams into one common pool. For him, the "Cosmic Christ" was the spark of conscious evolution, a process destined to culminate in the "spirit of one earth" uniting all human beings with one another, and with God, through spiritual love.

A similar vision of human consciousness evolving toward universality was held by Sir George Trevelyan (1906–1996), called "the father of the 20th century movement for spiritual regeneration in Britain." Sir George, like Teilhard, recognized that the world's religions shared the same core truths. He, too, had a mystical realization that "all life is of God and everything is of Divine origin."[9] The Cosmic Christ was, for him as well, central to the process of evolution. He defined this divine presence as both a principle—"the heart principle of Divinity"[10]—and a universal force of love being released on Earth to propel human evolution toward unity.

In addition, however, Sir George was a strong proponent of the role of the individual in the planet's evolution. "Change man and you change society," he wrote.[11] In his view, spiritual awakening was crucial to humanity's survival and evolution. An apostle of self-transformation, he stressed the need to address the unconscious dimension of human beings—particularly "the shadow," often overlooked by spiritual teachers. For him, facing the unredeemed contents of the human psyche was as essential to spiritual growth as were meditative experiences of higher states of awareness. Through a holistic approach to transformation, he envisioned *homo sapiens* evolving into *"homo-universalis."*

Still other visionaries, sensing the direction of human evolution, had glimmerings of a new kind of religion. They foresaw the emergence of a new religion at a higher turn of the evolutionary spiral whose nature would be universal. One such individual was Richard Bucke, who had predicted the rise of "cosmic consciousness."[12] Bucke sensed that in the future, religion would become a living *expression* of this higher stage of consciousness—"every minute of every day of all life." He envisioned it as a spiritual *force* entering the world and pervading all aspects of human experience.

Saying little about the form of this new religion, he ruled out what it would *not* be:

> It will not depend on tradition. It will not be believed and disbelieved. It will not ...[belong] to certain hours, times, occasions. It will not be in sacred books nor in the mouths of priests. It will not dwell in churches and meetings and forms and days... It will not teach a future immortality nor future glories, for immortality and glory will exist in the here and now. The evidence of immortality will live in every heart as sight in every eye. Doubt of God and of eternal life will be as impossible as is now doubt of existence.[13]

A few generations after Bucke's, on the other side of the world, a mystic imprisoned in the gulag of Soviet Russia had an elaborate vision of a new universal religion. Daniel Andreev (1906–1959)— poet, student of history, and spiritual visionary—intuited the impending dawn of a new era of spirituality that would blossom into a new religion. Calling it the "Rose of the World," he described it as "an *inter*religion" that will be "a teaching that views all religions that appeared earlier as reflections of different layers of spiritual reality...and different segments of our planetary cosmos." He wrote:

> If the older religions are petals, then the Rose of the World will be a flower: with roots, stem, head, and the commonwealth of its petals.[14]

The heart of Andreev's vision was an "interreligious, global church of the new Age...the sum total of the spiritual activity of many people...standing beneath the shower of...revelation."[15] This new religion would be born of a living relationship between spiritually conscious human beings, sensitive to higher impression, and spiritual Beings from higher realms. It would function as "a receptor, fosterer, and interpreter of...the collective mystical consciousness of all living humanity."[16]

Like Bucke, Andreev envisioned that religion would become thoroughly integrated with all aspects of life. He perceived an inti-

mate link between individual spiritual growth and social justice—
"two parallel processes that should complement each other."[17] In
Andreev's vision of the future, inner growth and its outer manifestation would culminate in a global federation of peoples and religions under the guidance of the wisest human beings—the "finest
representatives of all nations, all faiths, all social classes, and all
specialties."[18] These wise beings would become "the mystical links
between humanity and the other worlds, the revealers of the will of
providence, the spiritual guides of billions."[19]

The guidance of genuinely wise beings would supplant old
methods of rule, in Andreev's new global federation. The system of
governance would be neither theocracy, nor hierocracy, nor mon-
archy, but

> ...something qualitatively different from all that has
> come before...a global-wide social system working to-
> ward sanctifying and enlightening all life on earth... Its
> essence will consist of work in the name of spiritual-
> izing individuals, all of humanity, and nature.[20]

From a certain angle, visions like these are not entirely new.
The core of the mystical insight of Bucke and Andreev—that religion will evolve into a spiritual consciousness pervading all dimensions of life—is similar to visions of earlier mystics. One example
is Symeon the New Theologian (949–1032), an Eastern Orthodox
Christian who professed that God was not only a transcendent being, but could also be known here and now through direct personal
experience, and that those who had this experience could live "a
heavenly life here on earth...not just in caves or mountains or monastic cells, but in the midst of cities."[21]

What separates the more recent mystical visions from earlier
ones is a matter of scale. Symeon more than likely anticipated that
only a few souls would ever reach that transcendent state of awareness, whereas Bucke, Andreev, Teilhard, Trevelyan, and many others have anticipated the flowering of a whole new era—a new kind
of human civilization growing out of the evolution of many souls
toward a higher stage of consciousness. Mystics of recent times

have envisioned a segment of humanity reaching a higher stage of awareness and becoming agents of transformation in religion, culture, politics, education, and all other facets of society.

The wisdom teachings have also set forth the vision of a new civilization, flowing from a higher stage of consciousness, with religion at its core. The Tibetan master's concept of religion in the new age, as portrayed in the books of Alice Bailey, is remarkably similar to the mystical perceptions mentioned above. The picture presented in these books, however, is vastly amplified. Scattered throughout the twenty-four volumes are gems of insight into the ways in which religion and the whole planetary civilization are likely to evolve.

Of all the differences between religions past and future, as outlined by the Tibetan, the most fundamental one was foreseen by both Andreev and Bucke: religion will not be relegated to a separate sphere of life, but will become the conscious expression of higher awareness in every aspect of daily life. Moreover, it will grow out of direct *experience* of the divine. When the soul awakens, religion will no longer be based on belief, or on faith, but on firsthand knowledge and experience of spiritual realities. The Tibetan master states:

> In the new world order, spirituality will supersede theology; living experience will take the place of theological acceptances. The spiritual realities will emerge with increasing clarity and the form aspect will recede into the background; dynamic, expressive truth will be the keynote of the new world religion.[22]

The most fundamental of the new spiritual realities will be a conscious realization of the soul's true nature and its inherent potential to enter into contact with the spiritual kingdom. It is said that the new universal religion will be born of a living relationship between the human and spiritual realms. The fabric of this relationship will be woven one thread at a time as individual souls awaken, set foot on the spiritual path, and undertake the practices that reorient the life and lead inexorably, over time, to contact with the divine.

At present, it requires a stretch of the imagination for most human beings to fathom the possibility of such relationships. Yet many seekers are now beginning to realize that the Buddha, the Christ, and other avatars not only inspired world religions, they forged paths into the next kingdom for others to follow. Moreover, their lives served to create a vital bridge in consciousness between the human and spiritual worlds. In more recent times, Beings on the other side of that bridge have been "drawing closer to humanity," according to the Tibetan master, in preparation for the next stage of planetary evolution.

The most tangible evidence of the spiritual hierarchy's approach to humanity is the body of Ageless Wisdom teachings now available. In certain of these teachings,[23] the forging of relationships between the kingdoms is explained. The seeker on the Path of Return is actually building a bridge in consciousness to the spiritual kingdom. Inevitably, progress on this path results in the establishment of such a link. Spiritual relationships flow from expansions of consciousness, called "initiations," that begin with the soul's awakening. With each further step into the realm of spirit, guidance from the inner kingdom becomes more accessible, reinforcing and enhancing the soul's apprehension of subtle realities.

As the new age unfolds, and as growing numbers of souls forge such inner linkages, a new culture and civilization will arise. Insight and inspiration from the spiritual guides of the human race will travel across this collective bridge of light into the realm of human activity, raising the level of consciousness of humanity as a whole. Once humanity is sufficiently resonant to a higher vibrational frequency, it will be possible for Masters of Wisdom to return to earth—for the first time since the days of Atlantis.[24] Though not identified as such, they will be recognized as enlightened individuals and will rise to the fore in their respective fields of service, becoming leaders of humanity.

With the spread of soul consciousness—variously called Christ consciousness, Buddha nature, the indwelling Atman—it is predicted that the Being called the Christ will again appear on

Earth. However, this Being will not be known as the representative of one religion, but as the most advanced "unit of consciousness" in the 18-million year stream of human evolution. Known within the spiritual hierarchy as the "Master of Masters,"[25] this individual will emerge as the World Teacher to "inaugurate" a new religion, which will in turn inspire a new world civilization.[26]

It is said that Christ's last incarnation, 2,000 years ago, served an important esoteric function—that of anchoring the first threads of the Kingdom of God on Earth.[27] The purpose of the coming incarnation will be to fully *establish* the Kingdom of God on Earth, by fostering conscious awareness of spiritual realities on the plane of material living. According to the wisdom teachings, human civilization will become "spiritualized" during the course of the Aquarian Age. The main "instrument" for achieving this aim will a new world religion, to be initiated by the coming World Teacher.

At the heart of this new religion is *the binding back* of the human soul to God, by means of the spiritual path. The goal of aligning human will with divine purpose for our planet will be accomplished through the self-transforming process by which awakening souls reorient their lives to the spiritual plane, purify the dross of the separative persona, and learn to work co-creatively with the spiritual kingdom in service to the divine plan. Souls treading the path will *live* the new religion by bringing spiritual awareness into daily life, while fulfilling their own unique part in the plan. For the unawakened, religious ceremonies will focus on fostering soul consciousness: awareness of and identification with the One Life of God.

Like all religions, the new religion will present teachings to humanity. Unlike previous religious doctrines, however, these teachings will consist of "unalterable truths that have stood the test of time" and that comprise "the inner structure of the One Truth upon which all world theologies have been built."[28] They will neither negate the fundamental truths of earlier religions nor depart significantly from them, but will expose "the reality underlying all dogmas and doctrines"[29]—a reality that in the past was either obscured or misinterpreted. The new teachings will explain and expound upon timeless truths that have remained largely veiled until now.

The cardinal truth of all religious truths is that there *is* a God—"God, or whatever word anyone may employ to express the Originator of all that exists," in the words of the Tibetan master.[30] God is seen as the "all-embracing Life" as intimated in a well-known quotation from the *Bhagavad-Gita*: "Having pervaded this whole universe with a fragment of Myself, I remain." The Tibetan explains:

> God is here, present among us and in all forms of expression; He includes, pervades and remains beyond. He is greater than all appearance. He reveals Himself progressively and cyclically as man gets ready for further knowledge.[31]

This depiction of God represents a fusion of traditional Eastern and Western perspectives. Although Christ taught that "the kingdom of heaven is within you," Western religions have stressed the *transcendent* dimension of deity—the Creative Force that gave birth to the world but is believed, by many, to have largely remained outside of human history. Eastern religions, by contrast, have emphasized God *immanent*—the inner divine spark that is fanned into a flame on the spiritual path. In the future, as these perspectives are synthesized, God will be understood as *both* the force that "guarantees the plan for our world"[32] through an ever-unfolding evolutionary purpose, and also the germ of consciousness *within* all life forms, evolving and expanding through time.

All other fundamental religious truths spring from one of these two aspects of divinity. Flowing from the immanence of God is the truth that human beings are inherently related to the divine source and to one another. The notion that we are all "children of God" belonging to a "brotherhood of humanity" has become increasingly accepted over time. Less clearly understood is the basis for this interrelationship: *the human soul*, pure spirit at the subtlest level.

The divine spark that brought each individual soul into manifestation was born of the one Spirit that connects all living beings to one another.

As for the transcendent dimension of God, "greater than all appearance," there is much that lies beyond the reach of human comprehension. There are, however, certain principles that we can grasp intellectually. One is that God, whose attributes include will or purpose, is the First Cause of an ongoing evolutionary process. This process works out in time and space through an array of forces under the impress of divine will, all of which influence the planet's evolution in ways that conform to divine purpose. At present, these forces are focused on the evolution of consciousness *within* forms— a phenomenon increasingly apparent to awakening souls.

The notion that consciousness evolves, and that it does so over time, is linked to yet another fundamental religious truth: the immortality of the soul. But in contrast to the traditional doctrines of Western religions, the wisdom teachings hold that the soul's immortality plays out through a long chain of human incarnations. Over the course of lifetimes of experience, the forces of evolution serve to awaken the soul to its spiritual nature and ultimately transform it into a divinized human being—a "God-man"—an embodiment of higher consciousness. The life of Christ 2,000 years ago is emblematic of the spiritual journey of every awakened soul: from spiritual birth to purificatory tests, illumination, surrender to God's will, and finally union with God.

There is still another fundamental truth that will be paramount in the coming era: the existence of a *path* to God. Historically, the path—the middle Way of the Buddha; the Way of Life of the Tao; the Truth, the Way and the Life personified by Christ—has been seen as the province of mystics, saints, and sages. Its nature remained obscure to all but the initiated, who generally lived apart from the world while engaging in practices shrouded in secrecy. In the universal religion to come, by contrast, the requirements of spiritual transformation will be widely known.[33] An understanding of the soul's evolutionary journey—from the descent of the divine spark into matter to its ascent toward *realized* divinity—will be integral to the new culture.

The availability of such knowledge will foster a growing realization of the universality of spiritual truth, a realization that in the past was attained by only the few who walked the path. Yet the testimony of those few, from all cultures and religious faiths, confirms the reality that the path is one and the same. The Tibetan master states:

> The testimony to the existence of this Path is the priceless treasure of all the great religions and its witnesses are those who have transcended all forms and all theologies, and have penetrated into the world of meaning which all symbols veil.[34]

One of the most extraordinary witnesses to the universality of the spiritual path was a Hindu saint seen by many as a "prophet for the new age"—Sri Ramakrishna (1836–1886). Ramakrishna's search for enlightenment was deeply rooted in the Hindu tradition, yet he openly explored the path to God in other forms. For a time he became immersed in the Sufi tradition; years later he had a mystical vision of the Christ, whom he came to revere as a divine avatar. Reflecting on his experience toward the end of his life, Ramakrishna stated:

> I have practiced all religions—Hinduism, Islam, Christianity—and I have also followed the paths of the different Hindu sects. I have found that it is the same God toward whom all are directing their steps, though along different paths... Wherever I look, I see men quarreling in the name of religion... But they never stop to reflect that He who is called Krishna is also called Shiva, and bears the name of the Primal Energy, Jesus and Allah as well.[35]

In the coming age, the wisdom teachings say, the universal truths of religion will be embraced globally, while sacred customs and rituals rooted in different cultures will continue to be practiced locally. The oneness or sameness of the path leading into the Kingdom of God will be accepted along with celebrations honoring each religion's history, traditions, prophets, saints, and avatars. In essence, the soul of religion—all that constitutes its inner core— will be widely acknowledged, while the outer forms will continue to be clothed in robes of many colors.

Even now, though the religious forms of the old age still appear largely in tact, the spirit of the new religion is coming into expression. A poignant example emerged in the year 2000, at an event held in New York City, which was captured in a film entitled *Five Masters of Meditation*.[36] Several hundred people attended this historic gathering of diverse religious leaders on the theme of meditation—the core practice of every spiritual path. Christian, Sufi, Buddhist, Hindu, and Jewish teachers discussed their own tradition of meditation, its principles and techniques, and then led the participants in a unique meditative experience.[37]

What made this event remarkable was its underlying premise. These five spiritual teachers shared the view that encouraging seekers to meditate—to experience a higher state of awareness—was more important than gaining adherents to their own particular faith. One of the five teachers, Swami Satchidananda, put it like this: "The idea of 'the only way' is long gone. Go home and think: Which method is best suited for me, my temperament, my taste? Choose the way you feel will satisfy your hunger."

In describing the purpose of meditation, the words of these teachers sounded a common theme. "When we meditate," said Father Laurence Freeman, a Christian monk, "we come into communion with our own true self," adding, "and also with those who wish to be in communion with us." "My true home is my Self, my Buddha nature," said Sister Annabel Laity, a Buddhist nun. "In meditation I have arrived, I am home." The Sufi leader Pir Vilayat Khan asserted: "We are a condition of God, like a wave is a condition of the sea. Meditation establishes a connection with the reality we call God."

Father Laurence also spoke of the value of individuals from different religions meditating together as a means of fostering human understanding. Calling interfaith meditation "the great discovery of our time," he contrasted the sharing of inner *experience* with the verbal dialogue of most interfaith meetings and conferences.

> Meditation is a spiritual practice found in all the world's religious traditions. From the spiritual core or contemplative heart, all religions are able to relate to each other and work together ultimately for the good of the world. If there is to be real dialogue and understanding, it has to come out of this depth of shared meditation.[38]

From an esoteric perspective, the value of meditation is that it brings the soul into the foreground of consciousness. In the meditative state, the outer form cloaking the soul (in this particular lifetime) fades from awareness. All the differences that have historically separated human beings—race, religion, nationality, gender, age, socio-economic status—fall away. What remains is soul consciousness, the dimension of awareness in which there is no separation. The evolutionary goal of the new age is to turn this meditative awareness into a condition of spiritual unity that will permeate the life of our planet.

A vivid example of the power of meditative awareness—soul consciousness—materialized in 2008 at a gathering in Jaipur, India held by the Global Peace Initiative of Women. The "Jaipur Summit" brought together women spiritual leaders from around the world to discover how to harness qualities often considered feminine—inclusiveness, compassion, receptiveness, relatedness—for the benefit of the world community. It focused on ways "to foster global transformation by embracing the spiritual realities of the oneness of life, compassion that flows from the awareness of oneness, and ahimsa (non-harm), our natural state of living in awareness of the Divine essence in all."[39]

Women (and men) attended the meeting from over forty countries, and from religious backgrounds including Christian, Jewish, Muslim, Buddhist, Hindu, Sikh, Jain, and traditional African. The convener, Dena Merriam, described it as "probably the most significant multi-religious gathering of women spiritual leaders that has ever taken place." Reflecting on the four-day event, Merriam wrote, "Although words were spoken, it was not the words that left a lasting impression." More important was the experiential space of oneness that had been created, at a level deeper than words, through a sharing of prayer, meditation, and sacred song from diverse traditions.

Remarkably, the energy field created by this event had immediate practical benefits. From Jaipur, the facilitators moved on to a gathering they had organized for young Iraqi community leaders, mostly men, held in Dharamsala, India. The purpose was to reduce conflict between the Iraqis, who arrived wounded, angry, polarized, and mistrustful of one another. At the beginning, it was a struggle for the women spiritual leaders to sustain the healing, unifying energy field generated in Jaipur. However, Merriam reported, "slowly the energy transformed and locked minds began to open." Having witnessed the potential of women to engender spiritual unity, she concluded: "The work of the feminine is just beginning."

The *idea* of spiritual unity, formulated in terms of a human ideal, is actually not new. During a chapter of history little known to much of the world, this notion came to flower in a largely social context. Leading writers and philosophers of pre-revolutionary Russia, deeply rooted in Russian Orthodoxy, articulated a new ideal inspired by spiritual experience. It became encapsulated in the word *sobornost*. Often translated as "brotherhood" or "togetherness," the literal meaning of *sobor-nost* is "cathedral-ness"—a word that evokes a communion of souls in the presence of God under the soaring dome of a cathedral.

During the 19th century, the Russian soul was closely identified with the ideal of *sobornost*. Dostoyevsky referred to it as "Russia's unspoken word," and though he lamented the social and political upheaval in which his nation was embroiled, he never lost faith in its latent potential to become a force for spiritual brotherhood in the world. A friend of Dostoyevsky, the visionary philosopher Vladimir Solovyov (1853–1900), was also a proponent of the *sobornost* ideal, but expressed it in more purely religious terms. For Solovyov, the entry into history of Christ—"God-man"—had initiated the transformation of humanity into "Godmanhood," which he saw as the ultimate manifestation of *sobornost*. Christ's transfiguration by divine light was, for Solovyov, the prelude to the transfiguration of life on Earth.

However, the means of realizing Godmanhood, the actual processes by which life on Earth would be transformed, was never directly addressed by Solovyov. Like other spiritual visionaries, he implicitly believed that religious faith and inspiration alone would suffice. It was only with the appearance of the modern wisdom teachings that the actual processes of spiritual transformation— the methods and requirements—were clearly and explicitly made known. These processes constitute the spiritual Path—the very heart of the religion of the future.

In the past, as previously mentioned, treading the path was a solitary venture. The practice of religion, by contrast, traditionally involved a gathering of souls—in churches, synagogues, mosques, and temples—to collectively invoke the presence of the divine. In our time, the throwing off of religious doctrine in favor of the inner quest for spiritual experience has led many seekers to experience an uncomfortable sense of isolation. But that isolation has, in turn, begun to engender a yearning for spiritual community that is reminiscent of the spirit of *sobornost*.

There are signs that the current widespread experience of spiritual isolation may actually be preparing the soil for a new *form* of religion. A hint of this appeared in a 2005 article entitled "Spiritual But Not Religious: Moving Beyond Postmodern Spirituality." The author, scholar and journalist Elizabeth Debold, cited the rise of "individualized spiritual paths...outside the context of religion" as characteristic of our time and posed a provocative question: "Does this uniquely postmodern spirituality—each one of us in a religion of one—have the capacity to bind us into a true global culture? Or do we need something more?"[40]

Her own answer to this question is a mystical invocation of a new religion born of awakening souls:

> Rooted in mystical depth...we can create a new religious
> context for an awakening world. A religion that calls

us to realize our deepest collective purpose, bound together as the living expression of the mind and heart of God in a cosmic act of mutual Self-creation.[41]

NOTES

1   In the wisdom teachings conveyed by Alice Bailey these two wars are viewed as one extended conflict.
2   *Time* magazine, April 8, 1966.
3   Ferguson, *The Aquarian Conspiracy*, 368. The theologian was Anthony Padovano.
4   From Huston Smith's introduction to *The Illustrated Rumi*, 7.
5   Rumi, *The Illustrated Rumi*, 23.
6   *Ibid.*, 78.
7   King, *Christian Mystics*, 210.
8   *Ibid.*
9   Farrer, *Sir George Trevelyan and the New Spiritual Awakening*, 126.
10 *Ibid.*, 155.
11 *Ibid.*, 119.
12 See Chapter 3.
13 Bucke, *Cosmic Consciousness*, 5.
14 Andreev, *The Rose of the World*, 21.
15 *Ibid.*, 20.
16 *Ibid.*, 23.
17 *Ibid.*, 21.
18 *Ibid.*, 30.
19 *Ibid.*, 29.
20 *Ibid.*, 30.
21 King, *Christian Mystics*, 177.
22 Bailey, *The Externalisation of the Hierarchy*, 202.
23 Certain of the books of Alice Bailey, conveyed by the Tibetan master, focus specifically on this knowledge.
24 There is a belief (dating back to Plato's time) that a continent named Atlantis, which occupied an area of what is now the Atlantic Ocean, was destroyed by violent eruptions between 50,000 and 10,000 BCE.
25 See Chapter 9 for an exploration of the Spiritual Hierarchy and the Christ.
26 For more on this subject see Alice A. Bailey, *The Reappearance of the Christ* and *From Bethlehem to Calvary*.
27 Bailey, *The Reappearance of the Christ*, 53.

28 Bailey, *The Externalisation of the Hierarchy*, 405.
29 *Ibid.*, 415.
30 Bailey, *Esoteric Psychology*, vol. 2, 277.
31 Bailey, *The Externalization of the Hierarchy*, 289.
32 Bailey, *The Reappearance of the Christ*, 144.
33 See Chapters 5 and 9.
34 Bailey, *The Externalisation of the Hierarchy*, 405.
35 Schiffman, *Sri Ramakrishna*, 78.
36 Hartley Film Foundation, the Temple of Understanding, and the Tibet Center, *Five Masters of Meditation: Renowned Spiritual Leaders of Five World Religions Offer the Keys to Their Spiritual Practice*, DVD, 2002.
37 The teachers were: Father Laurence Freeman, Christian monk and author; Pir Vilayat Inayat Khan, Sufi leader and author; Sister Annabel Laity, Buddhist nun and abbess of the Green Mountain Dharma Center; Sri Swami Satchidananda, Hindu leader and head of the Integral Yoga Institute; and Marcia Prager, rabbi of the Philadelphia Jewish Renewal Community and author.
38 *Ibid.*
39 Dena Merriam, "Making Way for the Feminine for a Better World," *Kosmos* journal, Spring/Summer 2008, 50-51.
40 Elizabeth Debold, "Spiritual But Not Religious: Moving Beyond Postmodern Spirituality," *What is Enlightenment?* magazine, Dec–Feb 2005–6, 56.
41 *Ibid.*, 62.

CHAPTER NINE

SAINTS AND MASTERS

When all the race...
As man...has tended to mankind,
...in completed man begins anew
A tendency to God...
For men begin to pass their nature's bound.

~Robert Browning

IN THESE FEW SPARE lines, with a touch of the poet's magic, Robert Browning (1812–1889) describes the origins of a saint. The journey toward holiness begins with a "completed" human being—one who has surpassed the bounds of "animal-human" nature, or human nature circumscribed by the visible, physical reality. As the soul of such a person awakens, there unfolds a new cycle of lifetimes impelled by "a tendency to God." When that tendency blossoms into a full-fledged union with God, a saint is born. Abilities to heal the sick and "read" souls, to change hearts and shape human events, are the outer signs of this inner attainment.

Saints have appeared throughout history in virtually all cultures as a source of inspiration and hope for humanity. Having transformed themselves by the power of spiritual aspiration and the force of self-discipline, they emerge as links between the human and the divine. Still human, they have been cleansed of the baser nature of our species, imbued with sacrificial love, and endowed with superhuman capacities. Such holy beings have been viewed by other human beings, depending on their own stage of consciousness, as objects of worship, veneration, or emulation.

In our postmodern Western culture, it would be easy to dismiss the notion of a saint as anachronistic and anomalous. Despite the fact that the late pope, John Paul II, canonized more saints than had been canonized by all previous popes combined,[1] the image of our species reflected in the mass media leans conspicuously toward the "sinner" side of the human polarity. When saintly beings do appear on our television screens, such as the late Mother Teresa of Calcutta or the Dalai Lama, they come across to many viewers as fossils of a distant past, if not members of a different species.

And yet, to the seeker on the Path of Return, saints are actual role models. Both individually and collectively, whether alive or deceased, they stand as beacons of light at the end of the road that lies ahead for us all. Esoterically, they represent the outcome of the soul's natural progression from the human kingdom into the spiritual kingdom. Genuine saints are individuals who have reached the end of the cycle of human lifetimes—the chain of incarnations into the physical world necessitated by karmic debt. Though still in human form, they have evolved to the point of exhibiting aspects of divinity.

In pre-modern societies, the fact that divinity could be made manifest on Earth through holy beings and "god-men" was widely accepted. With the age of scientific materialism, however, religious skepticism set in among the educated classes. All phenomena that were not provable by science, particularly religious phenomena, were subject to suspicion and doubt. Despite the long historical record of the existence of saints, the very notion that human nature could be so radically transformed became suspect.

William James was among the visionaries at the turn of the last century who served to narrow the chasm between reality as perceived through the lens of modern science and the reality of saintly beings, those who had transcended ordinary human experience. A scientist as well as a philosopher, James used the scientific method in his quest to determine whether religion had any pragmatic value. His research led him to conclude that saints were the embodiment of "the best fruits of religion" and that "the best fruits of religious experience are the best things that history has to show."

By way of introducing his lectures on saintliness,[2] James quoted the esteemed 19th century French literary figure, Charles Augustin Sainte-Beuve, who describes the state of saintliness as a universal "condition of the soul":

> There is veritably a single fundamental and identical spirit of piety and charity, common to those who have received grace; an inner state which before all things is one of love and humility, of infinite confidence in God, and of severity for one's self, accompanied with tenderness for others. The fruits peculiar to this condition of the soul have the same savor in all, under distant suns and in different surroundings, in Saint Teresa of Avila as in any Moravian brother of Herrnhut.[3]

For James, the scientist, whatever it was that transformed an ordinary human being into a saint remained unexplained. The actual means by which such a metamorphosis occurs was not something that he focused on unduly. Assigning it to "psychological or theological mystery," he proceeded to examine what interested him most—the *fruits* of the condition of saintliness—"no matter in what way they may have been produced."

Having extensively studied the lives of saints, James created a composite picture of "universal saintliness...[essentially] the same in all religions." The condition of saintliness, he concluded, has four main features:

- an experience of being part of a greater life that transcends selfish interests,
- a living relationship with an Ideal Power, or God, and a "willing self-surrender to its control,"
- feelings of elation and freedom produced by breaking out of the narrow confines of ego identity, and

- a transformation of emotional orientation from antipathy toward others, born of narrow ego identity, to a love of all beings.

While these qualities are common to saints the world over, their individual legacies have tended to accentuate one or two particular features. Francis of Assisi (1181?–1226), for example, came to personify a love for all beings. His "Canticle of the Creatures," celebrated through the ages, is an offering of thanks to the Most High—for "Master Brother Sun, who illuminates the day for us," for "Sister Mother Earth, who nourishes and sustains us all," for the moon and stars, the wind and water, for those who pardon, and those who live in peace. Its expression of intimate love for all creatures, as members of the Creator's family, continues to inspire over eight centuries later.

The fact that Francis' words have profoundly touched the human spirit for such an exceedingly long span of time is a testament to the radiance of his soul. And yet, very little is known about the life of the individual who became Saint Francis. In fact, so little is known about saints in our contemporary culture that they tend to be seen, when they are seen at all, as cardboard characters born into perfection. But when they are viewed, instead, as the flowering of human evolution—products of a long cycle of lifetimes—their stories take on new significance.

The Dalai Lama alludes to the process of evolution in the foreword to *Mystics, Masters, Saints and Sages: Stories of Enlightenment*.[4] In an effort to make the accomplishments of highly evolved beings more accessible to readers, he states: "It is important to understand that each of these saints and sages was born an ordinary person." He adds, however, that while some achieve enlightenment through the spiritual practices and disciplines undertaken in a given lifetime, others awaken spontaneously "as a result of positive spiritual merit accumulated from previous births."

In the story of Saint Francis, we find a life that began in a seemingly ordinary way. There were, in fact, episodes from his early years that could be interpreted as the kind of "antipathy toward others" referred to by James. But Francis' life was almost instantly transformed when he was still a youth. The suddenness of the "conversion," plus the age at which it occurred, point to what the Dalai Lama described as accumulated spiritual merit. The level of consciousness attained in prior lifetimes appears to have been rapidly regained.

The son of a prosperous merchant in Assisi, Francis was born into a life of privilege. As a student, he spent evenings at lavish banquets in the company of a "merry gang" of lads. With aspirations to knightly heroism, he enlisted eagerly when Assisi declared war against neighboring Perugia. Captured and imprisoned for a year, having suffered severe illness, he was nonetheless on the verge of embarking on another military campaign when he experienced an awakening: he heard the voice of God urging him to turn back. On returning home, he gave all his possessions to the poor, to the dismay of his father and Assisi's upper class. Shortly thereafter, while meditating in an old and dilapidated church, he again heard God's voice saying, "Go and repair my house which has fallen into ruin."[5]

Thus began a life of obedience to God's will, a life that epitomized "poverty in spirit"—owning nothing and entrusting all things to God. As a mendicant friar and preacher, the holiness he exemplified rapidly attracted others. It has been said that 3,000 friars were drawn to Assisi within a decade.[6] Following Francis' way of life and preaching his ideals, they quickly spread throughout Europe, giving rise to a worldwide movement of Franciscan religious orders and lay people that has endured for eight centuries. Francis also inspired some of the world's greatest religious art—portrayals of his love for the poor and the sick, his communion with birds and animals, and the miracles he performed.

The impact of Francis of Assisi upon Italy, which enshrined him as a patron saint,[7] parallels the impact of Sergius of Radonezh (1314?–1392) upon Russia. While Francis personified spiritual love, Sergius personified spiritual authority. He alone has been credited with salvaging Russia from the Mongol Yoke and rekindling the spirit of "Holy Rus." When the ancient capital of Rus, Kiev, was ravaged by the Mongols in the years 1238–1240, the people scattered across the desolate northern territory, living in abject poverty and submission to their conquerors. The princes, whose internal feuds had led to the downfall of Rus, continued fighting even when forced to kneel before the khans. It was the spiritual power of Sergius that united them sufficiently to loosen the Mongols' stranglehold.

The life of Sergius was unusual from the start.[8] As a child he had preferred the solitude of nature to attending school, a preference that led to a troubling inability to read. His reading problem was instantly overcome, legend holds, by the miraculous intervention of an old monk whom he met in the forest—one of several such incidents in Sergius' early life. Throughout his youth, he had yearned to live in the forest as a hermit, leading a life of solitude and prayer. At age twenty, freed of family obligations, he set out to create a hermitage with his older brother, a monk. When the cold winters and scarcity of food became unbearable for his brother, Sergius remained in the forest alone.

Wandering monks who came upon him in their journeys were always struck by his purity of spirit. As word of his holiness spread, other monks sought him out, pleading with him to become their spiritual director. Sergius refused, shunning positions of authority for the spiritual ambition they fueled, and preferring the life of solitude. But the monks petitioned his religious superiors to intervene on their behalf, setting in motion a pattern that was repeated throughout his life: he first resisted but ultimately acceded to orders to become an abbot, a priest, and finally director of a flourishing monastic center. At one point, repelled by internal politics, he set out on his own again for the forest. It took four years to persuade him to return to what became, and has remained, the spiritual center of Russia—the Holy Trinity Lavra at Radonezh.

Years later, the dying head of the Russian Orthodox hierarchy, the Metropolitan, implored Sergius to become his successor. For the first time, Sergius flatly refused, declaring, "You will not find what you are looking for in me. I am only a sinner and least among men."[9] Within two years, the destiny of Russia was placed in his hands. As the Mongol Horde threatened to invade Moscow, the new capital of Rus, the Grand Prince, whose forces were vastly outnumbered, appealed to Sergius for spiritual guidance. With his blessings, Russia waged war against the Mongols for the first time in over a century. Sergius, clairvoyantly aware of each stage of the battle, was found offering prayers of thanksgiving for the victory when a courier arrived to deliver the news to him.

It would be hard to overestimate the influence of Sergius on Russia—both in his own time and thereafter. Just as the light of his soul had attracted monks to establish monasteries around him, many of his disciples set out on their own and replicated the pattern. The spiritual light of these monasteries, arising after a long period of darkness, attracted lay people who then built towns around them. It has been estimated that between the late 14th and 16th centuries—the golden age of Russian spirituality—the spark lit by Saint Sergius had kindled the founding of 150 monasteries in the forests and 104 more in towns.[10] On the 600th anniversary of his death, in 1992 (one year after the fall of the atheistic communist regime), his memory was celebrated across the vast territory of Russia.

Though the legacies of Francis and Sergius remain alive to this day, the little that is known about them pertains largely to their outer lives as observed by others. The same is true of the lives of countless other saints, documented to greater or lesser degrees. Far more rare are records of the *inner* lives of saintly beings, and among the best of these are the records left by women, often at the urging of their superiors. A prime example is Teresa of Avila (1515–1582), whose writings are considered among the most lucid Christian works on the subject of the mystical path.

In her *Autobiography*, Teresa depicts the stages of spiritual growth through the creative use of metaphor. Likening prayer to "watering the garden of one's soul," she outlines four stages, each of which becomes progressively easier as human effort is offset by divine grace. The first stage—stilling the senses and concentrating the mind—is likened to the heavy labor of drawing water from a well. She compares the second stage—contemplation and the development of intuition—to turning the crank of a waterwheel, far easier than the first. By the third stage, water flows freely into the garden of the soul as if from a natural spring and the soul, in grateful surrender to God, begins to bear fruit in the world through service to others. The fourth stage, divine union, is likened to a copious rainfall.

This final stage is described by Teresa as "heavenly water that in its abundance soaks and saturates the entire garden."[11] The soul, thoroughly infused with divine grace, becomes emboldened to carry out God's will no matter how great the sacrifice exacted by "the world." Writing of the soul's boundless courage at this stage, she declares: "Such prayer is the source of heroic promises...the beginning of contempt for the world."[12] Her words evoke the lives of many who have trod this path, fearlessly obeying the dictates of their souls—from the disciples of Christ to Mahatma Gandhi and Martin Luther King, Jr.

The writings of other women saints—past and present—also contain vivid descriptions of the latter stages of the path. There are two accounts of the soul's acquiescence to divine will, left by women who lived six centuries apart in completely different cultural and religious milieus, which serve to underscore the point made by James that saints of all times and places exhibit the same characteristics. Both women, like Saint Sergius, desired only to lead the contemplative life. Yet they yielded to the inner voice calling them into the world, where they manifested extraordinary powers of healing.

The first of the two, chronologically, was Catherine of Siena (1347–1380). Drawn to religious life from early childhood, Catherine entered a period of silent retreat in communion with Christ at age sixteen. She subjected herself to severe self-purification and testing, particularly with regard to learning discrimination between visions received from God (those leading to "greater knowledge of truth in the soul" plus greater humility) and apparitions of evil origin (those resulting in self-pride). After three years of seclusion, Christ appeared to her, indicating that it was time to break her silence and reenter the world to serve others. The voice she heard instructed her to learn to see her Beloved in everyone, saying, "Your neighbors are the channel through which all your virtues come to birth."[13]

In the remaining thirteen years of her brief life, Catherine became a spiritual mother, healer, and advisor to circles of people radiating outward from her own family to the reigning pope. Able to see into souls, she offered guidance and healing that attracted multitudes of the sick in body and spirit. The lives of many were converted to God simply by being in her presence. At one point, she stopped breathing for four hours, conscious that her soul was freed from its body, only to be returned "for the good of souls."[14] Witnesses said that for years thereafter, she lived virtually without food or sleep, oblivious to her own physical suffering, while continuing to share her spiritual gifts with the "rivers of men and women" who sought her out.

A woman of a similar destiny appeared 600 years after Catherine's time in a tiny fishing village near the southern tip of India. She would become, to her followers, a living embodiment of the Divine Mother and the ideal of unconditional love. Mata Amritanandamayi (b.1953), called Ammachi and known as "the hugging saint," has held in her arms untold thousands of souls around the globe in search of healing. Those who have experienced the love flowing through her—to the endless streams of men and women who wait patiently to receive her blessings—claim that it is an actual force that heals. So long were the queues of people waiting for several hours to see her in Washington, DC, in 2005, that *The Washington Post* gave her visit front page coverage.

Like Catherine, Ammachi also had to be pried loose from the contemplative life. In an attempt to convey something of the ineffable experience of mystical union, she wrote about what transpired inwardly when she surrendered her life to the Divine Mother who, "Smiling...became a Divine Effulgence and merged in me." Entering into a prolonged state of bliss thereafter, she withdrew completely from human contact until she heard an inner voice, whose message was strikingly similar to the voice heard by Catherine:

> My child, I dwell in the heart of all beings and have no fixed abode. Your birth is not for merely enjoying the unalloyed Bliss of the Self but for comforting suffering humanity. Henceforth worship Me in the hearts of all beings and relieve them of the sufferings of worldly existence.[15]

The love expressed by saintly beings is distinctly different from the love of ordinary human beings. Whereas the latter is an emotion that ebbs and flows in response to the behavior of others, the former is a force. Like the rays of the sun, it radiates outward from the soul to embrace all others. This force of love dissolves boundaries between human beings and has the power to heal. In the view of William James, it is the essence of brotherly love, which springs from the realization of the fatherhood of God—a unifying state of mind "in which the sand and grit of the selfhood incline to disappear and tenderness to rule."[16]

One of the most legendary exemplars of brotherly love and human tenderness was a Russian Elder, Amvrosy of Optina (1812–1891), best known through the fiction of Dostoyevsky as Elder Zosima.[17] A biography of *Saint* Amvrosy, canonized by the Russian Orthodox Church in 1988 as communism was dying, contains descriptions of the man rendered by those who knew him. The author of one firsthand account said this:

> To love his neighbor so that he wished him every happiness that God may bless... that was his life and breath. And there was such power in this flood of love that poured on all who came to [him] that it could be felt without any words or actions. It was sufficient only to approach [him] in order to feel the strength of his love; and in response to this love one's heart opened up, and a complete trust and utter kinship was born.[18]

Dostoyevsky traveled to Optina to meet this elder, a renowned "reader of souls," during a time of personal tragedy and grief. After several days in Amvrosy's presence, feeling consoled and healed, he returned home to work on what would be his last work, *The Brothers Karamazov*, in which he immortalized the elder's spirit in the character of Zosima. The tender love of Zosima resounds in the homilies he gave to his fellow monks, humbly addressing *them* as "Fathers and Teachers." In one talk, epitomizing the mystic's all-embracing love, he exhorts his listeners to:

> Love all of God's creation, both the whole of it and every grain of sand. Love every leaf, every ray of God's light. Love animals, love plants, love each thing. If you love each thing, you will perceive the mystery of God in things. Once you have perceived it, you will begin tirelessly to perceive more and more of it every day. And you will come at last to love the whole world with an entire, universal love.[19]

The spirit of Elder Zosima recalls that of Saint Francis, so well known to the Christian West. Turning to the East, we find a parallel expression of the consciousness of mystical union in the *Autobiography of a Yogi* by Paramahansa Yogananda (1893–1952). Describing an early experience of cosmic consciousness, which occurred in the presence of his Hindu master, Yogananda writes:

> All objects within my panoramic gaze trembled and vibrated like quick motion pictures. My body, Master's, the pillared courtyard, the furniture and floor, the trees and sunshine...all melted into a luminescent sea; even as sugar crystals, thrown into a glass of water, dissolve after being shaken. The unifying light alternated with materializations of form... An oceanic joy broke upon calm endless shores of my soul. The Spirit of God, I realized, is exhaustless Bliss; His body is countless tissues of light... I cognized the center of the empyrean as a point of intuitive perception in my heart.[20]

Yogis, saints, and sages have appeared among us through the ages as manifestations of human perfection—seen as the ultimate state of being. And yet, according to the Ageless Wisdom, there is an even higher stage of evolution: that of a Master of Wisdom.[21] In the scheme of evolution described in esoteric teachings, a saint is one who has fulfilled the human experience, while a master has taken a further step, one that leads into the next kingdom. A saint is one who has renounced everything of a separative nature, living only to serve God, yet still experiencing the "I–Thou" duality. A master is one who has left behind his human identity, having merged his soul with the One Life known as God.[22]

One of the names that the masters have given themselves in the wisdom teachings is "the elder brothers." This name reflects the way they see their relationship to those who are at earlier stages of the Path. We tend to think of them as having arrived at a place in consciousness so removed from ours that we are of no significance to them. But in fact, once we step onto the path, they take responsibility for our adaptation to the spiritual world much as elder brothers in human families help younger siblings adapt to the material world. By guiding the spiritual development of seekers, they are training aspirants to become conscious co-workers in carrying out the divine Plan.

Two other designations for masters also reflect the chain of consciousness extending from their kingdom to ours: "Custodians of the Plan" and "Guides of the Race." The masters know the substance of the divine plan of evolution and are entrusted with its execution by the planetary Logos, the Lord of our world. Yet actualizing the plan requires the participation of humanity. It was to prepare us for our destined role as cooperators with the divine plan that the "elder brothers" brought forth the Ageless Wisdom for our time. "Humanity is coming of age," writes John Nash, author of *The Soul and its Destiny*, "and the Hierarchy of Masters...has extended a unique invitation to participate in the work of implementing the Divine Plan."[23]

The Plan of God, "the One in whom we live and move and have our being," involves the "spiritualization" of life on Earth during the course of the Aquarian Age. It will be the task of awakened souls to help anchor divine purpose on Earth through the use of our minds. As spiritual evolution proceeds and human consciousness becomes increasingly receptive to telepathic impression from masters and their inner plane groups, sensitized humanity will manifest the *intelligence* of God on the physical plane, just as the spiritual hierarchy manifests the *wisdom and love* of God on the spiritual plane.

What links us to the masters, quite literally, is the spiritual path. Every "unit of consciousness" that now belongs to the spiritual hierarchy was once an ordinary human being. Each of them struggled through every phase of human evolution, as we do, and every phase of spiritual development. They all advanced from the stage of spiritual aspirant to that of disciple, becoming affiliated with the *ashram*[24] or group of one of the masters of wisdom, and ultimately making conscious contact with that inner group. Step by step, they moved through each initiation, progressively unfolding the divine nature, developing enhanced spiritual faculties and the higher virtues of saints. Finally, upon reaching the end of this path, they advanced from the human kingdom into the kingdom of souls.

The passage between these two kingdoms, which *is* the spiritual path, consists of five discrete stages. There are five major milestones or "initiations," three of which were mentioned earlier and will be briefly touched on here.[25] Each initiation brings an expansion of consciousness that is likened to passing through a doorway. At the first doorway, the "birth" initiation, the soul awakens to its true nature and experiences the spiritual livingness of the universe. With the opening of the heart that occurs at the birth of soul awareness, the life of the seeker becomes reoriented towards the welfare of others.

Signs of this stage of awareness now exist everywhere. A remarkable aspect of our time is that large numbers of individuals find themselves either at or approaching the stage of spiritual rebirth. Evidence that initiation is no longer limited to the rare individual, as in the past, lies in the conspicuous rise of altruism.[26] The Latin word *altrui* means *others*. Concern for others, increasingly visible since the middle of the 20th century, has surged to new heights since the start of the new millennium—with an unprecedented degree of responsiveness to victims of natural disasters and human catastrophes. The intensification of world need has given rise to an expanding pool of individuals who are moved to respond to calls for help.

There now exists a global body of altruists and idealists who have been identified by the Tibetan master as "the new group of world servers." The "members" of this group are scattered across the globe in virtually every nation. What unites them is a state of consciousness that embraces humanity as a whole and expresses itself by serving world need. The Tibetan predicted that "millions" of individuals would reach this stage of awareness by the year 2025.[27] Interestingly, at the turn of this new century, the combined worldwide memberships of NGOs at the United Nations—groups actively serving humanity—had already reached the millions.

An active concern for others is a sign that an individual is approaching the first initiation, yet that alone does not allow for passage through this doorway. Other requirements include the ability to function responsibly in the world, by controlling instinctual urges and appetites, plus consistent adherence to high moral and ethical standards. When these requirements are met, the first doorway opens. From that point onward, the path of ascent becomes narrower and steeper. Far fewer individuals meet the qualifications of the second portal, though according to the Tibetan master, growing numbers will be prepared to do so as the new age unfolds.[28]

The second initiation, symbolized by the ritual of baptism, involves purifying the emotions and controlling the desire nature. Overcoming the inner struggles of this stage can take several lifetimes. The disciple learns not only to control powerful emotions and passions, such as anger and the desire for revenge, but also to modulate the swing of emotions between extremes such as love and hate, attraction and repulsion, ecstasy and despair. Calm of the "astral body" is a prerequisite to quieting the mind and developing the intuition, both of which are essential to discovering the soul's purpose. To establish this emotional calm and, more generally, to foster spiritual growth, three tried and true methods have been used since ancient times: meditation, study, and service. By focusing the mind through meditation, the seeker learns to still the emotions, becoming aware of the circumstances that trigger them, and creating an opening to the realm of intuition. The study of spiritual truth fosters dispassion and detachment, while kindling insights into the causal nature of life experience. Service to others—the "urge of the soul"—instills a sense of contribution to the greater life, while placing one's personal struggles in right proportion.

With the establishment of these practices in the life of a seeker, there occurs a steady reorientation from the material to the spiritual plane of reality. As the individual's identity shifts from that of a human personality with a soul, to that of a soul incarnate in a human vehicle with a higher intention, the spiritual aspirant is gradually transformed into a disciple. The purpose of incarnation is increasingly understood as an opportunity to balance the scales of karma and contribute to the evolution of our planetary Life. As such understanding grows, the disciple enters into telepathic rapport with a master's ashram and the soul's unique avenue of service comes into clearer focus.

The purification process that occurs between the first and second initiations brings the soul increasingly further into the foreground of consciousness. The dross of personality that masks the soul is removed over time by the requisite passage through "battlefields" and "burning-grounds"—crucibles of spiritual learning intended to sublimate emotional desires, dispel glamours and illusions, and annihilate personal ambitions. Near the end of this cycle comes a series of tests and trials designed to prove whether the personality is free of self-interest and worldly temptations. When these tests are passed the second portal opens. At this point, the disciple is of genuine use to the spiritual hierarchy.

With the third initiation, the incarnate soul becomes a functioning member of a master's inner group, having constructed the inner bridge of consciousness to the kingdom of souls. The persona, now controlled by the soul, becomes an instrument of service to humanity under a master's guidance. Having demonstrated that the misuse of power is no longer possible, the disciple becomes a full-fledged "initiate" of the spiritual kingdom, gaining access to spiritual will. Along with a growing capacity to perceive God's plan for humanity, the soul perceives with clarity the task for which it has been prepared over lifetimes. Carrying out this task, in co-operation with a master's group, becomes the central focus of the initiate's life.

At this third or "transfiguration" initiation, "the personality is irradiated by the full light of the soul."[29] The inner light of the soul illumines the outer mask of the persona and becomes the directing force of the life. The personality's threefold "vehicle"—body, emotions, and mind—is consecrated to fulfilling the soul's task in the world. These outer vehicles have become "simply forms through which spiritual love may flow out into the world of men in the salvaging task of creation."[30]

From this point onward, the soul increasingly becomes an embodiment of divinity on Earth—less human than divine. In earlier times, the divine light that emanated from holy beings was depicted in works of art through the device of a halo of radiant light surrounding the head. In the coming age, as more individuals on Earth arrive at this stage of divinization, and as the pathway into the spiritual kingdom is better understood, the light of such souls will indicate (to those with eyes to see) their identity as representatives of the spiritual kingdom in the midst of the human kingdom, serving the Plan in their chosen field of endeavor.

The final two initiations, those of saints and masters, are more difficult for spiritual students to fathom.[31] Technically, a saint is one who is approaching the fourth initiation—the "renunciation" or "crucifixion."[32] What is to be renounced is the soul's identity with the material plane. The individual who takes this initiation, called an *arhat*, no longer needs to reincarnate in physical form. In esoteric terms, the soul is ready to release the causal body, the body of causes that has given coherence to the evolving unit of consciousness over the course of countless cycles of rebirth. No longer needed, the soul's subtle body is "crucified." As it breaks apart, the germ of Spirit that gave life to the individual soul, now fully conscious, is free to reunite with its Source.

At the final initiation, marking the completion of the passage between the human and spiritual kingdoms, a Master comes into being. The perfected being, fully enlightened and identified with its spiritual nature, now dwells on the spiritual plane in a body of purely spiritual substance, while retaining the ability to take on a physical form as needed in service to the Plan. As a "citizen" of the spiritual kingdom, such a being works to further the will of God by guiding the evolution of humanity, while continuing its own evolution toward still higher planes of consciousness, under the guidance of the Christ and the Buddha, who have attained even higher levels of awareness.

At present, it is said that the vast majority of masters of wisdom exist in spiritual realms. However, a few enlightened beings, scattered across the earth, have taken on physical bodies in recent times and more will do so as the consciousness of humanity evolves. When a large enough segment of humanity has undergone the first initiation—the birth of Christ or Buddha consciousness in the heart—it is predicted that many members of the spiritual hierarchy will return to Earth for the first time since the destruction of Atlantis. Christ, the head of the spiritual hierarchy, the Presence overseeing the evolution of human consciousness, will then return as the World Teacher in fulfillment of the Divine Plan.

In the near-term future, the plan involves the awakening of many souls and their setting foot upon the spiritual path. This path that leads to mastery—the esoteric path to union with God involving the application of spiritual law—builds upon the mystic's apprehension of truth perceived by the heart. The way of conscious evolution amplifies the wisdom of the heart with the illumination of the mind, helping the seeker to grasp the broader scheme of evolution. In the process, the higher intuition awakens—"the synthetic understanding which is the prerogative of the soul."[33] Ultimately, this higher intuition serves to bridge the gap between the material and spiritual dimensions of existence.

Intuition is essential to spiritual transformation. Once the necessary foundation has been laid, the soul encounters a realm of subtle energies within which it must learn to navigate. It does so by means of the intuition. As this faculty develops and the soul gains the capacity to perceive subtle realities, spiritual presences make themselves known. The seeker becomes aware of inner plane teachers whose role it is to offer guidance. They are "citizens" of the spiritual kingdom, members of a master's ashram to which the seeker is attracted by a shared soul quality and purpose. The intuitive recognition of these inner relationships gradually transforms a seeker from an aspirant into a disciple of one of the masters.

A master first recognizes a disciple by the quality of the disciple's thoughts. The more refined the thoughts, the more they reflect spiritual values and intentions, the more they emit light. When the soul's light reaches a certain degree of radiance, it attracts the notice of a master. From that point onward, the disciple undergoes preparation to become an integral part of an inner plane group. A subjective relationship is established through which members of the master's ashram provide guidance to the disciple on the path, and the disciple begins to serve the specific purposes of the master, helping to fulfill part of the unfolding evolutionary Plan.

NOTES

1   Cunningham, A Brief History of Saints, 121. The number of John Paul II's beatifications and canonizations was close to 900 by 2003.
2   James' lectures became the chapters of his book, The Varieties of Religious Experience.
3   James, The Varieties of Religious Experience, 231.
4   Ullman and Reichenberg-Ullman, Mystics, Masters, Saints, and Sages, xiv.
5   This message was widely interpreted as a reference to the state of moral decay of the Church at that time.
6   Cunningham, A Brief History of Saints, 39.

7   Catherine of Siena, who appears later in this chapter, is the other patron saint of Italy.

8   There are tales of women in church hearing cries from the babe while still in his mother's womb.

9   Kovalevsky, *Saint Sergius and Russian Spirituality*, 115.

10 *Ibid.*, 133.

11 Flinders, *Enduring Grace*, 179.

12 *Ibid.*, 179.

13 *Ibid.*, 114.

14 *Ibid.*, 117.

15 Ullman and Reichenberg-Ullman, *Mystics, Masters, Saints, and Sages*, 250.

16 James, *The Varieties of Religious Experience*, 246.

17 Elder Amvrosy was actually one of two principal sources of Dostoyevsky's inspiration for Elder Zosima. The other was Saint Tikhon of Zadonsk (1724-1783).

18 Chetverikov, *Elder Ambrose of Optina*, 215.

19 Dostoyevsky, *The Brothers Karamazov*, 319.

20 Yogananda, *Autobiography of a Yogi*, 167.

21 The substance of the remainder of this chapter is a synthesis of the teachings transmitted by the Tibetan Master through Alice Bailey.

22 The masculine pronoun is used in reference to masters, as it is said that souls achieving the stage of mastery have done so in male bodies up to the present.

23 Nash, *The Soul and Its Destiny*, 241.

24 "Ashram" is a Sanskrit word that refers to a spiritual "center" where a master gathers disciples for training and for the execution of cooperative endeavors, and from which more advanced disciples provide guidance to those who are newer to the path.

25 See Chapter 5.

26 See Chapter 7.

27 Bailey, *The Rays and the Initiations*, 571.

28 Bailey, *The Reappearance of the Christ*, 86.

29 Bailey, *The Rays and the Initiations*, 278.

30 *Ibid.*

31 "Final" here refers to the final two initiations that complete the path of spiritual evolution. There are said to be further expansions of consciousness awaiting Masters of Wisdom at a still higher turn of the evolutionary spiral.

32 In common usage, the word "saint" refers to a wide spectrum of spiritual attainment. In this chapter, it is specifically used with reference to the individual who takes the 4th initiation, technically called an "arhat."

33 Bailey, *Glamour*, 2.

CHAPTER TEN

THE SOUL OF HUMANITY AND THE DIVINE PLAN

First we receive the light,
Then we impart the light,
Thus we repair the world.

~The Kabala

AS WORLD EVENTS UNFOLDED in this new millennium, an idea long dismissed as part of the radical fringe of fundamentalist Christianity began to penetrate mainstream American culture. In 2006, the notion of the "end-time" finally breached the invisible media firewall designed to keep out "the irrational." As that year was ending, a writer for a popular cosmopolitan magazine observed, "Apocalypse is on our minds."[1] A major TV network reported that nearly two out of three Americans believed that end-time events described in the Book of Revelation were already taking place.[2]

A cascade of global events, accelerating and intensifying since September 11, 2001, has given rise to an increasingly palpable sense that a world era is ending. What is often overlooked by forecasters of doom, however, is that endings give rise to new beginnings. Embedded in the natural order of our universe is the principle of cycles. When one cycle ends, another begins—night passes into day, one month follows another, an old year gives way to a new one. And just as days, months, and years are determined by the rotational cycles of our planet in relation to other celestial bodies, so too, on a larger scale, are longer cycles called *ages* influenced by the course of the stars.[3]

The cyclical notion of ages has long been accepted by much of humanity. It is a notion held in some form by all major religions, along with the idea that in times of chaos a great Teacher is sent forth to bring needed light to humanity and to restore the law. Presently, within Christianity, Judaism, Buddhism, and Islam, various sects and denominations are actively anticipating the end of this age as the prelude to a new one. Christians are expecting the return of Christ and a thousand-year reign of peace, Jews are awaiting the Messiah, Buddhists are anticipating the appearance of the Lord Maitreya, and Muslims are looking to the golden age of the Imam Mahdi.

There is yet another prophecy of cyclical change that has captured widespread attention. This prophecy dates back several thousand years to the ancient Mayan civilization. Mayan astronomers, priests, and seers— using methods that remain shrouded in mystery—produced a "long count" calendar spanning a "Great Cycle of Creation." This cycle, etched into sculptures, pyramids, and other monuments of stone, was calculated to last for 5,125 years—a great turning of the wheel of time that is now coming to a close.

The final year of the Mayan calendar is 2012, a year that many have come to see as the time when "life as we know it will pretty much end."[4] While history shows that "end-time" predictions tend to proliferate and spread like wildfire in periods of chaos, the Mayas' date for the end of this cycle has gained unusual currency around the globe, fueling a vast array of books, articles, web-sites, and even a Hollywood film.

In the lead-up to this portentous year, a number of serious scholars have labored feverishly to break the code of the Mayan calendar, which is said to have been an accurate predictive tool in the past. Some interpreters of the end-date of December 21, 2012 have viewed it mainly as an augury of catastrophe on a planetary scale. Others, delving more deeply into the cultural underpinnings of the Mayan worldview, have seen the calendar's end as the precursor to a new world age that will usher in a higher dimension of consciousness.

One of the foremost proponents of this latter view is John Major Jenkins, author of *Maya Cosmogenesis 2012: The True Meaning of the Maya Calendar End-Date* and other books on the subject. Jenkins' exploration of this ancient culture, largely destroyed by the Spanish conquistadors and later pieced together, led him to conclude that: "The early visionary prophets of the Maya were astronomers, shamans, and calendar-priests [who] gazed deeply into cosmic mysteries that we are just beginning to unravel."[5]

By all accounts, the Mayas' vantage point of the cosmos dwarfs our current one. Their prophetic vision of the dawn of a new age flowed from an astronomical perspective in which the earth was viewed *both* in relationship to our solar system as a whole *and* to the center of our galaxy—the point in the sky which they saw as "the cauldron of creation," the "God of all gods," the source of life, consciousness, and time. They based their calculations not only on the rotation of the planets around our Sun, but also on the rotation of our solar system around the center of our spiral galaxy—the densest portion of the Milky Way, visible at night as a band of light arching across the sky. Presumably their observations were made with the naked eye, over a thousand years before Galileo's telescope revealed that the sun, not the earth, is the center of our universe.

What these Mayan "calendar-priests" predicted long ago was that an extraordinary celestial event would occur on the winter solstice of December 21, 2012, in the constellation Sagittarius. Their "long count" calendar ends as both our planet and Sun align with the center of our galaxy, a cosmic event so rare (occurring once every 26,000 years) that it signaled to them the start of a radically new cycle. According to Jenkins, these ancient seers intuited that the union between *the sun*, a mythical symbol of the father principle, and *the womb of the galaxy*, symbolizing the mother principle, would give birth to a new cycle of evolution in which human awareness will become attuned to the larger cosmos. "In a sense," Jenkins writes, "a doorway will open between the local reality on earth and the transcendent, eternal reality of our cosmic source."[6]

Amazingly, in 2002, astronomers discovered some highly unusual bursts of energy that appeared to emanate from the center of our galaxy—26,000 light-years from Earth. The cause or source of these bursts remains unknown. As first reported in the science journal *Nature*, in 2005, astrophysicist Scott Hyman discovered radio waves from an unidentifiable source appearing to come from the densest part of the Milky Way, in the constellation of Sagittarius. The properties of these mysterious transmissions, referred to as cosmic bursts, were so noticeably different from those previously identified by scientists that Hyman termed this anomalous type of burst "a radio rebel" and "a real oddball."

This unique event consisted of a series of radio waves that occurred over a seven-hour period between September 30 and October 1, 2002. During that time, five separate bursts of equal brightness occurred at regular intervals of seventy-seven minutes, each lasting about ten minutes. The uniqueness of this "object," as scientists refer to it, gave rise to speculations that it might be linked to a mysterious, unknown intelligence. A *National Geographic News* reporter mused: "The transmission's intriguing characteristics beg the question: Might the source be intelligent?"[7]

It remains to be seen whether or not this initial discovery will bear out the Mayan prophecy of a conscious link between Earth and the heart of our galaxy. But the ancient seers were so certain of this event and its timing that a monument was built to mark its occurrence. As the sun sets over the main pyramid at Chichenitza on December 21, 2012, its rays will project a pattern of light and shadow moving, in serpentine fashion, down the stairs.[8] Upon reaching the bottom of the pyramid, the sun will illuminate the sculpted head of the feathered-serpent god, Quetzalcoatl, who represents the union of sky and earth—or spirit and matter—as well as death and resurrection. The visual depiction of Quetzalcoatl's return to Earth was intended to signify the start of a new era in which matter will be infused by spirit.

Whether one views this prophecy as pure mythology or potentially valid symbology, human consciousness clearly does not change in a single day or year. In this regard, John Major Jenkins counseled his readers to view the year 2012 as the midpoint of an *era of change* spanning roughly a century—from fifty years before 2012 to fifty years thereafter. Strikingly, the start of this hypothetical "2012 era" (circa 1962) is synchronous with events that signaled "the dawning of the age of Aquarius." From an astrological perspective, the events of the 1960s can be viewed as manifestations of the emergent influence of the constellation Aquarius, which "governs" both a new 26,000-year cycle—a "Great Year" or precessional age—into which our solar system is entering, and a new 2,200-year cycle for our planet.[9]

It was, in fact, the early 1960s when a wave of Aquarian consciousness began to break upon the shores of the U.S. and other Western nations. Characterized by a sense of universality, it gave birth to new expressions of spirituality beyond the bounds of traditional religion, a budding fascination with higher dimensions of consciousness, and a nascent realization of the interconnectedness of life on our planet. For some people, the new energies sparked a mystical awakening that led to a spiritual quest; others experienced a heightened sense of human brotherhood that led to involvement in movements for progressive change. The first photos of Earth—pictures of a small, blue sphere devoid of manmade boundaries[10]—came to symbolize the "paradigm shift" that was underway.

The shift in consciousness that occurred in the 1960s and 70s was brilliantly chronicled in a ground-breaking book, *The Aquarian Conspiracy*, published in 1980. The author, Marilyn Ferguson, a journalist in the field of brain-mind research, captured the excitement generated by discoveries of previously unimagined dimensions of human consciousness. Moreover, blighted as the 1960s were by national tragedy, they had also produced great progress in the realm of civil liberties, and in the field of space exploration. The book reflected the profoundly new *zeitgeist* of human possibility that colored those years. Faith in American democracy had been restored, in the 70s, by the toppling of a president who had threatened to subvert the U.S. Constitution, and by the ending of a long, brutal war in Southeast Asia. There was a widely shared sense, however ephemeral, that good *could* conquer evil and that peace *was* possible.

Against the backdrop of those times, Ferguson documented emergent perceptions of invisible realities. These perceptions, the product of both spiritual experience and mind-altering chemicals, were revealing subtle interconnections, unifying wholes, and transcendent levels of reality. There was a growing awareness of the illusory nature of the barriers that had kept humanity divided—by nation, religion, race, and gender—and engaged in perpetual conflict. The same mental barriers had divided the human being into disconnected compartments of body, mind, and spirit. The falling away of these unreal walls of separation, in the minds of people in varied professions and geographical regions, had sparked new hopes for the healing of human beings and our world.

A spirit of optimism permeated *The Aquarian Conspiracy*, based in part on Ferguson's research and in part on logical deduction. On the strength of evidence that "human hearts and minds were being transformed," she concluded, "We are changing because we must"—alluding to the consequences of our failure to change in an era of proliferating nuclear weapons. The book pointed toward a consensual vision of "an evolution of consciousness as significant as any step in the long chain of our biological evolution." Ferguson asserted that the Aquarian "conspirators" collectively viewed

> ...this transformation of consciousness as the moment anticipated by older prophecies in all the traditions of direct knowing—the death of one world and the birth of a new, an apocalypse, the "end of days" period in the Kabbalah, the awakening of increasing numbers of human beings to their godlike potential. "The seed of God is in us," Meister Eckhart said. "Pear seeds grow into pear trees, nut seeds into nut trees, and God seeds into God."[11]

To illustrate how individual seeds of God might undergo a transformation into full-fledged spiritual beings, and thus become agents of *social* transformation, Ferguson closed her book with an account of a project aimed at ending world hunger. Founded in 1977, the Hunger Project had set out to eliminate world hunger in the span of two decades—prior to the start of the new millennium.[12] Its premise was that the knowledge and capacity to feed the world already existed. What was lacking was sufficient awareness of the problem on the part of those with the resources to help, plus the necessary will.

In the goal of raising awareness of world hunger, a number of celebrities threw their support behind the project. Among them was the late John Denver, singer, song-writer, and activist. In a statement reflecting the nascent soul awareness of that time, Denver said to a newspaper reporter:

> We're at a point in this planet where we're going to have to make a specific shift in attitude... Up until now it's been, 'If this were the last cup of grain, my very survival depends on my keeping it for me and my own.' Now we're at a time when we will shift to 'My survival depends on my sharing this with you.'[13]

Although the Hunger Project enlisted 750,000 supporters in its first two years, the vision soon became a mirage. Within two decades, by which time the project had aimed to *end* world hunger, the World Food Summit of 1996 had settled on the goal of reducing world hunger by half—over the *next* two decades. This more modest target became a core element of the UN's Millennium Development Goals, ratified in 2000 by 189 nations. Within only a few years, many of the wealthiest nations had reneged on their commitments. In 2006, one child died of hunger and related diseases every five seconds, as weapons purchases soared into the trillions of dollars. In that year, nearly one of every six human beings went to bed hungry, as the "club" of billionaires doubled in size.

What occurred, shortly after the Hunger Project was launched, was the rise of a countervailing trend in the United States and other wealthy nations. Instead of a sharing of resources, there was a sharp surge in conspicuous consumption and self-indulgence. The culture of shopping malls grew to epic proportions, along with the threats it posed to many species—toxic by-products of over-consumption—including our own. In a film of the era, a trenchant exposé of the violence bred by unbridled self-interest, the anti-hero proclaims, "Greed is good," and "Greed captures the essence of the evolutionary spirit."[14] By the 90s, that counter-evolutionary drift toward greed was seen by some as a form of addiction, masking a longing for fulfillment that material things can never satisfy.

Paradoxically, this unabashed trend toward selfishness occurred in tandem with the resurgence of religion and spirituality. Rather than the latter balancing the former, however, the two often became intertwined. The traditional religious emphasis on charity, compassion, and concern for the poor gave way to churches espousing "prosperity consciousness." New Age spiritual teachers began charging lavish fees for seekers to attend seminars held in luxurious venues. The universal spiritual ideal of sacrifice for the greater good was displaced by an ever-intensifying quest for material comfort, relief from anxiety, and fleeting moments of transcendence. There came a time when even spiritual gurus, themselves the primary beneficiaries of this trend, began to decry its narcissism.

By all appearances, the first wave of spiritual consciousness to spread across the globe at the start of the "2012 era" had vanished almost without a trace by the late 90s. Many "Aquarian conspirators" were left wondering what had happened to the sixties' vision of wholeness and unity. Not only had our world *not* been transformed as many had anticipated, but divisions—with some notable exceptions—had grown into widening cleavages of culture, religion, and class by the early 21st century. In an environment of escalating violence, ideas like "give peace a chance" had the hollow ring of naïve, romantic sentiments belonging to a distant past.

To her credit, Marilyn Ferguson, whose book gave voice to that first Aquarian wave, had been aware of the dangers of overstating the case for personal and social transformation. She revealed that in the process of writing the book, she had initially shied away from even using the word "transformation," a buzz-word of the time, for fear that it would exaggerate the scale of change that was actually taking place. Presciently, she stated her concern that "the trappings and symbols of transformation [would] be mistaken for *the difficult path*."

Mindful of the wrenching change involved in genuine transformation, Ferguson underscored the consistent failure of human beings, throughout our collective history, to materialize utopian ideals. In making this point, she quoted Dostoyevsky:

> I have seen the truth. It is not as though I had invented it with my mind. I have seen it, seen it, and the living image of it has filled my soul forever... In one day, one hour, everything could be arranged at once! *The chief thing is to love.*[15]

The need to love, Dostoyevsky went on to say, was a truth that had been spoken "a billion times" (alluding to Christ's injunction to "love one another") yet had failed to transform human societies. In the century since Dostoyevsky's time, the consequences of this failure have become far more menacing: conflict continues to escalate, and weapons of mass destruction continue to proliferate, as our world shrinks into an ever more tightly knit whole. And still we are left with the question, why? Why have our staggering wealth and breathtaking advances in science and technology failed to make us more compassionate and generous? Why has the instant availability of the world's repositories of knowledge failed to make us more wise?

From another angle we might ask: What became of the first blush of Aquarian consciousness? Why did the early signs of awakening that once held such promise largely disappear from our culture? The answer, it would seem, revolves around what Ferguson called "the difficult path." In the Ageless Wisdom, it is explained that the soul's initial glimpse of the oneness of life, upon first awakening, does not constitute transformation. The perception of a higher reality, in itself, is little more than an insight. Only when such an insight is vitalized by intense aspiration can it gather enough momentum to become a catalyst for transformation. As that happens, the individual steps onto the difficult path of spiritual evolution.

The difficulty of the path, as discussed earlier,[16] is tied to the nature of metamorphosis—the process of turning one type of being into another. Starting out with an identity circumscribed largely by material reality, the seeker is gradually transformed into a being identified with spiritual Reality. By treading "the narrow, razor-edged path," the personality, long entrenched in patterns of separativeness, is forced through a process (directed by the soul) that results in the higher Self moving into the foreground of consciousness. Over time, through persistent struggle, that emergent Self—aware of being part of the ocean of Life—grows strong enough to *remain* in the foreground and thus transform the life of the persona.

At its core, the path that transforms involves a conscious erosion of the isolating walls of personality—the separative patterns of perception and behavior produced by the concrete mind, reinforced over a long stream of lifetimes. As the soul gains control of the life, these inner walls begin to dissolve. Just as it is instinctual for the persona to grasp what it has and to desire still more, it is instinctual for the awakened soul to give freely, to serve others, and to seek to mitigate human suffering. Sharing resources—one of the evolutionary goals of the coming age—is as natural to the fully awakened soul as it is unnatural to the personality, the separative ego, before it enters the crucible of transformation.

From an esoteric perspective, material conditions are reflections of states of consciousness. It is not surprising, therefore, given the present state of human awareness, that we live in a world where most people have barely enough food and water to stay alive while a wealthy minority discard staggering amounts of material excess. Ironically, in the wake of September 11, 2001, "a failure to share" was the constant refrain of those who analyzed what went wrong. They were referring to the failure of government agencies to share intelligence. But the failure to share resources, and the growing gap between rich and poor, has been widely recognized as a major source of present world conflict.

As consciousness evolves, the wisdom teachings foresee the time when human beings will voluntarily, willingly, share their resources. As Aquarian energies intensify and the love of the soul flowers into expression, it will be apparent that we are all part of an interconnected and interdependent planetary life system whose health depends upon the free flow of energy, just as the health of any living organism depends upon the unimpeded circulation of vital energy. According to these teachings, the sharing of resources in the new age will result from an expansion of consciousness—an evolutionary departure from the past that will occur voluntarily and peacefully.

By contrast, human progress has lurched ahead in recent epochs by means of violence. Revolution has been the chief mechanism by which human beings have sought to bring about greater justice and equality since the 18th century. The goal of all revolutions has been fundamentally the same: to redistribute power and resources, concentrated in the hands of the few, to the many. However, the call to revolution has been sparked by two divergent ideals: (1) the freedom of the individual, and (2) the good of the community. In the future, it is predicted that a synthesis of these ideals will bring forth a new civilization. But until quite recently, our world was divided into nuclear-armed camps on the basis of the *ideologies* born of these two ideals—capitalism and communism.

In the light of esoteric knowledge, the ideals that spawned these opposing ideologies are *both* organic to our development as a species. However, while one of the ideals was in tune with the evolutionary flow, the other was not. The ideal of freedom, at the core of capitalism's free enterprise and free markets, has been central to the present stage of human evolution. The pursuit of individual liberty, beginning with the American and French revolutions, was intrinsic to this current cycle. Therefore, though force was used to overthrow the old order, the use of force was largely unnecessary to

204 • *WHEN THE SOUL AWAKENS*

preserve the peace that followed, since the new republics reflected the will of the majority of the people.

The Russian revolution, by contrast, began as a struggle for an ideal reflecting a *future* stage of evolution. Humanity was not yet prepared to create a society based on contributing to the greater good *voluntarily*. Thus the ideal, as it worked out on the material plane, became grossly distorted. Force was used not only to remove an oppressive ruling class, as in all revolutions, but also to impose a corrupted version of the ideal—construed as the welfare of the collective *over* the rights of the individual. The result was the imprisonment, torture, and death of tens of millions of Russians and citizens of other communist bloc nations in order to create "a happy life for everyone."

And yet, despite the ignominious fate of communist ideology, the actual roots of the Russian revolution form an important "missing link" in the unfolding story of humanity. The initial inspiration behind the revolutionary movement was a visionary spiritual ideal first articulated by writers and philosophers of Russia's 19th century Golden Age of literature. "Tolstoy and Dostoyevsky were the mouthpieces of a revolution of the spirit," wrote Nikolai Berdyaev (1874–1948), the illumined philosopher of Russian thought. "They would have been horrified at the Russian communist revolution with its denial of the spirit, and yet they were its forerunners."[17]

In *The Origin of Russian Communism*, Berdyaev asserts that communism was an outgrowth of Russian history and religion, despite the fact that it became a worldwide phenomenon. Prefacing his exposition for Western readers, he warns, "A knowledge of Marxism will not help."[18] The actual source of the communist revolution, states Berdyaev, was the culture of Orthodox Christianity in which the great Russian minds of that time had been steeped. From the belief that the kingdom of God would one day become a reality on Earth—in a new era of freedom, brotherhood, and love—sprang a vision of *spiritual* communism that bore no resemblance whatsoever to the totalitarian version of communism that came to be.

Among the 19th century Russian intelligentsia there was a be-

lief that the Russian peasantry, untouched by Enlightenment no-
tions of material progress, had a unique destiny tied to "the end
of history." Idealistically, these thinkers clung to the hope that
Russia could somehow bypass Western capitalism and its brand
of Christianity—seen as compromised by accommodating to "the
kingdom of this world"—and give birth to a genuinely spiritual
culture. In their eyes, Western capitalism was a temporary phase of
history destined to be superseded by an era of the Holy Spirit. To
them the evils of capitalism were obvious: the exploitation of workers; the amassing of wealth by the few while the many groveled
for crumbs; the transformation of human beings into consumers
of goods.

In *The Russian Idea*, the last and best-known of Berdyaev's
works, he describes Russians as "a people of the End"—a people
who lived with a messianic expectation of the end of time, as we
have known it, and the birth of a new age. Likening them to pilgrims "in search of truth, in search of the Kingdom of God," he
observes the salience of spiritual pilgrimage in Russian life:

> The masses of the people have always produced pil-
> grims from their ranks, but in spirit, the most cre-
> ative representatives of Russian culture were pilgrims:
> Gogol, Dostoyevsky, Tolstoy, Solovyov and the whole of
> the revolutionary Intelligentsia were pilgrims. Not only
> physical but spiritual pilgrimage exists; it is the striv-
> ing toward infinity...the expectation that to everything
> finite there will come an end, that ultimate truths will
> be revealed, that in the future there will be something
> extraordinary.[19]

And yet, it was Berdyaev who trenchantly exposed the Russian
character as being riddled with contradictions and polar extremes.
On the one hand, Russians saw themselves as genuine bearers of
the Christian idea, which had given rise to the Russian nation in
988 with the collective baptism of the people of Kievan Rus. It was
widely believed that the Christian spirit had taken root more deep-

ly in Russia than elsewhere, particularly among the peasantry. In the simple people, the Russian masses, the intelligentsia discerned a purer expression of the Christ-inspired idea of universal brotherhood than they observed in the West. Nearly a millennium after the birth of the Russian nation, many of its people still lived with the expectation that "in the end" both humanity and the world would become transfigured by divine light.

On the other hand, noted Berdyaev, the messianic idea had been "clouded by the imperialistic idea, by the will to power" throughout the course of Russian history. The *idea* of the Kingdom of God had taken root along with the cruelest forms of tyranny and brutality. In a paradoxical twist difficult for the Western mind to grasp, Berdyaev depicts Russian communism as a distortion of the Russian messianic idea. It was the "Russian quest for the kingdom of right," or righteousness, corrupted by "the will to power" that had caused the idea to pass into a "non-religious and anti-religious form." This anti-religious form, which had sought to "annihilate God," extinguished not only the spirit of the idea but also the spirit of the people— by the end of the communist regime.

Significantly, however, those enlightened souls of 19th century Russia had glimpsed a genuine human potential—albeit a potential destined to unfold at a future time. The evolutionary goal of the coming era, as portrayed in the Ageless Wisdom, is to establish a kingdom of souls on Earth that will bring about a spiritual form of communism. The ideal of *sobornost*[20] was one of its first articulations. Although this spiritual ideal became twisted into a materialist ideology applied by force, faint echoes of it lingered in the communist slogan "from each according to his means, to each according to his need." The shift from past to future appears to hinge on supplanting revolution with conscious *evolution*—replacing violence aimed at changing external circumstances with the self-initiated process of inner transformation.

Looking back on the 20th century through the prism of esoteric wisdom, the Cold War can be seen as a conflict over two ideas of divine origin—freedom and community. We are told that "ideas held in the Mind of God" become progressively distorted as they descend from the plane of spirit to the plane of matter. Divine ideas are first "stepped down" into ideals by human beings. Next, they are stepped down into ideologies—crystallized thought-forms destined to die like all concrete material forms. The divine idea of *freedom* was turned into the ideology of free-market capitalism by America's individualistic persona (masking its soul). Likewise, Russia's persona turned the divine idea of *community* into the totalitarian ideology of communism.

The first to die, paradoxically, was communism—chronologically the newer and the one pointing toward the future. The reason for its death baffled many members of the late 20th century Russian intelligentsia, who clung to the communist ideal in the belief that it was more spiritual than capitalism. A humorous anecdote of that time asserted that the Soviet "experiment" had not totally failed; it had shown the world what *not* to do. Yet many remained mystified by the real cause of failure. From an esoteric perspective, not only had the ideal become a crystallized ideology, its imposition by force was a violation of the human spirit.

In the eyes of many, American capitalism is now in its death throes. The drive for individual freedom became crystallized into the ideology of capitalism, often forcibly imposed upon other nations. Thus is freedom's own light being snuffed out. The American pursuit of individual happiness—translated into a quest for newer, bigger, better material objects—has resulted in astonishing *un*happiness. Individual liberty became sacrosanct to the degree that self-restraint and concern for the greater good are frequently held in disdain. In its distorted form, the idea of freedom grew into a destructive force now ravaging our planet.

And yet, the divine idea of freedom has been the driving force of human evolution for the past five centuries, and will continue to be such a force in the future. According to the Tibetan master, divine ideas such as freedom and community are actually "building blocks in the plan of God." Issuing from the mind of our planetary Logos, the Lord of our world, these ideas are subtly transmitted to humanity by the spiritual hierarchy. Such ideas become evolutionary tools for the implementation of divine purpose on Earth—a purpose that must be worked out *in* and *through* the human kingdom.

By spiritual law, however, human will must always remain free. The teachings hold that the spiritual hierarchy is not permitted to interfere with the free will of humanity, even if it causes the plan of God to be delayed. The only means available to the "custodians of the divine plan" in executing their work is cooperation with awakened human beings—those who are sensitive to higher impression, attuned to the evolutionary flow, and able to act under the authority of their own souls. Working telepathically, the guides of the race seek to impress the minds of these individuals with divine ideas that will implement the plan of God.

At present, poised on the brink of the greatest leap in consciousness that collective humanity has ever made, a new divine idea is rapidly spreading around the globe—the idea of "the one humanity."[21] For the first time in our long evolutionary journey, humanity is starting to become aware of itself as one species, one kingdom in nature, one family, with a shared history and destiny. The realization is also dawning that consciousness is not fixed and unchanging, but that it evolves separately from the form side of life, and that it evolves in a particular direction. The current direction is toward a greater sense of wholeness and universality, along with greater awareness of complexity and diversity.

The magazine *What is Enlightenment?* devoted an entire issue to this topic in 2007, sketching the broad spectrum of evolutionary thought—in essence, tracing the evolution of our understanding of evolution. The issue included a timeline for the development of "evolutionary spirituality" that highlighted theories of illumined thinkers about how and why consciousness evolves.[22] Interestingly, this timeline dovetails significantly with efforts of the spiritual hierarchy, as described by the Tibetan master, to impress sensitive minds with the evolutionary "building blocks" of the coming age.

According to the Tibetan, members of the Hierarchy, in their role as custodians of the divine plan, began seeding the mind of humanity in preparation for the Aquarian Age six centuries ago—a mere wrinkle in time given the grand sweep of human evolution. One of the first divine ideas sent forth, essential to throwing off the shackles of the Dark Ages, was the idea of freedom. This idea flowered first in the creative explosion of the Renaissance and then in the Age of Enlightenment—the Age of Reason. In the light of reason, it became self-evident that it was not divinely decreed for a few human beings to oppress the vast majority, a realization that ignited the revolutions of the 18th century.

The *idea* of freedom and the revolutions it spawned radically changed the course of human history. Yet this idea was interpreted by minds steeped in the perception of separateness. It took root at a stage of consciousness where values were shaped by sense perceptions and the concrete mind—a level of mind that focuses on divisions and distinctions between physical forms. What sparked those revolutions was the *ideal* of freedom (from oppressive monarchs). In actuality, however, liberties won through America's revolutionary war were initially reserved for white male property-owners only. The struggle for freedom was carried out under a social hierarchy—based on distinctions of race, gender, and class—that rewarded only those at the top.

The promise of the coming age lies in the evolutionary emergence of the soul. In the new world order, as awareness of the consciousness *within* the form expands, freedom will be understood in spiritual terms. The vision of Martin Luther King, Jr.—that human beings would some day be judged by the content of their character and not by the color of their skin—is a vision of spiritual freedom. The soul sees past the outer "cloak," as Rumi put it, to the inner being wearing that cloak, sensing that all of us have worn an array of different cloaks—black and white, male and female, rich and poor, Jew and Muslim, Christian and Hindu—in the succession of lifetimes preceding the present one.

And thus, another kind of freedom struggle looms before us. Although the battle to overcome external oppression is far from being won for most of humanity, another battle lies ahead for those who are awakening spiritually: an inner struggle for freedom from imprisoning personality patterns. This is the heart of "the difficult path," also known as the Path of Liberation. The transformative power of this path will in time make manifest "the one humanity"—the divine idea for the Aquarian Age. When this idea flowers into expression, at a higher turn of the spiral of consciousness, individuals will discover freedom *within* the context of community, as the part recognizes its place within the whole.

In recent times, traces of this new consciousness have surfaced at the United Nations, our lone world body. Despite the habitual clinging to sovereignty of member states, an official event occurred in 2006 that was a harbinger of change. Quietly, unnoticed by the media, the Aquarian idea was given voice in a program entitled "Our Common Humanity in the Information Age." Its central message was: "the global community is one family with common values."[23] Like the muffled sounds of church bells floating above the cacophony of a busy marketplace, new voices are being heard at the UN, particularly within the community of NGOs—now the most trusted institutions in the world.[24] Their recognition of the oneness of humanity is a tangible sign that the soul of our species is awakening.

The change underway in our world body is exemplified by the Millennium Development Goals (MDGs)—the UN program aimed at helping the poorest half of humanity. Interestingly, the founder of an NGO, writing to coworkers around the world, noted parallels between the MDGs and the divine plan of evolution as outlined in the wisdom teachings. Viewing these compassionate goals in the light of a new world order based on "relations that reflect the spirit of the One Humanity," he observed, "We are as a species learning to choose to govern ourselves in such a way as to foster the values of sharing, cooperation, and right relations. And we are doing this on a grand, planetary scale." [25]

Outside of the UN, numerous groups around the globe offer similar testimony to the awakening Soul of humanity, increasingly becoming aware of itself as a single organism. Among the newer groups with a global consciousness is the World Wisdom Council, which issued a statement about the human condition in 2006. An excerpt reads:

> Our present is fear-based; the great teachings were love-based... Fear breeds scarcity, greed, dominance, racism, hate, violence, fundamentalism and all other "us or them" divisions. The wisdom of love is in connection, kindness, caring, sharing, and inclusion.
>
> We find great hope in the sea change of positive actions people engage in all over the world as they green deserts; conserve water; invent alternative energy and sustainable technologies; dialogue instead of debate; practice non-adversarial politics; reinvent their communities; and awaken to their spirituality, the oneness of the human family, and the sacredness of all life. This is wisdom in action. Each of us individually has a vital role to play in changing our world from one of fear to one of love.[26]

To transform the foundation of our world from fear to love is the evolutionary purpose of the coming age. In the esoteric wisdom, world change begins within the individual who steps onto the path leading from the isolated experience of the lower self, the ego, to the inclusive reality of the higher self, the Soul. Those who tread the path invariably discover that fear, the demon of the alienated self, gives way to love—the inherent quality of the soul. It is the love of the soul that knows the oneness of all souls, and that "widens our circle of compassion and embraces all living creatures," as Albert Einstein phrased it.

In the Kabala it is written: "First we receive the light, then we impart the light, thus we repair the world." Redeeming the world, some Kabalists say, is the work of the soul, which receives the light of God and uses it to heal the world. The goal of the path of spiritual evolution as presented in the Ageless Wisdom reflects this idea. A fusion of the Buddhist way of the Bodhisattva and the teachings of

Christ, "the avatar of sacrificial love," the aim of this path is to free the soul from material attachment in order that it may serve to "repair" the world. Liberation is sought not to escape from this world, but rather to contribute to its spiritual regeneration.

In *A New Earth: Awakening to Your Life's Purpose,* the popular spiritual teacher Eckhart Tolle writes: "It is our purpose and destiny to bring a new dimension into this world by living in conscious alignment with universal intelligence."[27] We do this, he says, by aligning our inner purpose—the awakening consciousness of our true Being—with our outer purpose, our work in the world. When this alignment occurs:

> Then comes the reconciliation of outer and inner purpose: to bring that essence—consciousness—into the world of form and thereby transform the world. The ultimate purpose of that transformation goes far beyond anything the human mind can imagine or comprehend. And yet, on this planet at this time, that transformation is the task allotted to us. That is the reconciliation of outer and inner purpose, the reconciliation of the world and God.[28]

The evolutionary purpose of the age we are now entering, according to the Tibetan master, is *the fusion of spirit and matter through the evolution of human consciousness.* The full scope of this purpose, involving the redemption and transfiguration of the material world, stretches our current capacity to comprehend. But we know that the process begins with spiritual awakening and the emergence of the soul—the dimension of consciousness through which the light, love, and purpose of God pour into our world. Souls treading the Path of Liberation are transforming their personas into vehicles through which Spirit can infuse the material world.

As an old age wanes and a new one looms on the horizon, we are faced with symptoms of a dying civilization. Hindu teachings say that we are moving out of a dark age, the Kali Yuga, and toward a blessed age, the Satya Yuga.[29] In this transitional period, what is becoming most conspicuous is the destruction of form. However, destruction can also serve an evolutionary purpose. From a higher perspective, "In the destruction of form lies hid the secret of all evolution."[30] With the breaking apart of old and crystallized forms of civilization, the consciousness within those forms is released, exposed to greater light, and freed to take on new forms that are more appropriate to the currently unfolding stage of evolution.

Less visible than the destruction of form, but no less real, is the new consciousness permeating the "noosphere"—the mental field of our earth. For those with eyes to see, humanity has reached a watershed. Millions of souls have begun to turn from the path of human evolution onto the path of *spiritual* evolution. In *Promise Ahead,* scientist and visionary Duane Elgin likens this moment to the labor pains that precede physical birth. For Elgin, the crises we are facing are "part of our initiation" into new relationships with each other and our planet. He calls this time "a period of stress and testing in which we will be challenged to discover ourselves as a single family with responsibilities to one another, the Earth, and future generations."[31]

This collective discovery of who we really are will evolve, over time, transforming initial flickerings of soul awareness into a steady state of spiritual perception. As a critical mass of souls awaken, step onto the path of liberation, and dissolve densely encrusted walls of ego, the outlines of a kingdom of souls will slowly emerge. When significant numbers of us recognize our inseparability from the One Life of Earth and freely find our field of service within that Life, the long-prophesied Kingdom of God will finally be established on Earth "as it is in heaven."

Though it may remain beyond our own present imagining, there is inspiration in the words of the wise who have seen what lies ahead:

> We stand at the gateway of the new world, the new age,
> and its new civilization.[32]

This is...the most amazing period in the history of humanity.[33]

~*Djwhal Khul, the Tibetan Master*

A new revelation is hovering over mankind... A new heaven and new earth are on their way.[34]

~ *Alice A. Bailey*

And I saw a new heaven and a new earth: for the first heaven and the first earth had passed away.[35]

~*Saint John the Divine*

NOTES

1 Kurt Andersen, "The End of the World As They Know It," *New York*, October 2, 2006, 24.
2 The poll, conducted by CNN, was cited in the program "What is a Christian?", which aired December 27, 2006.
3 The names of ages, based on zodiacal constellations, are derived from astronomy, while the meaning attributed to the ages comes from astrology.
4 Andersen, "The End of the World As They Know It," 24.
5 John Major Jenkins, "The Union of Cosmic Mother and Father on the Maya Calendar End-Date in A.D. 2012," www.alignment2012.com/mothfath.html (accessed December 27, 2006).
6 *Ibid.*
7 Brian Handwerk, "Radio Waves Detected Coming from Center of Galaxy," *National Geographic News*, March 3, 2005, www.news.nationalgeographic.com/news/2005/03/0302_galactic_radio.html (accessed December 26, 2006).
8 Hector Carreon, "Strange Rumblings at the Center of our Galaxy," *La Voz de Aztlan*, October 18, 2005, www.aztlan.net/rumblings_center_galaxy.html (accessed October 30, 2006).
9 According to some astrologers, the shorter cycle is, more accurately, 2,160 years long while the longer cycle is 25,920 years.

10 These photos were taken by the Apollo 8 astronauts who first orbited the moon in December 1968.

11 Ferguson, *The Aquarian Conspiracy*, 385.

12 The Hunger Project was initiated by the founder of est, Werner Erhard.

13 Ferguson, *The Aquarian Conspiracy*, 415.

14 "Wall Street," 1987.

15 Ferguson, *The Aquarian Conspiracy*, 402. Source not given.

16 See Chapter 5.

17 Berdyaev, *The Origin of Russian Communism*, 88.

18 *Ibid.*, 7.

19 Berdyaev, *The Russian Idea*, 197.

20 See Chapter 8.

21 This idea is central to the Ageless Wisdom teachings transmitted by the Tibetan master through Alice Bailey.

22 Tom Huston, "A Brief History of Evolutionary Spirituality," *What is Enlightenment?* magazine, Jan.-Mar. 2007, 77-84.

23 Ida Urso, e-mail letter to the Aquarian Age Community, November 30, 2006.

24 Nancy Roof, "Media Between Citizens and Power: A World Political Forum Seminar," *Kosmos*, no. 1, 2007, 8-9. Based on data from Pew Institute and Edelman surveys in 2005.

25 Steve Nation, e-mail letter to the Intuition in Service network, November 1, 2005.

26 World Wisdom Council Press Release, "Humanity is in Great Danger," September 9, 2006, published in *Kosmos*, no. 1, 2007, 34.

27 Tolle, *A New Earth*, 277-78.

28 *Ibid.*, 280.

29 A metaphysical definition of "satya" is consciousness, or soul consciousness. By some accounts, the Satya Yuga remains several hundred thousand years in the future.

30 Bailey, *A Treatise on White Magic*, 371.

31 Elgin, *Promise Ahead*, 8.

32 Bailey, *Esoteric Astrology*, 148.

33 Bailey, *The Externalisation of the Hierarchy*, 567.

34 Bailey, *The Reappearance of the Christ*, 148-49.

35 Revelation 21:1.

GLOSSARY OF TERMS

FROM THE WISDOM TEACHINGS

Ageless Wisdom

The Ageless Wisdom is a body of ideas, laws, and truths that have guided spiritual seekers throughout human history. It consists of the great underlying metaphysical principles that have been "recognised in all lands down through the ages."[1] In the esoteric tradition, this knowledge has been called "the secret doctrine of the world" and "the ancient wisdom." Starting in the late 19th century, more recent teachings regarding the next stage of human evolution were added to the established body of wisdom teachings.

Consciousness

Consciousness is awareness or developed sentiency. It exists within all life forms, to varying degrees, and evolves from stage to stage through experience. The human soul is a "unit of consciousness" on an evolutionary journey proceeding from mass consciousness, to self-consciousness, to group or soul consciousness, and ultimately to universal or cosmic consciousness. Esoterically, consciousness and soul are essentially the same. They represent the middle principle of esoteric trinities such as: spirit, soul, and matter; life, consciousness, and form.

Dweller on the Threshold

The Dweller is a term used to designate the sum total of the forces of the lower nature—all aspects of the unredeemed personality that serve to impede spiritual contact. It is the mask of the persona veiling the true Self. Its presence is experienced acutely at the point when the awakened individual has set foot on the Path and seeks direct impression from the soul. Facing the dweller involves a conscious struggle between personal desires and ambitions and the higher impulses of the soul.

Etheric Vision

Etheric vision is the power to see the subtler grades of matter with the strictly physical eye. People with fully developed etheric vision are able to register "all forms of divine manifestation as light units of varying degrees of brightness."[2]

Guides of the Race

The Guides of the Race are the senior members of the 5th kingdom—the Spiritual Kingdom or Kingdom of Souls—who guide humanity on the Path of Evolution. Having evolved beyond the limitations of physical form, they serve from the inner worlds as teachers or guides, overseeing the evolution of humanity and the other kingdoms of life on Earth. They are also known as Masters of Wisdom and members of the Spiritual Hierarchy.

Initiation

Initiation is an inner experience that marks an expansion of consciousness—an increased understanding of the nature of reality and an enhanced ability to serve the processes of evolution. It involves the opening of centers within the human energy (or etheric) body, through which it becomes possible to make contact with the subtle energies of spiritual realms.

There are five major initiations in the unfoldment of human consciousness. Together they form a line of approach from the human to the spiritual kingdom.

1. Rebirth: the soul's awakening to the spiritual realm, or the mind's first conscious apprehension of the inner dimensions of life.
2. Baptism: the purification of motives, resulting from mental control over the desire nature and a growing apprehension of spiritual reality.
3. Transfiguration: the manifestation of the love of the soul fused with the light of the mind, through an illumined or soul-infused personality.
4. Crucifixion or renunciation: the soul's sacrifice of form life, as seen in genuine saints and holy beings, resulting in an "arhat"—one who no longer needs to reincarnate in form.
5. Mastery: a state of consciousness that represents perfection of—or mastery over—the human evolution. It is characterized by total freedom from form identity, and identification with the kingdom of souls. A Master of Wisdom is a liberated adept[3] with "the power to wield light as the carrier of life to all in the three worlds."[4]

Master of Wisdom

A Master of Wisdom is described as an "Elder Brother"—one who has passed before us on the path of evolution and has become a full-fledged member of the spiritual kingdom. As an initiate of the 5th degree, a master has achieved liberation from the world of form but has chosen "to stay upon our planet to help His fellowmen."[5] In conscious rapport with the Divine Mind, he serves as a custodian of the Divine Plan in cooperation with—and service to—the One Life.

Old souls

Old souls are individual "units of consciousness" who have garnered the fruits of many lifetimes in the schoolhouse of Earth. Having been tested and tried in the crucible of human experience, they have progressed beyond the point of ordinary human evolution. Symbolically, they have turned on "the wheel of life" and have mounted the Path of Return to the spiritual Source from which all souls have come.

Oversoul

The Oversoul is the "world soul...revealing the character of God."[6] It is the ocean of self-existent, self-engendered consciousness that "permeates, animates and integrates the entire solar system."[7] The Oversoul is the overshadowing, all-embracing, universal presence that contains all human souls, which are said to be "identical with the Oversoul."[8] Individual souls are sometimes depicted as "sparks of light within an ocean of light."

Path of Return

The word "return" embodies an essential truth about the nature of human evolution: the soul on the spiritual path is returning to the source of divine life from whence it came. Just as the soul enters into incarnation on the Way of Descent into matter, to learn needed lessons, the awakening soul mounts the Path of Return and follows the Way of Ascent back to the spiritual source. "Every human being in the course of time works his way back on the Path of Return.[9]

Ring-pass-not

Ring-pass-not is a symbolic term designating a limited sphere of consciousness. It is a circumscribed arena of awareness, appropriate to a given cycle of development and entered into for purposes of growth. For some incarnating souls it may be the emotional (or astral) body; for others, the concrete mind. For highly integrated personalities, the limiting influence is the personality itself, whose dominance keeps the lower self temporarily cut off from the light of the soul.

Soul

Soul is another word for consciousness itself. (See Consciousness above.) "Soul is an aspect of every form of life from a Logos to an atom."[10] In human beings, the soul—the evolving unit of consciousness—technically consists of two aspects: the spiritual soul and the human soul. The *spiritual* soul is the divine Self, aware on its own plane of reality. Standing free from the world of form and illusion, it is self-existent and self-aware. It knows itself to be an integral part of the One Life.

The *human* soul is the aspect of the self that awakens after many lives in the schoolhouse of Earth experience. It is the soul incarnate, the fragment of the spiritual Self that enters into cyclic rebirth by taking on a persona, an extension of the spiritual soul in the world of form. Called *"the imprisoned splendor,"* the human soul is identified with form, asleep to its true nature until it approaches the end of the evolutionary journey, when it awakens to its divine essence.

Spiritual Hierarchy

The spiritual Hierarchy is the 5th or spiritual kingdom in nature—also referred to as the Kingdom of God or the Kingdom of Souls. It is the culmination of the evolution of consciousness on Earth, which passes sequentially through the mineral, plant, animal, and human kingdoms. Entry into the spiritual kingdom is the ultimate destiny of every evolving human soul.

Contact with the spiritual kingdom begins at the 1st initiation, when the soul in incarnation awakens to spiritual Reality and steps onto the spiritual path. It expands through the 2nd initiation of purification, as the desire nature is brought under the control of the mind. At the 3rd initiation, the "soul-infused personality" knowingly enters into the Kingdom of Souls to consciously cooperate with members of the Spiritual Hierarchy.

NOTES

1   Bailey, *The Unfinished Autobiography*, 282.
2   Bailey, *A Treatise on White Magic*, 334.
3   An adept is one who has mastered five stages of consciousness: the physical-etheric, the astral or emotional nature, the mental nature, the soul or buddhic nature and the spiritual directing will, or atma.
4   Bailey, *The Rays and the Initiations*, 643-44.
5   Bailey, *Letters on Occult Meditation*, 262.
6   Bailey, *A Treatise on White Magic*, 36.
7   Bailey, *The Destiny of the Nations*, 47.
8   Bailey, *A Treatise on Cosmic Fire*, 7.
9   Bailey, *A Treatise on White Magic*, 197.
10 Bailey, *A Treatise on Cosmic Fire*, 7.

BIBLIOGRAPHY

Andreev, Daniel. *The Rose of the World*. Lindisfarne Books, 1997.
Bailey, Alice A. *A Treatise on Cosmic Fire*. Lucis Publishing Company, 1925.
————. *A Treatise on White Magic*. Lucis Publishing Company, 1934.
————. *Discipleship in the New Age*. 2 vols. Lucis Publishing Company, 1955.
————. *Education in the New Age*. Lucis Publishing Company, 1954.
————. *Esoteric Astrology*. Lucis Publishing Company, 1951.
————. *Esoteric Healing*. Lucis Publishing Company, 1953.
————. *Esoteric Psychology*. 2 vols. Lucis Publishing Company, 1942.
————. *From Bethlehem to Calvary*. Lucis Publishing Company, 1937.
————. *Glamour: A World Problem*. Lucis Publishing Company, 1950.
————. *Letters on Occult Meditation*. Lucis Publishing Company, 1922.
————. *Telepathy and the Etheric Vehicle*. Lucis Publishing Company, 1950.
————. *The Destiny of the Nations*. Lucis Publishing Company, 1949.
————. *The Externalisation of the Hierarchy*. Lucis Publishing Company, 1957.
————. *The Light of the Soul*. Lucis Publishing Company, 1927.
————. *The Rays and the Initiations*. Lucis Publishing Company, 1960.
————. *The Reappearance of the Christ*. Lucis Publishing Company, 1948.
————. *The Soul and Its Mechanism*. Lucis Publishing Company, 1930.
————. *The Unfinished Autobiography*. Lucis Publishing Company, 1951.
Berdyaev, Nikolai. *The Origin of Russian Communism*. The University of Michigan Press, 1960.
————. *The Russian Idea*. The Macmillan Company, 1948.
Besant, Annie. *A Study in Consciousness: A Contribution to the Science of Psychology*. The Theosophical Publishing House, 1975.
————. *A Study in Karma*. The Theosophical Publishing House, 1975.
————. *Esoteric Christianity*. Quest Books, 2006.
Blavatsky, H.P. *Isis Unveiled*. 2 vols. Theosophical University Press, 1998.
————. *The Secret Doctrine*. 3 vols. Theosophical University Press, 1974.

————. *Collected Writings.* comp. Boris de Zirkoff. 15 vols. Theosophical Publishing House, 1950-1995.

Brunton, Paul. *The Secret Path: A Technique of Spiritual Self-Discovery for the Modern World.* E.P. Dutton, 1935.

Bucke, Richard Maurice. *Cosmic Consciousness: A Study in the Evolution of the Human Mind.* E.P. Dutton, 1969.

Carroll, Lee and Jan Tober. *The Indigo Children: The New Kids Have Arrived.* Hay House, 1999.

Cerminara, Gina. *Many Mansions: The Edgar Cayce Story on Reincarnation.* Signet, 1999.

Chetverikov, Sergius. *Elder Ambrose of Optina.* St. Herman of Alaska Brotherhood, 1997.

Cousineau, Phil. *Soul: An Archaeology.* HarperSanFrancisco, 1994.

Cunningham, Lawrence S. *A Brief History of Saints.* Blackwell Publishing, 2005.

Dalai Lama. *The Universe in a Single Atom: The Convergence of Science and Spirituality.* Random House, 2005.

Dostoyevsky, Fyodor. *The Brothers Karamazov.* Vintage Books, 1991.

Elgin, Duane. *Promise Ahead: A Vision of Hope and Action for Humanity's Future.* HarperCollins, 2001.

Emerson, Ralph Waldo. *The Best of Ralph Waldo Emerson: Essays, Poems, Addresses.* ed. Gordon S. Haight, Walter J. Black, 1941.

Emoto, Masaru. *The Secret Life of Water.* Atria Books, 2005.

Farrer, Frances. *Sir George Trevelyan and the New Spiritual Awakening.* Floris Books, 2002.

Ferguson, Marilyn. *The Aquarian Conspiracy: Personal and Social Transformation in the 1980s.* J.P. Tarcher, 1980.

Flinders, Carol Lee. *Enduring Grace: Living Portraits of Seven Women Mystics.* HarperSanFrancisco, 1993.

Frank, Joseph. *Dostoyevsky: The Mantle of the Prophet, 1871–1881.* Princeton University Press, 2002.

Frank, Philipp. *Einstein: His Life and Times.* Alfred A. Knopf, 1947.

Hall, Manly P. *The Secret Teachings of All Ages.* The Philosophical Research Society, 1977.

Head, Joseph, and S. L. Cranston., eds. *Reincarnation: The Phoenix Fire Mystery.* Crown, 1977.

Hoeller, Stephan A. *Gnosticism: New Light on the Ancient Tradition of Inner Knowing.* Quest Books, 2002.

James, William. *The Varieties of Religious Experience: A Study in Human Nature.* Barnes & Noble Classics, 2004.

Jenkins, John Major. *Maya Cosmogenesis 2012: The True Meaning of the Maya Calendar End-Date.* Bear & Company, 1998.

John Paul II. *An Invitation to Joy: Selections from the Writings and Speeches of His Holiness John Paul II.* Simon & Schuster and Callaway Editions, 1999.
———. *The Private Prayers of Pope John Paul II: The Loving Heart.* Atria Books, 1993.
Keating, Thomas. *Open Mind, Open Heart: The Contemplative Dimension of the Gospel.* Continuum, 2004.
Keats, John. *The Complete Poems of John Keats*, ed. John Barnard. Penguin Books, 1988.
Kelly, Kevin W., ed. *The Home Planet.* Addison-Wesley Publishing Company, 1988.
King, Ursula. *Christian Mystics: The Spiritual Heart of the Christian Tradition.* Simon & Schuster, 1998.
Kovalevsky, Pierre. *Saint Sergius and Russian Spirituality.* St. Vladimir's Seminary Press, 1976.
Lossky, Vladimir. *The Mystical Theology of the Eastern Church.* St. Vladimir's Seminary Press, 1976.
Macquarrie, John. *Mediators Between Human and Divine: From Moses to Muhammad.* Continuum, 1996.
Nash, John. *The Soul and Its Destiny.* AuthorHouse, 2004.
Oken, Alan. *Soul-Centered Astrology: A Key to Your Expanding Self.* Bantam Books, 1990.
Plato. *The Symposium.* The Liberal Arts Press, 1956.
———. *The Republic.* Penguin Books, 1959.
———. *The Timaeus.* The Bobbs-Merrill Company, Inc., 1949.
Reagan, Michael, ed. *The Hand of God: Thoughts and Images Reflecting the Spirit of the Universe.* Templeton Foundation Press, 1999.
Redfield, James. *The Celestine Prophecy: An Adventure.* Warner Books, 1993.
Rumi. *The Illustrated Rumi: A Treasury of Wisdom from the Poet of the Soul.* HarperSanFrancisco, 2000.
Rutter, Owen. *The Scales of Karma.* Samuel Weiser, 1975.
Sahtouris, Elizabet. *Gaia: The Human Journey from Chaos to Cosmos.* Pocket Books, 1989.
Schiffman, Richard. *Sri Ramakrishna: A Prophet for the New Age.* Paragon House, 1989.
Shroder, Tom. *Old Souls: The Scientific Evidence for Past Lives.* Simon & Schuster, 1999.
Silva, Freddy. *Secrets in the Fields: The Science and Mysticism of Crop Circles.* Hampton Roads, 2002.
Skilton, Andrew. *A Concise History of Buddhism.* Barnes & Noble Books, 1994.
Smith, Huston. *The Religions of Man.* Harper & Row, 1965.
Smoley, Richard. *Inner Christianity: A Guide to the Esoteric Tradition.* Shambhala, 2002.

Steinsaltz, Adin. *The Thirteen Petalled Rose: A Discourse on the Essence of Jewish Existence and Belief.* Basic Books, 1980.

Stevenson, Ian. *Twenty Cases Suggestive of Reincarnation.* The University Press of Virginia, 1974.

Sutton, Jonathan. *The Religious Philosophy of Vladimir Solovyov.* St. Martin's Press, 1988.

Tanner, Florice. *The Mystery Teachings in World Religions.* The Theosophical Publishing House, 1973.

Tejasananda, Swami. *A Short Life of Swami Vivekananda.* Advaita Ashrama, 1971.

Teresa of Avila. *Interior Castle.* ed. and trans. E. Allison Peers. Image, Doubleday, 2004.

Timms, Moira. *Beyond Prophecies and Predictions.* Ballantine Books, 1994.

Todeshchi, Kevin J. *Edgar Cayce on the Akashic Records.* A.R.E. Press, 1998.

Tolle, Eckhart. *A New Earth: Awakening to Your Life's Purpose.* Dutton, 2005.

Tolstoy, Leo. *The Portable Tolstoy.* ed. John Bayley. Viking Penguin, 1978.

Ullman, Robert and Judyth Reichenberg-Ullman. *Mystics, Masters, Saints and Sages: Stories of Enlightenment.* Conari Press, 2001.

Yogananda, Paramahansa. *Autobiography of a Yogi.* Self-Realization Fellowship, 1979.

INDEX